SOME 20 TH-CENTURY HISTORIANS

Contributors

JAMES L. CATE

HENRY R. WINKLER

GORDON H. McNEIL

HAROLD T. PARKER

RICHARD H. BAUER

S. WILLIAM HALPERIN

JOHN EDWIN FAGG

DONALD F. LACH

WILLIAM H. MAEHL

FRED L. HADSEL

PALMER A. THROOP

SOME 20TH-

ESSAYS ON EMINENT EUROPEANS

ENTURY HISTORIANS

EDITED BY S. WILLIAM HALPERIN

 THE UNIVERSITY OF CHICAGO PRESS

LIBRARY OF CONGRESS CATALOG NUMBER: 61-5608

THE UNIVERSITY OF CHICAGO PRESS, CHICAGO 37
THE UNIVERSITY OF TORONTO PRESS, TORONTO 5, CANADA

© 1961 BY THE UNIVERSITY OF CHICAGO. PUBLISHED 1961
COMPOSED AND PRINTED BY THE UNIVERSITY OF CHICAGO PRESS
CHICAGO, ILLINOIS, U.S.A.

S. WILLIAM HALPERIN

INTRODUCTION

The contributors to this volume are former students of Bernadotte E. Schmitt. All of them attended one or more of his courses at the University of Chicago; some went on to write Ph.D. dissertations under his supervision. They profited greatly by the experience, and the passage of time has not dimmed their awareness of this. They offer these essays as a token of their appreciation. In so doing, they wish to pay homage to a good friend, a valued teacher, and an admirable scholar.

On first acquaintance Mr. Schmitt seemed cold, aloof, almost unapproachable. At the beginning of a term, a visit to his office was something of an ordeal. From behind his desk he would glower and say nothing. His interlocutor, already in awe of him and petrified by this reception, would grope unsuccessfully for an opening gambit. For what seemed an excruciatingly long time, the silence would remain unbroken. These encounters and others like them gave Mr.

Schmitt a rather fearsome reputation. However, as his students got to know him better, they discovered how misleading such first impressions could be. His manner concealed a genuine interest in others and a capacity for loyal and lasting friendship. Long after they had left his classroom and gone their several ways, his students found him ready to give of himself generously and graciously. Today he is "Uncle Bernadotte" to many of them. This side of his personality has been even more evident since his marriage to Damaris Ames, whose companionship is a source of endless joy.

As a teacher, Mr. Schmitt displayed an amazing knowledge of his subject and the ability to present it with extraordinary clarity and cogency. His lectures were remarkably compact, beautifully organized, and elegantly phrased. Moving with ease from one topic to another, he exhibited an analytical power honed to razor sharpness. Always careful, precise, and thorough, he instilled an ineradicable sense of the importance of these qualities. In the graduate courses and seminars which he gave on the Midway, his students received in the use of the scientific method a training so rigorous that they could never again look at a source, especially a diplomatic document, without thinking of him. Quite palpably, therefore, they have carried into their own work as historians the imprint of what he had taught them.

In the meanwhile his reputation as a scholar steadily grew, thanks to a succession of publications. He authored several books. He edited several others, including collections of documents and the excellent volume on Poland in the "United Nations series."[1] He wrote brochures and articles and read papers at meetings of learned societies. Over the years, at home and abroad, many honors came his way. The

[1] Bernadotte E. Schmitt (ed.), *Poland* (Berkeley, 1945).

most recent has been the presidency of the American Historical Association. But to go back: from the outset, as a
very young man, Mr. Schmitt showed a predilection for
diplomatic history. To this predilection his three-year so-
journ at Oxford as a Rhodes scholar contributed appreciably.
He became interested in Anglo-German relations, which
had deteriorated so markedly since the days of Bismarck. He
gave the matter a good deal of attention while he was
abroad. On his return to the United States he continued to
ponder it while he held a fellowship and then an assistant-
ship at the University of Wisconsin. There, in 1910, when
he was twenty-four, he received his Ph.D. after writing a
thesis that marked the beginning of his career as a diplomatic historian. The subject of his dissertation was "British
policy and the enforcement of the Treaty of Berlin, 1878–
1887."

To this period he was to return repeatedly during the next
three and a half decades, when he taught first at Western
Reserve and then at the University of Chicago. But like so
many people from various walks of life, he became increasingly absorbed after August 1914 in the question of why
Europe was at war. His preoccupation with Anglo-German
relations dovetailed with this new interest and reinforced it.
Inevitably, therefore, he found himself drawn into the controversy over the *Kriegsschuldfrage*. A host of scholars entered the fray; he was one of the first.

As early as September 1915 he completed his *England
and Germany, 1740–1914*. It appeared the following year.
The title notwithstanding, it was mainly a study of the
decade or so that preceded the outbreak of hostilities. To be
sure, as he himself pointed out, the book was not "entirely"
a product of the war; almost all the evidence on which his
conclusions were based had been collected before August

1914.[2] Nevertheless, the influence of the struggle then in progress showed clearly. Mr. Schmitt's approach reflected the harrowing anxiety felt in those American circles that were strongly pro-Entente. He did not claim to be free from partisanship. "I have tried," he explained, "to present the subject of Anglo-German relations from a historical point of view, and if I have taken sides it is because the available evidence seemed to warrant certain conclusions."[3] Needless to say, there were then, and there still are now, honest differences of opinion about some of the issues he discussed. But quite apart from questions of interpretation or judgment, the fact remained that he had written a pioneering work. The documentation testified to a prodigious amount of original research; the text, though extensive, represented the distillation of enormous quantities of data. Of course, the focal point of interest for him and his readers was the question of responsibility. On this he spoke out with characteristic clarity and vigor: the evidence, in his view, indicated that "Germany allowed the war to come—even precipitated it herself."[4]

In a remarkable essay which he published eight years later,[5] Mr. Schmitt again examined the diplomatic background of the war. Addressing himself to the question of why the conflict erupted when it did, he summed up his findings as follows:

There must have been some connecting link which acted as a chain of powder between the various accumulations of explosive material. And so there was. As one peruses the innumerable memoirs by politicians, soldiers, and sailors, from the German emperor to obscure diplomatists, or tries to digest the thousands

[2] Bernadotte E. Schmitt, *England and Germany, 1740–1914* (Princeton, 1916), p. vii.

[3] *Ibid.*, p. viii.   [4] *Ibid.*, p. 497.

[5] "Triple Alliance and Triple Entente, 1902–1914," *American historical review*, XXIX (1923–24), 449–73.

of documents published since 1918 from the German, Austrian, Serbian, Russian, French, Belgian, and British archives, the conviction grows that it was the schism of Europe in Triple Alliance and Triple Entente which fused the various quarrels and forces into one gigantic struggle for the balance of power; and the war came in 1914 because then, for the first time, the lines were sharply drawn between the two rival groups, and neither could yield on the Serbian issue without seeing the balance pass definitely to the other side.[6]

The evidence which Mr. Schmitt mustered was of course open to more than one interpretation, but his sheer mastery of it was in itself impressive. What he contributed was so basic that no serious student of the subject could afford to ignore it. Although he placed his main conclusion in a context that embraced all the leading powers, he did not hesitate to differentiate sharply between them. To be sure, he conceded, nobody wanted a European conflagration; everyone bluffed, and "for fear that his bluff would be called, sanctioned all military measures short of actual war. . . ."[7] Nevertheless, Germany was the chief culprit. The Russian mobilization, which was stressed by those who sought to shift the onus of responsibility away from Germany, had been ordered because "Austria refused all concessions";[8] and Austria was intransigent because she was "absolutely sure of German backing."[9] Thus the attitude of the Reich formed the base of this frightful pyramid. But the most serious charge that could be brought against Germany was not that she gave Austria a "blank check." Rather, it was that she declined to follow the lead of Sir Edward Grey. The British foreign minister "saw that the only escape from the impasse was to bring the Concert of Europe into action, and his proposal to that end was accepted by France, Rus-

6 Ibid., pp. 449–50.   8 Ibid., p. 472.
7 Ibid., p. 471.   9 Ibid.

sia, and Italy."[10] Germany's refusal to go along "before the diplomatic situation had been overtaken by military measures . . . prevented a compromise between the Alliance and the Entente, forced each group to maintain its position, and thus precipitated the war."[11]

The thoroughness and skill with which he could defend this thesis were magnificently displayed in his best-remembered work, The coming of the war: 1914.[12] Its two volumes, except for the introductory chapters, dealt primarily with the July crisis. Mr. Schmitt had interviewed some of the principal actors: William II, Berchtold, Poincaré. But oral testimony figured only slightly in his analysis. Thanks to some very recent documentary publications, he had at his disposal more evidence than had been available to any previous writer—over 35,000 items, according to his own calculation. Nonetheless, after working through this mountain of data, he found that it was not always easy "to determine precisely what happened."[13] As for "the motives of conduct," they could often be "only surmised."[14] On the highly controversial question of the Russian mobilization, he did concede that St. Petersburg could have waited another twenty-four hours "without serious disadvantage."[15] But he echoed his earlier contention that the Central Powers could not shirk the blame. In the last analysis, it was "as much upon them and their refusal to make any genuine concession, as upon the shiftiness of M. Sazonov, that the responsibility for the Russian mobilization rests."[16] The "blank check" to Austria came in for a most devastating appraisal. Emperor William and his government gave Vienna a free

[10] Ibid., p. 473.
[11] Ibid.
[12] 2 vols.; New York, 1930.
[13] The coming of the war: 1914, I, vii.
[14] Ibid.
[15] Ibid., II, 255.
[16] Ibid., pp. 255–56.

hand without bothering to check their hypothesis that Russia could be bluffed into staying out of an Austro-Serbian war. Their failure to do so was all the more noteworthy "in view of the fears which they had expressed, at the end of June, about the ultimate aims of Russian policy."[17] At this point Mr. Schmitt queried: "Can it be that they were reconciled to the idea of a general war?"[18] Some lines later he himself answered: "It cannot be said that the German Government was 'spoiling for a fight' with Russia, but evidently it was not unwilling to participate if one were offered or to run the risk of starting it."[19]

With the publication of the The coming of the war: 1914, Mr. Schmitt took his place beside Sidney B. Fay as one of the world's foremost authorities on the July crisis. Of particular interest, therefore, was Fay's appraisal of the new work. A leading "revisionist," it was inevitable that he should disagree with some of the conclusions in the book. In a lengthy review which he wrote for the Journal of modern history, he stated apropos of this:

Two travelers may approach a mountain from opposite sides. Each may describe very accurately and honestly what he sees, and yet the two pictures of the mountain—its outline, its wooded base and snow-capped peaks—may appear very different according to the point of view or the time of day at which each traveler makes his description. Mr. Schmitt seems to have looked at it from the west, from the Entente point of view, in the evening, when England and France appear in rosy colors and the deeds of Germany look dark. Some critics of the present reviewer believe that his approach was from the east in the morning, with a reversal of effects.[20]

To this picturesque explanation Fay prefixed the judgment that the work he was reviewing constituted "the most de-

[17] Ibid., I, 320.   [18] Ibid.
[19] Ibid., p. 321.
[20] Journal of modern history, III (1931), 147.

tailed, comprehensive, and up-to-date account of the immediate origins of the Great War which has appeared in any
language."[21]

This of course was high praise. But still more enthusiastic
was the reaction of Pierre Renouvin, author of The immediate origins of the war[22] and unquestionably France's leading authority on the crisis of 1914. Renouvin not only
agreed with Fay that Mr. Schmitt's study was the most
complete and detailed account of the subject that had yet
appeared; he also, unlike some American critics, discerned
a "rigorous impartiality" in Mr. Schmitt's approach[23]—a
view echoed by the eminent British historian of diplomacy,
R. B. Mowat.[24] Even a German authority on the crisis, Hermann Lutz,[25] parted company with most of his compatriots
and extolled the work. He underscored not only its exhaus-
tiveness but also Mr. Schmitt's "remarkable understanding
of the military requirements of the different nations."[26] In
addition, Lutz recorded his agreement with Mr. Schmitt's
strictures on the ultimatum to Serbia and the declaration of
war against that country. These two points, the German
scholar conceded, involved "a serious charge against the
Central Powers."[27] However, he strongly disagreed with Mr.
Schmitt's views on other matters, notably the Russian mobilization and Bethmann's moves at the end of July.[28] The
general acclaim which greeted the work was typified by its

[21] Ibid., p. 143.

[22] New Haven, 1928.

[23] Pierre Renouvin, "Histoire de la guerre (1914–1918)," Revue historique,
CLXVII (1931), 349.

[24] English historical review, XLVII (1932), 137.

[25] Author of Lord Grey and the World War (New York, 1928) and Die
europäische Politik in der Julikrise 1914 (Berlin, 1930).

[26] American historical review, XXXVI (1930–31), 596.

[27] Ibid., pp. 594–95.   [28] Ibid., pp. 595–97.

reception in the United States, where it received both the Pulitzer award and the George Louis Beer prize of the American Historical Association.

Mr. Schmitt wrote another monograph that represented years of unremitting work. This study, of far more limited dimensions than the one on the coming of the war, dealt with the famous Bosnian crisis of 1908–9.[29] Likewise exhaustive, it constituted the first systematic account of the subject. Mr. Schmitt relied mainly on the collections of diplomatic documents published by the Austrian, German, and British governments.[30] He also used Russian and Serbian documents. However, these sources were spotty and of unverifiable accuracy,[31] with the result that certain vital episodes could be reconstructed only fragmentarily. At all times master of the material he had assembled, Mr. Schmitt concluded the monograph with another carefully buttressed stricture on the Reich. Because on this occasion Germany threw her sword "into the scale of European decision," other nations sharpened their swords. Great Britain's decision to accelerate the construction of additional battleships and Russia's determination to undertake a large-scale reorganization of her armed forces were influenced by Germany's behavior during the Bosnian crisis.[32] Inasmuch as the relationship between the armaments race and the coming of the war was self-evident, there could be no mistaking the implication of this conclusion.

At the present time Mr. Schmitt is working on a study of broader scope—a treatment of the period of World War I for the Harper series edited by William L. Langer of Harvard. But more than twenty-five years ago, after the appearance of the two volumes on July 1914 and before the

[29] Bernadotte E. Schmitt, The annexation of Bosnia, 1908–1909 (Cambridge, England, 1937).

[30] Ibid., p. vii.   [31] Ibid., pp. vii–viii.   [32] Ibid., p. 252.

publication of his monograph on the Bosnian crisis, he put together a little book which ever since has given him particular satisfaction. Entitled *Triple Alliance and Triple Entente*[33] and comprising a text of only 115 undersized pages, it stood out as a beautiful job of compression, synthesis, and interpretation. Surveying the entire history of European diplomacy from 1871 to 1914 and doing so without a single superfluous word, it necessarily concentrated on highlights and trends. Roughly the first third dealt with the Bismarckian period. It was a model of clarity and insight. The tangled developments from 1890 to 1902—a most confusing and difficult subject—emerged with their inner logic succinctly and skilfully bared. The longest section covered the prewar decade, and here, quite naturally, the tragic denouement overshadowed everything else.

The qualities of this book and its usefulness were special. But no less so was the service Mr. Schmitt rendered his profession in a domain other than authorship. The *Journal of modern history* was founded in 1929. From that date until his retirement in 1946, he was its editor-in-chief. In this capacity he, together with his associates, made the *Journal* one of the world's outstanding periodicals. In any review of his career, this fact deserves to be emphasized.

So does yet another. During the twenty years of his affiliation with the Department of History of the University of Chicago, Mr. Schmitt contributed significantly to its traditional strength in the field of historiography. He conducted a course for Ph.D. candidates that concentrated mainly on noteworthy historians of the present century. A partial outgrowth of the course was the volume of historiographical essays he edited in connection with the fiftieth anniversary celebration of the University of Chicago.[34] The importance

[33] New York, 1934.

[34] Bernadotte E. Schmitt (ed.), *Some historians of modern Europe* (Chicago, 1942).

of the book was speedily recognized. Carl Becker hailed it as "a critical estimate of much of the best and the best-known historical scholarship and writing during the last two generations."[35] G. P. Gooch called it "a delight to members of the craft," pronounced all the essays "well worth reading," and declared the documentation to be "of the highest value."[36]

In view of his interest in this domain, it is altogether fitting that this volume of essays in honor of Bernadotte E. Schmitt should be concerned with the work of some twentieth-century historians. There are of course literally hundreds of historians who have done noteworthy things since 1900, and so the eleven men discussed here represent only a small part of this magnificent story. Nevertheless, they do reflect the infinite richness and variety that mark the historiography of our century. A wider knowledge and appreciation of what they have accomplished should therefore help to vitalize a significant aspect of our ever evolving Western civilization.

The writings of Bernadotte E. Schmitt, with the exception of book reviews and unpublished works, are listed below:

BOOKS

England and Germany, 1740–1914. Princeton: Princeton University Press, 1916.

An outline of modern European history. Cleveland: Western Reserve University Press, 1923.

The coming of the war: 1914. 2 vols. New York: Charles Scribner's Sons, 1930. Awarded George Louis Beer Prize, American Historical Association, 1930. Awarded Pulitzer Prize for History, 1931. French translation: *Comment vint la guerre, 1914.* 2 vols. Paris: Alfred Costes, 1931.

Triple Alliance and Triple Entente. New York: Henry Holt & Co., 1934.

[35] *Journal of modern history,* XIV (1942), 255.

[36] *English historical review,* LVIII (1943), 256.

The annexation of Bosnia, 1908–1909. Cambridge: Cambridge University Press, 1937.
The fashion and future of history. Cleveland: Western Reserve University Press, 1960. This volume is a collection of miscellaneous papers presented at various places between 1914 and 1959.

BOOKS EDITED

Some political problems of contemporary Europe. Williamstown, Mass.: Privately printed, 1925. Reports of the round table held at the Institute of Politics.
Some historians of modern Europe: essays in historiography by former students of the Department of History of the University of Chicago. Chicago: University of Chicago Press, 1942. A volume issued as a feature of the Fiftieth Anniversary Celebration of the University of Chicago.
Poland. ("United Nations series") Berkeley: University of California Press, 1945.
The United Nations Conference on International Organization, San Francisco, California, April 25 to June 26, 1945: selected documents. Washington, D.C.: Government Printing Office, 1946.
The Treaty of Versailles and after: annotations of the text of the treaty. ("Papers relating to the foreign relations of the United States. The Paris Peace Conference, 1919," Vol. XIII.) Washington, D.C.: Government Printing Office, 1947. Edited jointly with Denys P. Myers.

PAMPHLETS

Interviewing the authors of the war. Chicago: Chicago Literary Club, 1930. Privately printed.
From Versailles to Munich, 1918–1938. ("Public policy pamphlet," No. 28.) Chicago: University of Chicago Press, 1939.
What shall we do with Germany? ("Public policy pamphlet," No. 38.) Chicago: University of Chicago Press, 1943.
The origins of the First World War. ("Historical Association publication," No. 39.) London: Routledge & Kegan Paul, 1958.

OTHER WRITINGS

"Germany and international peace," *Nation*, XCII (1911), 444.
"President Wilson's Mexican policy," *ibid.*, XCVIII (1914), 460–62.

"Made in Germany," *ibid.*, XCIX (1914), 251–52.
"The Balkan Revolution, 1912–1914," *Western Reserve University bulletin*, XVII, No. 3 (1914).
"The diplomatic background of the war," *Mid-West quarterly*, III (1915), 27–33.
"La rivalité économique anglo-allemande," *Revue politique internationale*, No. 16 (1915), 3–21.
"The Balkan imbroglio," *Texas review*, I (1916), 201–9.
"The immediate causes of the war," *Nation*, CII (1916), 567.
"L'Angleterre moderne," *Revue politique internationale*, No. 25 (1917), 39–60.
"British policy and the Treaty of Berlin, 1878–1887," *Abstracts of theses*, Vol. I. Madison: University of Wisconsin, 1917.
"The diplomatic preliminaries of the Crimean War," *American historical review*, XXV (1919–20), 36–67.
"Historical study in English universities," *Historical outlook*, XII (1921), 109–13.
"Triple Alliance and Triple Entente, 1902–1914," *American historical review*, XXIX (1923–24), 449–73.
"Assessing the blame for the World War," *Current history*, XX (1924), 460–62.
"France's responsibility for the World War," *ibid.*, XXIII (1925–26), 796–803.
"Die grosse Politik der europäischen Kabinette, 1871–1914," *Die Kriegsschuldfrage*, IV (1926), 907–11.
"Where did the guilt lie?" *Saturday review of literature*, III (1926), 311–12.
"Germany's support of Austria in July, 1914," *Current history*, XXVII (1927), 395–98.
"Lord Haldane's mission to Berlin in 1912," in Louis J. Paetow (ed.), *The Crusades and other historical essays presented to Dana Carleton Munro* (New York, 1928), pp. 245–88.
"Diplomatic Europe," *Saturday review of literature*, V (1929), 721.
"Twenty-five years after (1904–1924)," *University of Tennessee Record*, XXXII, No. 5 (1929).
"Great German," *Saturday review of literature*, VII (1930), 7.
"Accomplished diplomat," *ibid.*, VII (1930), 450.
"The origins of the war," *National review*, C (1933), 37–56.
Section V, "World War period: 1914–1919" and section VI, "The postwar period: 1919–1933," *Webster's new international dic-*

tionary: with a reference history. 2d ed.; Springfield, Mass., 1934.
" 'War guilt' in France and Germany: resolutions adopted by a
Committee of French and German historians for the improvement
of textbooks in both countries," American historical review, XLIII
(1937-38), 321-41.
"The United States faces the world," University of Chicago Maga-
zine, XXXI (1939), 3-6, 21-22.
"The road to Munich and beyond," chapter xxii, in Robert J. Kerner
(ed.), Czechoslovakia ("United Nations series"). Berkeley: Uni-
versity of California Press, 1940.
"A visit to William II," Foreign affairs, XX (1941), 184-87.
"The Polish problem in international politics [during the world
war]," chapter xx, in Cambridge history of Poland, 1697-1935.
Cambridge: Cambridge University Press, 1941.
"History lesson: excerpts from address to National Council of So-
cial Sciences," Time, XXXVIII (1941), 57-58.
"Roosevelt-Churchill declaration," Vital speeches of the day, VIII
(1942), 312-18.
"What shall we do about Germany?" ibid., X (1943), 131-36.
"France will rise again," Current history, XLVII (1943), 163-71.
Encyclopaedia Britannica, 1943 ed.: articles on Europe 1914-1939,
Paul von Hindenburg, Pan-Germanism, the Rhineland, and the
Treaty of Versailles.
"July 1914: thirty years after," Journal of modern history, XVI
(1944), 169-204.
"Rebirth of Poland, 1914-1923," chapter vi, in Bernadotte E.
Schmitt (ed.), Poland ("United Nations series"). Berkeley: Uni-
versity of California Press, 1945.
"Serbia, Yugoslavia, and the Habsburg Empire," in Robert J. Kerner
(ed.), Yugoslavia ("United Nations series"). Berkeley: University of California Press, 1949.
"1848: a hundred years later," Proceedings of the American Philosophical Society, XVIII (1949), 216-21.
"The Brookings Seminar at Lake Forest," American foreign service
journal, XXVI (1949), 32-33.
"July 1914: unfinished business." Paper read at the Tenth International Congress of Historical Sciences, Rome, September 1955,
Riassunti delle communicazioni, VII, 370-72; Atti del Con-
gresso, pp. 711-13.

"New evidence on the Sarajevo assassination: comment," *Journal of modern history*, XXVII (1955), 413-14.
"The first World War, 1914-1918," *Proceedings of the American Philosophical Society*, CIII (1959), 321-31.
"The peace treaties of 1919-1920," *ibid.*, CIV (1960), 101-10.
"The relation of public opinion and foreign affairs before and during the first World War," in A. O. Sarkissian (ed.), *Studies in diplomatic history and historiography, presented to G. P. Gooch* (London, 1961).

REVIEW ARTICLES

"The German war lords on their defense," *Political science quarterly*, XXXV (1920), 440-56.
"British foreign policy," *ibid.*, XXXIX (1924), 308-22.
"July 1914," *Foreign affairs*, V (1926), 132-47.
"British revelations on the outbreak of the World War," *Current history*, XXV (1926-27), 844-51.
"The origins of the war," *Journal of modern history*, I (1929), 112-19.
"National traits," *Virginia quarterly review*, VII (1931), 631-37.
"The origins of the war," *Journal of modern history*, VI (1934), 160-74.
"Russia and the war," *Foreign affairs*, XIII (1934), 133-53.
"American neutrality, 1914-1917," *Journal of modern history*, VIII (1936), 200-11.
"The eve of conflict: 1914-1936," *Southern review*, II (1936), 116-25.
"France and the outbreak of the World War," *Foreign affairs*, XV (1937), 516-36.
"July 1914 once more," *Journal of modern history*, XIII (1941), 225-36.
"The Peace Conference of Paris," *ibid.*, XVI (1944), 49-59.
"British foreign policy, 1919-1939," *ibid.*, XXI (1949), 320-26.
"British foreign policy, 1931-1932," *ibid.*, XXIII (1951), 153-57.
"The origins of the War of 1914," *ibid.*, XXIV (1952), 69-74.
" 'Munich,' " *ibid.*, XXV (1953), 166-80.
"Italian diplomacy, 1939-1941," *ibid.*, XXVII (1955), 159-68.
"1914 and 1939," *ibid.*, XXXI (1959), 118-23.

CONTENTS

JAMES L. CATE

HENRI PIRENNE

1862–1935

It is a privilege to be able to join other former graduate students in a work of homage to Bernadotte Schmitt, a privilege especially welcome to one who was attracted to his class by the reputation of the teacher rather than by any intrinsic interest in diplomatic history. Those of us who survived the rigors of his seminar felt instinctively that we had passed the crucial test that separated the men from the boys, and even after three decades I can still recall how awed we were at his intimate acquaintance with the sources, at the subtlety of his analyses, and at the lucidity with which he would describe an international crisis without seeming to lecture. One can only hope that we who worked with him absorbed in some small measure the skills he exhibited almost casually in the class.

When I left that class, I made a vow never again to open a volume of *Die grosse Politik* or to use such terms as

James L. Cate is professor of medieval history at the University of Chicago.

démarche or fait accompli, and the vow has not been ill kept. But fortunately for the occasional student from another field who felt persona non grata among the embassies and chancelleries of prewar Europe, Bernadotte Schmitt had one interest we could all share alike—a lively and informed concern with the contemporary European masters of the craft we were trying to learn. At the University of Chicago there had been from earliest days a heavy emphasis on historiography as a branch of intellectual history; within that tradition his courses on the recent historians of modern Europe rivaled in popularity those on the coming of World War I or on the succession states. It seems not inappropriate here to remark that the tradition continues in the History Department at Chicago, and to confess that this paper was first offered as a lecture in an introductory course on the history of historical writing. Nor, in the present context, should it be out of place to call attention to the dual role of the academic historian by describing briefly the career of one who was distinguished both as a scholar and a teacher. This was Henri Pirenne, sometime professor of history at the University of Ghent.

Pirenne has often been referred to as an economic historian, and it was in illustration of that approach to history that this paper was originally offered. Certainly, Pirenne was deeply interested in economic institutions, and he was acutely conscious of the effect of economic factors in the shaping of society, but there is a real danger that by overemphasizing this aspect of his work one might do grave injustice to the breadth of his interests and the quality of his mind. With equal pertinence his writings might be considered under others of the categories customarily listed in the handbooks on modern historiography: under Nationalism, since his most monumental work was a seven-volume history of the Belgium he loved so well; under Liberalism, since the theme of that and of other books was the gradual emancipation of the human mind and spirit. He was a product of a seminar conducted after the Rankean tradition, and his devotion to the scientific ideal was apparent in his writings and in his own seminar, as important for Belgium in the twentieth century as was Ranke's for Germany in the nineteenth. He was early linked with Lamprecht, a devotee of *Kulturgeschichte*. And long before James Harvey Robinson taught us to speak of the New History, Pirenne was practicing its principles.

In describing his own interpretation of the history of Belgium, Pirenne referred to "the great importance attributed to the economic movement and to the urban life which is its consequence, and which forms the distinctive mark of our history."[1] He was widely read in the German economic literature of the day, and on occasion he could make use of the broad theoretical patterns they affected, as in his essay called "The stages in the social history of capitalism"[2] wherein he challenged the theories of Bücher and Sombart. Pirenne had a gift for generalizations, and he is perhaps best known today, at least in the United States, for his sweeping theories of social change in the Middle Ages. But for all his interest in broad interpretations of society, Pirenne built on a solid substructure of historical fact, and he distinguished carefully between the method of the historian and of the social scientist:

For him [the historian], chance and the deeds of prominent personalities, of which the sociologist cannot take account, constitute the essential data of his subject. In other words, the sociologist seeks to separate the typical and the general, while for

[1] *Histoire de Belgique* (5th ed.; Brussels, 1929), I, xv–xvi.

[2] In *American historical review*, XIX (1913–14), 494–515, a translation of "Les étapes de l'histoire sociale du capitalisme," *Bulletin de l'Académie Royale de Belgique, Classe des Lettres*, 1914.

the historian the typical and the general are only the canvas upon which life has painted perpetually changing scenes.[3]

Perhaps it will be convenient enough if we consider Pirenne as one who could appreciate the significance of economic factors without neglecting things of the mind and spirit, and without subscribing to the inescapable logic of historical materialism after the fashion of the party-line hack. He was, then, no economic historian in the narrow sense but rather, as his follower Ganshof called him, "un savant complet," a total scholar.[4]

Henri Pirenne was born at Verviers in eastern Belgium on December 23, 1862. His father was a well-to-do industrialist, a Walloon by origin and a Liberal by political persuasion. As a boy, Henri showed some interest in his father's textile factory, and he must have seen something of the violence that accompanied the labor movement in that area. This interest in the textile industry and in the social and political conditions under which it had developed was to illuminate much of his life's work.[5] In 1880 he entered the University of Liége, intending to study law, but he turned to history instead, a less radical change in Europe then than it would be in America today. He studied under Godefroid Kurth, an authority on the early Franks, and under Paul Fredericq, who wrote on the history of the Low Countries in late medieval and early modern times and on the Inquisi-

[3] "What are historians trying to do?" in S. A. Rice, Methods in social science (Chicago, 1931), p. 436.

[4] F. L. Ganshof, "Henri Pirenne, historien" in Henri Pirenne, hommages et souvenirs (2 vols.; Brussels, 1938), I, 197: "Il y a peu de savants complets: Pirenne l'a été." These volumes contain a vast deal of information about Pirenne's life and work, and I have borrowed heavily from the articles printed therein.

[5] Among the dozen or so of his works that deal specifically with the textile industry, the most substantial was H. Pirenne and G. Espinas, Receuil de documents relatifs à l'industrie drapière en Flandre (4 vols.; Brussels, 1906–24).

tion. Pirenne took his Ph.D. in 1883 with a thesis on the medieval government of Dinant, an ancient industrial town in the neighboring province of Namur.

Both before and after obtaining the doctorate he studied abroad. At Berlin he took courses with G. Schmoller on the growth of medieval towns and from H. Bresslau in diplomatics. At Leipzig he studied under W. Arndt, the famous paleographer. At Paris he continued his technical training at both the École des Chartes and the École des Hautes Études. There he studied with M. Thévenin, Gabriel Monod, and A. Giry, all well-known medievalists. Giry was a celebrated expert in diplomatics whose handbook is still standard, but, more important for Pirenne's development, Giry was a student of medieval town life whose studies on St. Omer and Rouen intrigued the young Belgian as had Schmoller's studies on Strasbourg.[6] In both France and Germany Pirenne began lasting friendships among his contemporaries: at Paris with Maurice Prou, Henri Stein, Abel Lefranc; at Leipzig with Karl Lamprecht. Among Berlin students he earned the friendly nickname "Bierhenne." This wide acquaintance among foreign scholars—perhaps stimulated by his master Paul Fredericq's interest in contemporary historiography—was to be reflected later in Pirenne's activities in the International Historical Congress.

In the spring of 1884 Pirenne was called from Paris to teach at the École Normale des Humanités at Liége, but he had hardly begun his lectures when the Liberal Frère-Orban ministry fell and the new Catholic minister of the interior, Victor Jacobs, dismissed him. The lutte scolaire was at a critical stage and Pirenne's Liberal political views seemed to outweigh his sound technical training, his wide intellectual

[6] A. Giry, Manuel de diplomatie (Paris, 1895; rev. ed., 1925); Histoire de la ville de St. Omer et de ses institutions jusqu'au XVIe siècle (Paris, 1877); Les établissements de Rouen (Paris, 1883).

contacts, and the promise he had already shown. Fortunately, Liberal gains in the election of October 1884 brought about a shake-up in the cabinet; Jacobs was replaced by the more moderate Thonissen and at the instance of Godefroid Kurth, who had influence in the Catholic party, his student was again recalled from Paris whither he had gone after his dismissal. Thus, in the autumn of 1885, Pirenne began to teach at the University of Liége, and it is indicative of the breadth of his technical training as a medievalist that he was commissioned to organize the newly authorized course in paleography and diplomatics. In the following year he was called to Ghent as professor extraordinary of medieval history and of Belgian history; he attained the full rank in 1889. Save for a forced interruption during World War I, he remained at Ghent from 1886 until his retirement in 1930. From 1919 to 1921 he served as rector, the university's highest official, but in the European sense of a temporary representative of the faculty, not as a professional administrator.

Pirenne's first essay, on Sedulius de Liége (Brussels, 1882), a political theorist of the ninth century, had been published while he was still a student. This was followed by a rapid stream of articles; these and his first book, based on his dissertation and called Histoire de la constitution de la ville de Dinant (Ghent, 1889), gave some clue as to the general direction of his interests. In part these early studies were methodological and professional: he surveyed the current status of historical studies and of the auxiliary disciplines, edited medieval texts,[7] reviewed scholarly works, and wrote articles on local history. His concern with methodology was to continue: he compiled the standard bibliography

[7] E.g., Histoire du meurtre de Charles le Bon, comte de Flandre, par Galbert de Bruges (Paris, 1891); Le soulèvement de la Flandre maritime de 1323–1328 (Ghent, 1902); Chronique rimée des troubles de Flandre en 1379–1380 (Ghent, 1902).

of the sources and literature of Belgian history[8] and a useful manual of diplomatics for Belgian documents;[9] he wrote short notices on the work of contemporary historians, and historical and historiographical articles for various reference works, including the *Encyclopaedia Britannica* and the *Encyclopaedia of the social sciences;* and he wrote as well succinct statements on the historical method.[10] But unlike some of the social scientists, he looked on method as a means, not an end in itself. His most important end he had decided on early in his career.

The Romantic historians of the early nineteenth century had turned back to the Middle Ages in their search for the origins of modern society. Because modern Europe was predominantly urban and medieval Europe predominantly rural, their interests centered especially on two basic problems: how did the Roman world, in which the *civitas* was the basic form, change into the feudal agrarian society of the Middle Ages; and how did the towns with their free institutions revive in the high Middle Ages in the midst of unfreedom? Scholars brought to these twin problems all their national and political biases and their scholarly predilections, and for a while had very little in the way of monographic studies upon which to build, so that often their theories were more ingenious than sound. Germany was a particularly fecund source of theories of town origins. Omitting the discredited Romanist view that Roman urban institutions had persisted in some cryptic fashion, one might list the following: (1) the gild theory of Wilda (1831); (2)

[8] *Bibliographie de l'histoire de Belgique* (Ghent, 1893; 2d ed., 1902; 3d ed., with H. Nowé and H. Obreen, 1931).

[9] *Album belge de diplomatie* (Brussels, 1908).

[10] "De la méthode comparative en histoire," *Compte rendu du V⁵ Congrès International des Sciences Historiques* (Brussels, 1923); "La tâche de l'historien," *Le Flambeau,* August 1931, translated under the title cited in note 3 above.

the immunity theory of Arnold (1854); (3) the *Hofrecht* theory of Nitzsch (1859); (4) the *Landgemeinde* theory of Maurer (1854 *et seq.*) and Below (1885–91); (5) the *Markrecht* theory of Sohm (1890); and (6) the *Burgrecht* theory of Keutgen (1894).[11] And there were others.

In 1893 Pirenne published in the *Revue historique* (LIII, 52–83) an article called "L'origine des constitutions urbaines au Moyen Âge" in which he gave a critical appraisal of these theories, and in a continuation of the same essay in 1895 he sketched in briefly an explanation of his own (LVII, 57–98, 292–327), based largely on his investigation of early institutions of Belgian municipalities. He insisted that there was no single pattern into which all cities could be fitted, but there was one basic fact which underlay all juridical forms—that the town was essentially an economic unit whose commerce and industry formed a sharp contrast to the agriculture of the surrounding countryside. He received strong support from the German scholar Siegfried Rietschel, who had developed independently a similar view,[12] and Pirenne's own ideas crystallized as he studied individual towns and wrote fuller syntheses.

His explanation, usually referred to as the burg-mercantile theory, I shall describe later; here it is sufficient to say that it appears, in one guise or another, in a third article in the *Revue historique*, "Villes, marchés et marchands au Moyen Âge" (LXVII [1898], 59–70); in the first volume of his history of Belgium; in a little book called *Les anciennes démocraties des Pays-Bas*, printed in 1910 and translated in 1915 in response to Anglo-American sympathy after the German

---

[11] For a brief analysis of these theories, see C. Stephenson, *Borough and town* (Cambridge, Mass., 1933), pp. 3–21, and the same author in "The work of Henri Pirenne and Georg von Below with respect to the origin of the medieval town," in Rice, *Methods*, pp. 368–82.

[12] *Die Civitas auf deutschem Boden* (Leipzig, 1894); *Markt und Stadt in ihren rechtlichen Verhältnis* (Leipzig, 1897).

invasion under the title *Belgian democracy: its early history;* and elsewhere.[13] The thesis was given its classical form in *Les villes du Moyen Âge* (Brussels, 1927), a book based on lectures given at Princeton in 1922 and published first in English as *Medieval cities: their origins and the revival of trade* (Princeton, 1925).

Pirenne's original approach to this problem had been, as I mentioned, via the towns of Flanders, Hainault, Brabant, Namur, and Liége, and most of his detailed studies had been concerned with those Belgian provinces. Because Belgium was so highly urbanized in modern times and because it had experienced, with Italy, the earliest revival of town life in the Middle Ages, Pirenne saw there an intimate connection between urban and national history, and both were to find a place in his monumental *Histoire de Belgique.* In 1893 he had contributed to the co-operative *Histoire générale* edited by Lavisse and Rambaud a chapter on the Low Countries in the late Middle Ages.[14] Somewhat later he was invited by his friend Karl Lamprecht to do a book on Belgium for the series of national histories begun under the title of *Allgemeine Staatengeschichte* by A. H. L. Heeren and F. A. Ukert in 1829 and now continued under the direction of Lamprecht and W. von Giesebrecht. So it was that the first volume of the most massive history of Pirenne's native country was published originally in Germany, in a translation by his friend Fritz Arnheim, as *Geschichte Belgiens* in 1899, then in the original French as *Histoire de Belgique* at Brussels in 1900, and then in a Flemish translation as

13 Much of the substance is to be found in two later versions available in English: "Northern towns and their commerce," *Cambridge medieval history,* VI (Cambridge, 1929), 505–27; and in the economic and social history cited below in note 26.

14 "Les Pays-Bas de 1280 à 1477," in E. Lavisse and A. Rambaud (eds.), *Histoire générale du IVe siècle à nos jours,* III (Paris, 1894), 416–62.

Geschiedenis van België in 1902. This covered the period
from Roman times to about 1320.

Thereafter, successive volumes appeared in the three languages, the French editions now coming first: II, to 1477
(1902); III, to 1567 (1907); IV, to 1648 (1911). After the
fourth volume, publication was interrupted by World War
I, and though each had been well received in Germany they
were now stigmatized in that country as Belgian propaganda; accordingly, when the French edition was resumed
with Volume V (to 1793) in 1921 and VI (to 1830) in
1926, there was a Flemish translation but not a German.[15]
The seventh and final volume appeared in 1932, bringing
the story down to August 4, 1914, which date seemed to the
author to mark a turning point in the nation's life. Already,
however, he had gone beyond that date in an independent
study on *La Belgique et la Guerre mondiale*. From the first,
each volume had been based on a mass of particular studies
on the sources and on controversial points, though the
documentation was not so heavy as to frighten the ordinary
reader. Only in the last volume did the author feel it necessary to apologize for a less thorough command of the now
too abundant sources.

Pirenne wished to make his book "une œuvre d'ensemble
et de synthèse," and so it is: for all its length, the main currents of thought are never impeded by irrelevant detail. His
task was made difficult by the unique character of Belgian
history; his success derived from his concept of the Belgian
nation.

Modern Belgium was a product of the post-Napoleonic
period and the revolutions of 1830, its very name gaining

[15] The Flemish translation throughout was by R. Belbecq. There was a
long interval between the French edition of Volume IV (1911) and the
Flemish translation (1926). Most of the French volumes were reprinted in
several editions.

official sanction only then, after earlier usage by classical and Renaissance authors. It is significant that only Volume VII of the *Histoire de Belgique* deals with Belgium as an independent state, and that the previous volumes treat earlier periods with a like or even greater intensity; definitely they are not intended as an overlong introduction for the climactic Volume VII. As a reviewer pointed out,

It is neither in 1830, nor even in 1430, that our history begins, but in the mid-ninth century, and if one wishes arbitrarily to have it commence with a diplomatic event it is not the Conference of London that one should assign as the point of origin for the life of that "in-between" country—it is the Treaty of Verdun.[16]

Certainly this was Pirenne's view. In 1899 he had said, "Despite the difference of time and milieu, modern Belgium is indeed the continuation of the ancient Low Countries. It has not been given to us by diplomacy; we hold it as a very old heritage from our ancestors."[17]

In the millennium that lay between the creation of the middle kingdom of Lothair I in 843 and that of Leopold I in 1831, it was hopeless to seek any unifying principle in political events. Situated as a wedge between the more powerful states of France and Germany, owing political allegiance to each in relationships that were constantly changing and sharing the blood and language and culture of each, Belgium was the product of a history which could be understood only in the context of French and German history, "as a 'microcosm' of western Europe." If the rich provinces along the lower courses of the Scheldt, the Meuse, and the Rhine lacked geographic unity in terms understood by politicians, their inhabitants nevertheless had developed an economic unity. This unity, rooted chiefly in industry

[16] L. Leclère in *Revue de l'Université de Bruxelles*, XXXVIII (1932), 402–3.

[17] *Ibid.*, p. 403.

and commerce, Pirenne traces through the early weavers of Frisia and Flanders, through the rich tycoons of the Burgundian era and the vast changes of the sixteenth century that saw the transformation of the textile industry and the golden age of Antwerp, and on to the colonialism and industrialism of the reign of Leopold II. Pirenne shows, too, how the Belgians borrowed from the intellectual and artistic and literary life of both powerful neighbors, and with a genius for adaptation created something that was their own. But in the end what counted most was a spiritual unity, born of a long tradition of resistance to foreign domination —by the French, the Germans, the Spanish, the Austrians, the French again, and the Dutch—which expressed itself in a fierce and proud nationalism in a country divided racially and linguistically and culturally: Nordic and Mediterranean in stock, Flemish and French in speech, Flamand and Walloon in culture. And it was precisely in those bilingual provinces where the dualism was most apparent—Liége, Brabant, Flanders—that the national traits, too, were most apparent.[18]

German propaganda of the war era had labeled Belgium an "artificial nation" and with that judgment Pirenne agreed, though without the invidious connotation implied by the Germans. In 1925 he said:

In a certain sense, indeed, the Germans were right in saying that Belgium is an *artificial* nation. It is indeed if one understands by this that both geographical unity and linguistic unity are equally lacking. It has neither natural frontiers nor a language common to all its inhabitants. It is not a product of nature; it is a work of history, that is to say, a work of man. And note, I pray you, that all that man has done is artificial. Law, art, morals, civilization itself, as it has developed since the age of the cavemen, are artificial. It is in that respect that Belgium too is artificial.[19]

[18] *Histoire de Belgique*, I, xv.

[19] Address before La Ligue Nationale pour l'Unité Belge, in *Hommages et souvenirs*, I, 124–25.

13

What man had wrought in Belgium Pirenne found on the whole good. The history of the national period especially he thought "une belle histoire," but he had found as well much to admire in earlier times, even the most troubled, and one can sense something of the temper of the man as well as of the nation as he portrays both the creativeness and the violence of the sixteenth century. He thought that to love one's subject was an aid to its better understanding, but his love was not blind.[20] Marc Bloch called him a "national historian" in the best sense of the word and his book "truly unique": "The *Histoire de Belgique* has nothing of the *livre à thèse*. It is in the most rigorous sense of the term a book of good faith. Like its author."[21]

While working on the last two volumes of the Belgian history Pirenne had returned to the problems of early medieval history, particularly to that most fundamental of all such questions: when and how had the antique world given way to that of the Middle Ages? Other scholars had challenged the catastrophic interpretations of earlier historians who had pictured a sudden overthrow of the Roman Empire as a result of the barbarian invasions. Alphons Dopsch of Vienna in particular was stressing the continuity of some aspects of Roman economic life into Carolingian times.[22] Pirenne, too, believed in the late persistence of an urban economy, though he put its end before the Carolingian period and ascribed the change to the spread of Islam rather than to the Germanic migrations. So far as I can tell, he first suggested this thesis in a general history of medieval Europe written in 1917 but not printed until 1937. The substance of his arguments was later published in two bold articles

[20] *Histoire de Belgique*, VII, xv.

[21] In *Revue historique*, CLXXVI (1935), 675–76.

[22] *Die Wirtschaftsentwicklung der Karolingerzeit* (2 vols.; Weimar, 1912–13); *Wirtschaftliche und soziale Grundlagen der europäischen Kulturentwicklung* (2 vols.; Vienna, 1918–20).

which appeared in a journal he had just helped found, the *Revue belge de philologie et d'histoire:* in 1922, "Mahomet et Charlemagne" (I, 223–35); in 1923, "Un contraste économique: Mérovingiennes et Carolingiennes" (II, 77–86). The same ideas appeared briefly in the opening chapters of his *Medieval cities* in 1925 and more elaborately in a book, *Mahomet et Charlemagne*, published posthumously in Brussels in 1937.[23] This thesis, too, I shall reserve for analysis later.

It would be impossible to mention here all of Pirenne's writings. His interests were wide, being European as well as national and extending from antiquity to the twentieth century. He was typical of the modern scholar in that much of the substance of his best-known books had appeared first in tentative form in essays or papers or monographs, so that his total output was formidable; a bibliography compiled by his students listed 303 items, besides a number of short sketches for the *Biographie nationale*.[24] In the years after 1918 his interests turned naturally to the recent war[25] and in his later years he showed his very real talent for simplification in writing for a general as well as for a professional audience, as in a survey of medieval society in a volume of the Glotz series, later translated into English as the *Economic and social history of medieval Europe*.[26] One of the most interesting of these works of synthesis, a one-volume *His-*

---

23 An English translation appeared as *Mohammed and Charlemagne* (London, 1939).

24 Prepared by F. L. Ganshof, E. Sabbe, F. Vercauteren, and C. Verlinden, and printed in *Hommages et souvenirs*, I, 145–64.

25 *La Belgique et la Guerre mondiale* (Paris, 1928) and various articles and addresses.

26 H. Pirenne, G. Cohen, and H. Focillon, *La civilisation occidentale au Moyen Âge du XIe au milieu du XIVe siècle*. Part I, *Le mouvement économique et social*, pp. 7–129 (*Histoire du Moyen Âge*, VII [Paris, 1933], in *Histoire générale* publiée sous la direction de Gustave Glotz.

toire de l'Europe des invasions au XVIe siècle, mentioned
in the preceding paragraph, had grown out of his war experiences. This, too, has appeared in an English edition.[27] (I
may say parenthetically that we are fortunate that so many
of Pirenne's books have been translated into English, but
some of the translations have been mediocre to bad, sometimes including ludicrous mistakes one could not condone
in an undergraduate's term paper.) The circumstances were
as follows.[28]

When the Germans occupied Ghent in October 1914,
they interned Pirenne as a hostage. Part of their policy then,
as in World War II, was to try to split the Belgian nation
by aggravating the latent separatism between the Germanic
Flemings and the French Walloons. Ghent, located in the
Flemish province of East Flanders, seemed a profitable
place to promote discord, so the Germans proposed as a divisive measure to turn the University of Ghent, French
since its foundation in 1830, into a Flemish institution.
Most of the faculty resisted. Since the whole burden of
Pirenne's interpretation had been against a linguistic or
racial concept of the nation, his influence was especially
feared by the invaders, and in retaliation for their stubborn
resistance, he and the like-minded Paul Fredericq were
secretly arrested on March 18, 1916 and deported into Germany.

There is a wonderful cloak-and-dagger story of how the
news of the arrest was passed through rigid censorship to

[27] A history of Europe from the invasions to the XVI century (London,
1939). For a critique of the translations and an appreciation of Pirenne's
work, see G. C. Boyce, "The legacy of Henri Pirenne," Byzantion, XV
(1940–41), 449–64.

[28] The story of his captivity is told briefly by his son Jacques Pirenne in
the preface to History of Europe (pp. 11–20), and more fully by Henri
Pirenne in "Souvenirs de captivité en Allemagne," Revue des deux mondes,
LV (1920), 539–60, 829–58.

Holland by means of innocent scholarly correspondence on open postcards which contained fake passages from non-existent Latin chronicles,[29] and I call attention to this as a practical argument in favor of studying dead languages. From neutral Holland the news was sent abroad, bringing a vigorous, but ineffective, protest from Pope Benedict XV, President Woodrow Wilson, Alfonso XIII of Spain, and from scholars of many lands. More practical perhaps was the effort of friends and admirers to supply him through Holland with two scholarly necessities in an appeal labeled "L'œuvre du livre et de la cigarette du Professeur Pirenne."

Pirenne was shifted around several times. At Krafelt in the Rhineland he began studying the Russian language from Russian officers imprisoned there. In a concentration camp at Holzminden he taught his national history to his own compatriots and a course on economic history to several hundred Russian youths seized at Liége. Later transferred to Kreuzburg-am-Werra in Thuringia as a "dangerous man" and a lone internee, he set out to write a broadly interpretative history of Europe, primarily to relieve the tedium of captivity. Without access to any scholarly apparatus he was forced to depend on his own memory and reflection, comparing his situation to that of Descartes in his room with the Dutch stove. By the time of the armistice he had brought the story down to 1550 and there he left off, though the outline for the more modern section had been written. Later the completed section was published with some editing by his son Jacques Pirenne.

Thus, the *History of Europe* belongs to that select genre of works which have been written in prison, and though the book seems little likely to rank in popularity with that of Boethius or of Marco Polo or of John Bunyan or of Adolf Hitler, it is at least as interesting a product of the active

29 As told by J. Cuvelier, in *Hommages et souvenirs*, I, 62, 63.

mind turned reflective by circumstance as is Sir Walter
Raleigh's History of the world. Certainly, Pirenne was as
proud of this book as of any of his more scholarly works. He
once showed me, in the famous cabinet de travail in his
home in Ghent, the original manuscript in his own crabbed
script, so notoriously illegible that according to student
legend, at least, there was only one typesetter in Belgium
who could compose from Pirenne's handwritten copy; and
he referred to it without too much exaggeration as his "histoire sans dates." (In the published form, some dates were
supplied by the editor and printed in parentheses.)

Pirenne's courageous stand during the war and his renewed scholarly activity after the armistice brought him
universal fame and a host of honors. He resumed direction
of the Belgian Royal Commission on History and he was
the moving spirit and the first president of the revived International Historical Congress, which began its new series
of meetings with a session at Brussels in 1923. His own misfortunes during the war, including the loss of a son killed in
combat, had mellowed rather than embittered him, and it
was at his insistence that German scholars were allowed to
participate in the congress without disabilities. He taught
or lectured at a number of foreign universities on the continent, in Great Britain, and in the United States, accumu-
lating a list of honorary degrees that finally numbered at least
fifteen: there is an interesting photograph of the ceremony
at Oxford in 1919 showing him as the only scholar in a
group of doctores honoris causa comprising such war heroes
as Pershing, Joffre, Beatty, and Herbert Hoover.[30] He was a
member, active or honorary, of a score of scholarly societies.
He had the unusual distinction of having been honored by
the dedication to him of two collections of essays: a Fest-
schrift called Mélanges d'histoire offerts à Henri Pirenne

[30] Ibid., II, 370. This book contains other interesting illustrations.

(2 vols.; Brussels, 1926) commemorating his fortieth anniversary at Ghent, and a memorial volume called *Études d'histoire dédiées à la mémoire de Henri Pirenne par ses anciens élèves* (Brussels, 1937) brought out after his death. The table of contents in the former is almost a *Who's who* of those then writing in European history. Contributors to the latter were exclusively his students, those who had taken Ph.D.'s with him or had done advanced pre- or post-doctoral work at Ghent. It is indicative of the high esteem in which he was held in this country that of the thirty articles in that volume, five were by Americans, of whom I am proud to have been one. Later there appeared also an unusual work of necrology, a two-volume testimonial called *Henri Pirenne, hommages et souvenirs* (Brussels, 1938), which gathers together in convenient form a mass of information about Pirenne as a scholar, a teacher, and a man.

Because he was truly distinguished in each capacity, his death on October 24, 1935 was looked on as a great national loss. It would be hard to name in recent times a man who was in the same degree *the* historian of his country, unless it might have been Nicolai Iorga of Rumania, and Iorga's international repute, though considerable, was not so great as was Pirenne's. Where else might one find a historian who was a national figure in the same sense: a friend of one king (Albert I) and teacher of a king-to-be (Leopold III); known to the man in the street by name at least and to many who had never met him through a number of portraits, friendly caricatures, and a gold medal which pictured him, along with Cardinal Mercier, Burgomeister Max of Brussels and the Bâtonnier Théodor, as one of the great heroes of the war?

Part of Pirenne's influence derived from his writing, part from his teaching. In assessing the merits of our colleagues we sometimes make a distinction between ability as a teacher and as a scholar, and undoubtedly such distinctions must exist. But at advanced levels of instruction no amount of pedagogical technique can hide an absence of ideas, and conversely no great historian is apt to be lacking in those qualities of mind and of spirit which are required for stimulating and guiding the student. Pirenne possessed in notable degree that combination of technical skill, vast erudition, brilliance of mind, and warmth of personality best calculated to attract and to discipline serious young historians. Thus, he was truly the founder of a "school" of history and most of the important chairs in Belgian universities today are occupied by his students and their students.

I have heard Pirenne lecture brilliantly, exhibiting even in a routine class exercise something of his gift for generalization and for terse presentation of a complex problem. But he was at his best in a seminar, where even in the relatively small University of Ghent his fame might attract ten or a dozen advanced students in medieval history. When I attended that seminar in 1929–30 he was working on *Mahomet et Charlemagne*, and so we divided our time between the sources upon which that study was based and a minute examination of Dopsch's most recent book, *Naturalwirtschaft und Geldwirtschaft* (Vienna, 1930). We sat around a table in a spacious seminar room surrounded by shelves containing the basic medieval source collections and reference works—the sort of room one can find in a small European university but which we cannot afford in the United States. The student would read aloud the assigned passages in Pirenne's earlier essays, giving an *explication de texte*, and at each footnote Pirenne would send one of us to the shelves for some folio of the *Monumenta* or of Bouquet or of the *Acta Sanctorum*, in which the student must find and read, first in Latin and then in translation, the cited passages from some chronicle or charter or saint's life. Then would follow a minute analysis of the text and comments on its relevance to the argument; we must have spent one whole afternoon on the elucidation of a single brief document from the *Formulary of Marculf*, painstakingly identifying in Du Cange's glossary each item in a long list of exotic imports.

With the student's laborious construing of some of the worst Latin ever written, Pirenne was patient, but occasionally he might take over and then be off in his rapid, staccato style punctuated with gestures that were just short of violent, squeezing from the text its last drop of historical information or inference. At term's end he listened patiently, too, as we read our reports of our own research, but his criticism was as penetrating and as suggestive as it was kind.

That year was his last at Ghent and on the final day his *anciens élèves* came from all over Belgium for a surprise reunion. Characteristically he insisted on finishing the scheduled program of the seminar before allowing any ceremonies, and when the last paper was completed he paused only for a moment, as one might in leaving a room after an occupancy of forty-four years, and then led us in a body to a neighboring sidewalk café for the oratory and refreshments appropriate to such an occasion. And it was characteristic, too, that he made no reference then to the *flamandisation* of the University of Ghent which had persuaded him to leave, refusing in 1930 as in 1916 to lecture in Flemish where he had taught so long and so effectively in French. The loss to the academic world was not yet complete, for as a most active emeritus he continued until the eve of his death to offer short courses and lectures—at Brussels and at a number of foreign universities. His was a full life and he lived it with intensity, with courage, and with no little joy.

To attempt to describe briefly Pirenne's two great "theses," as I have promised, is presumptuous—both because they are so well known as to make my effort a work of supererogation, and because it is difficult further to compress his own succinct statements. But I may try.

First for *Mahomet et Charlemagne.* "Romania," the Roman world of imperial times, Pirenne pictures as a political, economic, and cultural unity, bound together by the Mediterranean, *Mare nostrum.* After the crisis of the third century, reforming emperors restored order at the expense of creating a new system of defense based increasingly on the use of "barbarian" soldiers. Pressure along the frontiers increased during the late fourth century, and thereafter various German tribes crossed the frontiers, not as conquerors but as *foederati,* a euphemism meaning "allies," or as mercenaries. Their motive was to share the wealth of Romania, not to destroy the empire. As each successive tribe found a homeland nearer the sea and established a kingdom, the new rulers almost without exception acknowledged that they ruled through authority delegated by the Roman emperor. Vastly inferior to the Romans in number, the newcomers settled on the soil according to the accepted system of *hospitalitas,* an early and prodigal form of southern hospitality in which a certain share of the land went to the "guests," but they displaced proprietors rather than cultivators and continued Roman methods of agronomy. Roman institutions, officials, and law existed side by side with the German; Latin was used even in the Germanic law codes. With Justinian's reconquest in the west (533–55), a semblance of political unity was restored.

In Romania a money economy persisted, with a common monetary system based on the gold coinage of Constantinople; international trade, chiefly in the hands of Syrians and Jews, flourished, as did local trade and industry; urban life and institutions remained characteristically Roman. Art, letters, and intellectual life had changed, particularly since the legalization of Christianity, but society still maintained its secular character. Thus until well into the seventh century the unity of Romania was unbroken and it was the Mediterranean, giving easy access to the most prosperous provinces and the largest cities, that made this unity possible.

It was the Muslim invaders, not the Germans, who brought an end to the antique world. From the death of the prophet Mohammed in 632 the Arabs spread with incredible speed through territories of the Persian and Roman empires. Syria, Palestine, and Egypt fell after short campaigns, and the trek across north Africa was interrupted only temporarily by dynastic disputes among the followers of the Prophet. Meanwhile, after seizing Egypt's navy and shipyards, the desert-born Arabs took to the sea and became almost overnight a naval power. They captured or harried the Aegean Islands, raided westward to Sicily, and mounted a series of attacks against Constantinople itself. After two decades of respite, the westward movement began again. By 698 Carthage had been won and a great Arab base was set up in its place; a few years later Morocco had been secured. Berbers, newly converted to Islam, entered Spain in 711, quickly overthrew the Visigothic state, and by 720 had swept north of the Pyrenees to capture Narbonne. The defeat of the Muslims at Tours in 732 checked without terminating their operations in Gaul.

From north African bases Muslim pirates raided Sicily throughout the eighth century, then in the ninth conquered that island, Pantelleria, Corsica, and Sardinia and won a lodgment in southern Italy. Long before that the conquest of north Africa and Spain had made of the western Mediterranean a Muslim lake. Gone was the unity once afforded by the great inland sea: its eastern, southern, and western shores were under Arab control and in the north Byzance could exert its influence only in Greece, Venice, and a few other Italian ports.

Commercial intercourse between the Levant and the western provinces was badly hurt by the Arab seizure of Syria, Palestine, and Egypt, through whose ports had flowed most of the products of the Near and Far East, then later had suffered from the constant raiding of the Aegean Islands and the conquest of north Africa, Spain, and southern Gaul. Thus, for Christians, traffic was closed—east of Sicily by 650, westward by 700—so that Pirenne could quote with relish ibn-Khaldun's later judgment that "the Christians could no longer float a plank in the sea."

International trade between Gaul and the Levant dried up; no longer did ships bring to Marseilles rich cargoes of spices, silks, wines, jewels, papyrus, and oil. Gold coins went out of use. Only between Venice and Constantinople was there important business, exactly in those areas where Muslim seapower did not prevail.

The decline of the Merovingian monarchy in Gaul after the death of Dagobert in 639 coincides chronologically with the progressive decline of commerce after 650, and Pirenne would account for the loss of royal power by the decline of the chief source of royal revenue—the *impôt* on foreign trade. The landed aristocracy, unhurt by the decline in commerce, increased in relative power, and their civil wars, which the crown was unable to check, added to the impoverishment of the realm. It was from that landed class that the new dynasty, the Carolingians, derived—first as mayors of the palace, then after Pepin's coronation in 752 as kings. Significantly, the Carolingians represented not only the great landowners but Austrasia as well, the northern part of Gaul, less Romanized and less urbanized than the south. The political center of gravity in the west had shifted from the Mediterranean northward to the region between the Meuse and the Rhine.

Moved by antagonism toward the Byzantines and by fear of the Lombards, the popes allied themselves with the Carolingians, giving sanction first to Pepin's kingship, then to Charlemagne's *imperium*. Some unity was to come briefly to the west under emperor and pope, but the old unity of Romania was gone, broken into three rival power blocs, each with its own distinctive civilization—Islam, Byzance, and the Carolingian Empire. And, wrote Pirenne, "Without Mohammed, Charlemagne would have been inconceivable."

It was here, then, with the early Carolingians, that Pirenne would begin the Middle Ages, a period he would contrast sharply with antiquity. Medieval economy was largely a closed one, agricultural in the main and based on production for local consumption. There was little commerce and little town life. Society became stratified, with only three important classes—nobles, clergy, and servile peasants. Feudalism provided the political structure, the manor provided a living for all, and the church provided salvation and such artistic and intellectual life as was to be found.

In Pirenne's concept of the Middle Ages, *Mahomet et Charlemagne* is the obverse of the coin, *Medieval cities* the reverse. In either case he is concerned with a fundamental change in the structure of society; in either case he ascribes great significance to the role, positive or negative, of commerce; and in the one he challenges accepted dates for the beginning of the Middle Ages, in the other for the beginning of a proto-capitalism that presaged the dawn of the modern world. At the St. Louis meeting of the American Historical Association in December 1956, a speaker facetiously predicted the demise of the Middle Ages, with Pirenne chiseling away at one end and the twelfth-century Renaissance folk at the other. In a different context he might well have left Pirenne as the sole villain, for although Pirenne continued to use the conventional norms of periodization, the picture he paints of Italian and Flemish towns in the thirteenth century is hard to reconcile with the usual sentimental image of the medieval synthesis.

Medieval cities begins like a continued story, with a résumé of the earlier instalment, in which Pirenne describes briefly the Europe of Merovingian, Carolingian, and post-Carolingian times, the last with its feudal states, agricultural society, and closed economy. Urban life as we understand it, or as the Romans did, no longer existed; such cities as remained had shrunk physically and in population, losing all economic significance and all truly municipal institutions, and surviving only as royal or feudal or ecclesiastical administrative centers, until the very term *civitas* becomes synonymous with bishop's see. Venice, with its commercial contacts with Byzance and the paynim in Egypt, was the exception that proved the rule. In northern Europe continuing attacks from Vikings and Slavs and Magyars added to the unsettled state of society.

By the beginning of the eleventh century, however, some political stability had been achieved and once again the trade in Oriental goods began to quicken, in items light in weight and heavy in value and subject to the sort of mark-up characteristic of a speculative traffic in luxuries. These goods came along three well-marked routes: from Constantinople and the Black Sea, up the Dnieper, across the low watershed in Russia, and by river and Lake Ladoga to the Gulf of Finland and thence to Baltic or North Sea ports—the famed Varangian route; or, up the Danube and down the Rhine; or from Constantinople to Venice through the Adriatic, and thence by the Po and its tributaries to the north Italian towns or over the Alpine passes to Germany and France.

Who the new merchants were is unknown, nor is it apparent whence came their first capital. But it is clear that they were no longer Syrians and Jews as in Merovingian times, but westerners, and many must have been runaway serfs. At first they were migrants, peddlers with a bag or a pack animal, and for security they banded into caravan groups the better to resist robber barons and bandits, sometimes adopting a guild organization. Eventually this migrant and periodic type of trade was supplemented by a more settled form of commerce, and it is with the sedentary mercantile community that the urban revival is associated.

The exact process must have differed from region to region, especially between Italy and the transalpine lands. In Italy there had remained some contact through Venice with the east and some faint traces of town organization, and hence the revival came first in the towns of the Lombard plain. In the north the rebirth began in the lower valleys of the Rhine and the Scheldt. There, according to Pirenne, merchants settled under the walls of those fortified places used as a defense against Viking and Slav and Magyar, a place called variously *burg, bourg, castellum, civitas, cité*. Some were remnants of old Roman towns with the walls patched up; some were log palisades and blockhouses not unlike our frontier forts in colonial America. Thus, the early commercial settlement was *at* the burg, but not *in* it; it was *forisburgum* or *suburbium* or *portus*, not the burg itself. As the settlement grew, it was necessary to extend the walls and the distinction between the old town and the new town, still observable in many European cities, was born. Those communities favored by geographical or political conditions grew rapidly. By the late eleventh or early twelfth century the new merchant class found intolerable the rule by feudal or ecclesiastical prince. Some revolted and formed communes—a word as abhorrent to the ruling classes then as is the word "communist" today. Others won their freedom in less violent fashion. Eventually, the burghers took over the rule of the town and their rights, or burghal liberties, were set forth in the town charter which, with the town wall, became the guarantee of a free government in the midst of a feudal-agrarian-clerical world.

It is not necessary here to describe, as Pirenne did, the proliferation of town charters by king and baron, who found in the new merchant class a source of new taxes, nor to repeat his masterful analysis of the early development of a capitalistic spirit among the great merchants and industrialists who eventually turned the democratic commune into an oligarchy and so brought on the bloody class wars of the thirteenth and fourteenth centuries. His most original contribution lay in his theory of the origins of town life, and with that we may rest content.

It is perhaps too early to pass final judgment on the lasting value of these bold conjectures. Of the two, the burg-mercantile thesis has worn better, partly at least because Pirenne did not try to make it universal for all towns in all regions. Some scholars have tried to apply the formula to individual towns with varying success, and Carl Stephenson in his *Borough and town: a study of urban origins in England* (Cambridge, Mass., 1933) attempted to transfer the pattern into Norman England, an effort which has found both support and rejection from other scholars.[31]

From the earliest reviews *Mahomet et Charlemagne* has been extravagantly praised and roundly condemned. Schol-

[31] J. Tait, *Medieval English borough* (Manchester, 1936); A. L. Poole, *Domesday Book to Magna Carta* (Oxford, 1951), p. 505; H. M. Cam, "The origin of the borough of Cambridge: a consideration of Professor Carl Stephenson's theories," *Cambridge Antiquarian Society's Communications*, XXXV (1935), 33–53. Cf. J. L. Cate, "A decade of American publication on medieval economic history," *Progress of Medieval and Renaissance studies*, No. 16 (1941), pp. 19–20.

ars have questioned alike his views of Roman society and of medieval society, as well as his explanation of the process whereby the one was transformed into the other. Hardly a step in his complex argument has escaped rigorous scrutiny, followed by modification or rejection. The list of critics is a long one, including among others a number of Pirenne's own students.[32] So many of a younger generation have challenged Pirenne, indeed, that one cannot help thinking of the boxing profession where no young contender amounts to much until he has had a go with the old champ.

All this would have delighted the master had he lived on to continue the scholarly debate he had begun years before with Alphons Dopsch. He did not look on *Mahomet et Charlemagne* as a final statement. Elsewhere he agreed that "every attempt at synthesis is necessarily provisory," but that it was through such attempts that knowledge was advanced.[33] Again, "Every effort at synthesis, however premature it may seem, cannot fail to react usefully on investigations, provided one offers it in all frankness for what it is."[34] This is precisely how he offered his theses, crisply and without the cautious hedging that is the hallmark of the aca-

[32] Some idea of the literature may be had from the following incomplete list of studies: H. Laurent, "Les travaux de M. Henri Pirenne sur la fin du monde antique et les débuts du Moyen Âge," *Byzantion*, VII (1932), 495–509; P. Lambrechts, "Les thèses de Henri Pirenne sur la fin du monde antique et les débuts du Moyen Âge," *ibid.*, XIV (1939), 513–36; R. Lopez, "Mohammed and Charlemagne: a revision," *Speculum*, XVIII (1943), 14–38; D. C. Dennett, "Pirenne and Muhammad," *ibid.*, XXIII (1948), 165–90; A. R. Lewis, *Naval power and trade in the Mediterranean, A.D. 500–1100* (Princeton, 1951); Anne Riising, "The fate of Henri Pirenne's theses on the consequences of the Islamic expansion," *Classica et Mediaevalia*, XIII (1952), 86–130; E. Perroy, "Encore Mahomet et Charlemagne," *Revue historique*, CCVII (1954), 232–38; W. C. Bark, *Origins of the medieval world* (Stanford, 1958).

[33] *Histoire de Belgique*, VII, xi.

[34] "The stages in the social history of capitalism," *American historical review*, XIX (1913–14), 494.

demic historian, but also without dogmatism and with such evidence as was appropriate to the form he chose to use. Few historians of our time have prompted a more lively or fruitful discussion, both in published studies and in historical conferences; even in this country the Pirenne theses almost rival the Turner thesis as perennial favorites in the programs of the American Historical Association.

As he finished the last volume of his *Histoire de Belgique*, Pirenne gave his professional credo: "My sole end has been to seek to understand and to explain."[35] What more could a historian wish?

[35] *Histoire de Belgique*, VII, viii.

GEORGE MACAULAY TREVELYAN

1876—

George Macaulay Trevelyan, a recent student of historiography has written, has done more than any other living writer to restore history to its earlier station as a literary art which instructs and entertains the general public and professionals alike.[1] With this verdict there can be little quarrel. In essays and addresses, and above all in his own historical narratives, Trevelyan has made the case for imagination and historical insight. Over the course of a career spanning more than half a century, his love for, indeed his almost personal identification with, the living past has never

Henry R. Winkler is professor of history at Rutgers, the State University (New Jersey).

[1] Fritz Stern (ed.), *The varieties of history from Voltaire to the present* (New York, 1956), p. 227.

flagged. Reflecting aloud, late in his career, he summed up his attitude in a few evocative sentences:

How wonderful a thing it is to look back into the past as it actually was, to get a glimpse through the curtain of old night into some brilliantly lighted scene of living men and women, not mere creatures of fiction and imagination, but warm-blooded realities even as we are. In the matter of reality, there is no difference between past and present; every moment a portion of our prosaic present drops off and is swallowed up into the poetic past.

The motive of history is at bottom poetic. The patient scholar, wearing out his life in scientific historical research, and the reader more idly turning the pages of history, are both enthralled by the mystery of time, by the mutability of all things, by the succession of ages and generations.[2]

Beyond the poetic appeal of history, beyond even the light it might throw upon the present, Trevelyan saw in it also a moral purpose. Properly presented, history should help remove prejudice and train the mind of a citizen to take a balanced view of political questions. It must be the basis of humane education, opening out the culture of a nation to all its people, enabling them to savor its literary heritage by a knowledge of the past in which that heritage is rooted. It should breed enthusiasm, a sense of intellectual passion, an identification even with ideals and heroes from other ages. But, and here is the heart of all Trevelyan's work, enthusiasm and passion can only be aroused if the findings of history are communicated to the reader with grace, power, and emotion.

At the turn of the twentieth century, it can be argued, history as literature seemed well on its way toward a none-too-graceful exit from the field of English letters. With the Germanophile "scientific" school in the ascendant, a reac-

2 "History and the reader," An autobiography and other essays (London, 1949), p. 60.

33

tion had set in against the "literary" historians—Carlyle, Macaulay, Froude. Their failure to use "modern" research techniques was deplored, while the richness of their prose and the insight of their intuitions were shrugged away. History as a *story* dealing with past events was not particularly popular, at least among the professional historians. That the trend was halted is in no small measure attributable to Trevelyan's influence and example.

This is not to say that he rejected the so-called scientific aspects of history. In a famous early essay, he identified three distinct functions of his craft. The accumulation of facts and the sifting of evidence, he agreed, can properly be termed scientific. It is the "day labour that every historian must well and truly perform if he is to be a serious member of his profession." This is, however, but part of the task. Next, the historian must exercise the imaginative or speculative function, playing with the facts he has gathered, selecting and classifying them, making his guesses and generalizations. Finally, but assuredly not least, Trevelyan lists the literary function, the exposition of the results of science and imagination in a form that will attract as well as educate.[3]

He had few illusions about the difficulty of the literary mysteries. From the beginning he stressed the problems no less than the importance of creating a powerful narrative of historical events, pointing out that the "idea that histories which are delightful to read must be the work of superficial temperaments, and that a crabbed style betokens a great thinker or conscientious worker, is the reverse of the truth. What is easy to read has been difficult to write."[4] But, he argued, the results would be worth the effort. For the main

[3] "Clio, a muse," in *Clio, a muse, and other essays, literary and pedestrian* (London, 1913), pp. 30–31.

[4] *Ibid.*, p. 34.

works of historical scholars should be written not merely for the perusal of brother historians, but for the more receptive portion of the general public.

The young student too could learn much from such writers as Clarendon, Gibbon, Macaulay—even Scott. Taking Carlyle as an example, he declared that while he "is not to be imitated as a model historian . . . he should be read and considered by all historical students, because of his imaginative and narrative qualities. While he lacks what modern historical method has acquired, he possesses in the fullest degree what it has lost."[5] In similar fashion, Trevelyan admired Macaulay's ability to convey the drama and sweep of historical events. Throughout his writings on English themes, many of them "snatched from the heart of Macaulay's territory,"[6] he found occasion to correct the great Whig historian on numerous points of fact and interpretation. Yet he left no doubt that he would gladly exchange one Macaulay, with all his faults, for twenty more scientific modern historians.

Trevelyan's conception of history as art as well as science was conditioned by his sense of the inadequacy of all research techniques fully to uncover the actuality of the past. In characteristic prose, he outlined his attitude in his inaugural address as Regius Professor of Modern History at Cambridge:

The totality of past experience and action among European men, or even in the English nation alone in a limited period of years, presents a theme so vast and so intricate that we can only discuss it at all by making certain formulae or historical generalizations, which cover and shroud the variety and richness of the past. On the shore where Time casts up its stray wreck-

[5] *Ibid.*, p. 11. See also his brief article, "Influence of Sir Walter Scott on history," *An autobiography and other essays*, pp. 200–205.

[6] "G. M. Trevelyan," in Richard Church, *British authors: a twentieth century gallery* (London, 1943), p. 80.

age, we gather corks and broken planks, whence much indeed may be argued and more guessed; but what the great ship was that has gone down into the deep, that we shall never see.[7]

Finally, there is a quality in all of Trevelyan's work which merits attention. Whether he is sketching his vivid word pictures of the English past or marching with Garibaldi across the hills of Italy, his pages are informed by a deep devotion to the liberal institutions and optimistic ideals of his late-Victorian boyhood. If at times his liberal tolerance is brushed by a tinge of old-fashioned English chauvinism, his enthusiasm is most often captured by those traits and actions which have, in his view, enhanced the dignity of man.

Trevelyan's dual commitment to history and literature came to him almost as a heritage.[8] Born on February 16, 1876, he was the third son of Sir George Otto Trevelyan, historian, biographer, minor poet, and in an equally minor way, Liberal statesman. The elder Trevelyan was the author of an able and sympathetic history of the American Revolution, a brilliant picture of a bygone aristocratic society in his *Early history of Charles James Fox*, and a lively, rich, if rather uncritical biography of Macaulay. The great Whig historian was Trevelyan's great-uncle. The road which led to history was clearly a natural one.

In 1882, after the murder of Lord Frederick Cavendish, Gladstone offered Trevelyan's father the post of Chief Secretary for Ireland. For two years young George was in Dublin with his family, absorbing "a sense of the drama of English and Irish history . . . through daily sights and experi-

---

[7] *The present position of history: an inaugural address delivered at Cambridge, October 26, 1927* (London, 1927), p. 8.

[8] Biographical information from "Autobiography of a historian," *An autobiography and other essays*, pp. 1–51; Church, pp. 79–80; and J. H. Plumb, *G. M. Trevelyan* (London, 1951), pp. 7–12.

ences," with his father as teacher and guide. During this period too he began to develop a love for military history, so evident in all his later work. Moving long rows of small lead soldiers across the floor of his room under the careful instruction of the busy Chief Secretary, he learned more perhaps than from military manuals studied later in life. A "queer, happy little boy," he grew up to be equally at home in the liberal, tolerant, vigorous atmosphere of Victorian middle-class culture and in the sunset glow of a declining aristocratic society.[9]

Aside from the influence of his father, Trevelyan's education followed the normal pattern for a wealthy young man. At Harrow, he was the earliest "history specialist," studying under George Townsend Warner, himself an excellent scholar, and Robert Somervell, who taught both Trevelyan and Winston Churchill the mastery of English. Harrow led naturally to Trinity College, Cambridge, which he entered in 1893. At Cambridge, the pioneer work of Maitland and Cunningham captured his imagination, but he was put off by Seeley, who infuriated him by telling him that Carlyle and Macaulay were charlatans. Above all, he was influenced by Lord Acton, Seeley's successor as Regius Professor. More than Trevelyan's other masters, the great Catholic historian imparted to his students a feeling for great issues and their significance, for right and wrong, for the moral drama in history. Trevelyan himself has related how the History School

was so small that he was able to come into personal contact with a very large proportion of its members. Each man could receive individual counsel and encouragement in his own work. And collectively we learned to hold our heads high; under Acton's leadership we did not care how proud we were, for he

[9] See his *Sir George Otto Trevelyan, a memoir* (London, 1932), pp. 113–14, and Plumb, pp. 9–11.

had excited the imagination of the whole University and indeed of the country at large.[10]

After taking a first in the History Tripos of 1896, Trevelyan began immediately to consider a dissertation for a fellowship. With no intention of becoming a medievalist, he nevertheless chose a medieval subject. He saw the fourteenth century as a great turning point in English history, a period in which while medievalism was sick almost to death, the ideas of the modern world were forming in the greatest minds of the day.[11] Wycliffe and the Lollards attracted him because they bore the brunt of the first struggle for liberty of thought against the power of the medieval church "in all the prestige of a thousand years' prescriptive right over man's mind."[12] And beyond his sympathy with the movement for individual freedom, he interpreted the Peasants' Rising of 1381 as an outburst of national energy, a sign of the independence and self-respect which the medieval peasant bequeathed to the national consciousness of the English people as a whole.[13] Awarded a Trinity fellowship in 1898, Trevelyan offered his study to the public the next year as *England in the age of Wycliffe*. Shortly later, he published with Edgar Powell *The Peasants' Rising and the Lollards*,[14] a small volume of documents upon which much of his account was based.

England in the age of Wycliffe was a remarkable performance for a young man scarcely twenty-three when it

[10] *The present position of history*, pp. 12–13.

[11] *England in the age of Wycliffe* (reprint of the 4th ed.; London, 1948), p. 2. The first edition appeared in London in 1899.

[12] *Ibid.*, p. 352.

[13] *Ibid.*, p. 255.

[14] *The Peasants' Rising and the Lollards: a collection of unpublished documents forming an appendix to "England in the age of Wycliffe"* (London, 1899).

was completed. The book is primarily a narrative, sweeping along on a tide of colorful description and acute generalization, sketching in the lights and shadows of institutions and society, peopled by men who appear as men and not as cardboard manifestations of "historical processes." Even Wycliffe, about whom so little is known as a flesh-and-blood person, seems to come to life as his writings are analyzed in the chapters on religion. Above all, the Peasants' Rising itself erupts across the pages of the volume, suddenly bringing to focus the conditions under which the emancipation of the peasant took place and turning, in Trevelyan's own words, the manorial roll of the fourteenth century into a record of real and stirring life.

There are no doubt flaws in this brilliant first work. George Kriehn, whose criticisms Trevelyan incorporated in subsequent editions, and James Tait pointed out the limitations in his knowledge of the Middle Ages. He tends to rely too heavily on Froissart and so falls into unnecessary errors of detail. His partisanship for the cause of Wycliffe, so central to the main strength of his analysis, leads him into an aggressive anti-Romanism and a propensity to judge the medieval church by standards of a later day. The very exuberance of his youthful style results in passages which are overdrawn and overdramatic, in getting "the lights too high and the shadows too deep."[15] But these are faults which cannot conceal Trevelyan's achievement. This is indeed Whig history at its best, emphasizing the struggle for personal freedom against established tyrannies, viewing the past through the glasses of a self-confident liberal faith. If subsequent scholars have declined to accept some of Trevelyan's judgments, the numerous reprintings of England

[15] Reviews by James Tait in English historical review (hereafter cited as EHR), XV (1900), 161–65, and by George Kriehn in American historical review (hereafter cited as AHR), V (1899–1900), 120–22.

39

in the age of Wycliffe attest the lasting value of his one medieval study. It is still probably the best general account of its period available in English.

In 1903 Trevelyan decided to leave Cambridge. He wanted to write literary history, and he felt that he could do so in greater "spiritual freedom" away from the critical atmosphere of Cambridge scholarship. J. B. Bury's inaugural lecture as Acton's successor in 1902 had insisted on the study of history as a science, and Trevelyan was soon to publish *Clio, a muse* as his polemical answer. Apparently dissatisfied with his lecturing and teaching, he wanted more ample time to write. As a young man of some means, he could afford to be out of a paid job and so left Cambridge after the Lent term in 1903. He did not return in any formal capacity until 1927, when he accepted the Regius Professorship of Modern History.

Before Trevelyan left Cambridge he had agreed to write the volume on the Stuart period in Methuen's *History of England* prepared under the editorship of Professor Oman. *England under the Stuarts*[16] appeared shortly. Designed for the general public, the book has served historical students as well. The formidable Wilbur C. Abbott growled that, unlike the work of Gardiner and Stubbs, it made no great original contribution to knowledge, but acknowledged its strength in social history and in reconstructing the tenor of the period.[17] Trevelyan's Liberal sympathies are clearly with Cromwell and the Roundheads, but he is able to see the case for the Stuarts and the ultimate tragedy of internecine war. His interpretation, seen from a perspective of over fifty years, appears as balanced as his prose, which marks a real leap forward over his Wycliffe volume in carefully con-

16 London, 1904.
17 Review in *AHR*, XI (1905–6), 378–81.

trolled style. His story flows along at an easy, graceful pace, vigorous when strength is demanded, picturesque in its descriptions of a bygone England. Avoiding a conventional catalogue of dates and facts, it tries to ferret out motives and sentiments and to reproduce the atmosphere of each period under analysis. Curiously enough for Trevelyan, it is occasionally vague in indicating how or when an event took place, but never in assessing why. The general theme which informs this account is the importance of the Stuart era in laying the foundations for later British liberty and toleration. As Trevelyan saw the pattern:

At a time when the Continent was falling a prey to despots, the English under the Stuarts had achieved their emancipation from monarchical tyranny by the act of the national will; in an age of bigotry, their own divisions had forced them into religious Toleration against their real wish; while personal liberty and some measure of free speech and writing had been brought about by the balance of two great parties. Never perhaps in any century have such rapid advances been made towards freedom.[18]

While the professional historians gave the book a cool reception,[19] Trevelyan's achievement was recognized elsewhere. Thus *The Spectator* unerringly fixed on his chapter dealing with social history as the best in the volume, predicting that he was more likely than any of the younger men to attain some day the rank of a great historian.[20] For the public, certainly, *England under the Stuarts* definitely established Trevelyan among English historians. It has gone through some twenty-two reprintings and remains today one of the few textbooks that can be read for study and for pleasure in equal measure.

18 *England under the Stuarts* (1957 ed.), p. 429.
19 Plumb (p. 17) points to the unperceptive review by Professor C. Sandford Terry in EHR, XX (1905), 403–4.
20 See, for example, the review in XCIII (1904), 947–48.

The year of the publication of *England under the Stuarts* Trevelyan married Janet Penrose, daughter of a well-
known Victorian novelist, Mrs. Humphry Ward. It was
a felicitous match. Mrs. Trevelyan shared his love of walking and of bird lore, and became an accomplished historian
in her own right. She accompanied him on his excursions
into Central Europe and Italy, going over areas later
brought into vivid focus by his volumes on Garibaldi and
the Marlborough wars.

It was a chance wedding gift that turned Trevelyan's interest to the part played by Garibaldi in the unification of
Italy. For some years he worked eagerly in the libraries of
England and Italy, presenting his findings to the public in
three instalments.[21] But the Garibaldi trilogy represented
more than mere research in the libraries. For Trevelyan literally traversed by foot every step of the ground covered by
Garibaldi in the unsuccessful days of 1848–49 and in the
course of the more fortunate exploits of 1860. It was a labor
of love, for Garibaldi was the kind of man to awaken Trevelyan's enthusiasm. His courage, his color, his single-
minded patriotism, even his weaknesses as a "practical"
politician, provided magnificent material for the type of
history Trevelyan loved to write—rich, warm narrative dealing with a heroic theme and a sympathetic personality.

The Garibaldi saga fully repaid Trevelyan's interest, and
here one senses the perfect subject for his sparkling prose.
His later English volumes, particularly those on the era of
Queen Anne, were perhaps more highly polished, fuller in
portraying a period of history, more carefully balanced between description and analysis. But in these pages one rides
with Garibaldi across the South American pampas, shares

[21] *Garibaldi's defence of the Roman Republic, 1848–9* (London, 1907);
Garibaldi and the Thousand (London, 1910); *Garibaldi and the making
of Italy* (London, 1911).

his fixity of purpose in the face of odds that would have discouraged a more practical or a more clever man, fights his battles on the walls of Rome or in the mountains of Sicily, suffers with him as he carries his dying wife in his arms during the agonizing retreat from Rome. Trevelyan's Liberalism was above all a liberalism of the spirit, a deep feeling of communion with men fighting for country and for liberty. His passion and enthusiasm convey the courage and high adventure of Garibaldi's exploits and give the reader a unique sense of participation in the events described.

The three volumes brought to the fore a characteristic of Trevelyan's prose which remained conspicuous through his later works—a genius for describing military action with clarity and with authority. The confused rambling of guerrilla warfare, such as most of Garibaldi's campaigns were, was brought to life by Trevelyan's pen in some of the best passages in the books. His personal familiarity with the scenes of action undoubtedly contributed much to the final result, but familiarity alone would not have been enough without other qualities. Military knowledge, love of detail, and a sure feeling for the portrayal of action were the added ingredients.

But the Garibaldi volumes were more than a romantic story. Trevelyan contributed considerable new knowledge of the issues connected with his subject. The outstanding example was in *Garibaldi and the Thousand*, where he made use of unpublished papers of Lord John Russell and English consular materials to reveal the motives which led the British government to permit Garibaldi to cross the Straits of Messina.[22]

In looking back over the volumes, it is possible to find

[22] *Garibaldi and the Thousand*, pp. viii–ix, 104–5, 305–15.

43

errors of interpretation, some of which were not so evident at the time of writing. Thus Trevelyan repeats the story which pictured Victor Emmanuel as refusing to abandon the famous *Statuto* at the insistence of General Radetzky.[23] Later research has shown this part of the legend of the *Re Galantuomo* to be false.[24] Trevelyan accepts Italian nationalism with little analysis, he is unduly critical of papal and French policy, and he is more than generous in assessing British policy.[25] But fifty years later the trilogy still maintains a firm place in the list of standard works on the unification of Italy, a position cautiously prophesied by the reviewers at the time of publication.[26]

Trevelyan's *Manin and the Venetian revolution of 1848*,[27] his last major volume on an Italian theme, was written in a minor key. Published in 1923, it did not gain the popular acclaim of the Garibaldi volumes, probably because Trevelyan felt less at home with Manin, the bourgeois lawyer, than with Garibaldi, the filibuster. The complexities of Venetian politics eluded him, but the story of the revolution itself is told in restrained measures, with no superfluous passages and only an occasional overemphasis of the part played by its leading figure.[28] If it is not one of his best books, it can only be considered unsatisfactory when compared with his own *Garibaldi*.

[23] *Garibaldi and the making of Italy*, pp. 96–97.

[24] Howard McGaw Smyth, "The Armistice of Novara: a legend of a liberal king," *Journal of modern history*, VII (1935), 141–71; and "Documents relating to the Armistice of Novara," *ibid.*, VII (1935), 172–82.

[25] Plumb, p. 21; *An autobiography*, p. 32.

[26] See, for example, reviews by W. Miller in *EHR*, XXII (1907), 816–17, XXV (1910), 206, XXVII (1912), 173–75; H. Nelson Gay in *AHR*, XIV (1908–9), 134–36; and W. R. Thayer in *AHR*, XV (1909–10), 613–15, XVII (1911–12), 376–78.

[27] London, 1923.

[28] Reviews by H. Nelson Gay in *AHR*, XXIX (1923–24), 552–53, and W. Miller in *EHR*, XXXIX (1924), 135–36.

Already Trevelyan had begun to parallel his nineteenth-century Italian studies with several works on English figures of the same period. First *The life of John Bright*[29] appeared and seven years later *Lord Grey of the Reform Bill.*[30] Of the two, the life of Bright is incomparably the better biography. Trevelyan centers too exclusively on Bright, is insufficiently appreciative of the views of Bright's opponents and critics, and makes light of the genuine difficulties faced by Peel. Yet he is right when he claims in his autobiography that he drew the real features of the man, his tender and selfless motives and his rugged fearless strength. In the story of Bright and the Corn Law agitation, the Crimean War, the American Civil War, and the franchise struggle Trevelyan reflects something of the moral power which enabled this independent man to exercise so immense an influence over his fellow countrymen for so long. Because Bright's speeches were so much a part of him, there are long and numerous quotations, which, far from making the biography diffuse, help to give us the feel of the man. Associated in a sense with the Manchester School through his mother's family, Trevelyan conveys in this biography something of its moral conviction and drive. Nineteenth-century virtues, however, seem somehow to have gone out of fashion and the Bright book has never been particularly popular.

The biography of Lord Grey is strictly speaking not a biography at all. It is a Whig history of the "Tory reaction" which preceded the Reform Bill of 1832, and it uses the figure of Grey to give some unity to the narrative. The volume is a piece of passionate special pleading, written with the heat—and often with the wisdom, it must be said—of a Liberal damning the shortsightedness of politicians from

[29] London, 1913. [30] London, 1920.

1782 to 1832. Characteristically, Trevelyan enjoyed writing the work. The theme of glorious summer coming after a long winter of discontent and repression was, he has told us, congenial to his artistic sense. And Grey's Northumberland background was close to Trevelyan's own.[31] But his concentration on personalities and his categorical assessment of their actions fail to convey the political complexities of a long generation harassed by world-wide war and confronted with the problem of adjustment to an unprecedented industrial and social transformation. Some historians have found his point of view not to their taste, others have complained that he makes the Tory tradition appear "contemptible rather than intelligible," while a sympathetic critic has remarked that the "intricate interplay of social dynamics and political activity of which, at times, politicians are the ignorant marionettes is not a field for the exercise of his talents."[32] The Liberal-Radical heritage which informs all of Trevelyan's interpretations of history here seems clearly to have distorted the issues and oversimplified the period. For once his touch deserted him.

Research in the period of Grey and Bright led naturally to a more ambitious work. *Britain in the nineteenth century*[33] is a textbook designed "to give the sense of continuous growth, to show how economic led to social, and social to political change, how the political events reacted on the economic and social, and how new thoughts and new ideals accompanied or directed the whole complicated process."[34] The plan is admirably fulfilled for the period up to 1832. More temperately than in the study of Grey and despite his Liberal bias, Trevelyan vividly sketches the England of pre–

[31] *An autobiography*, p. 34.

[32] Reviews by C. E. Fryer in *AHR*, XXVI (1920–21), 90–91, and W. Hunt in *EHR*, XXXV (1920), 457–60. Also, Plumb, pp. 22–23.

[33] London, 1922.   [34] P. vii.

French Revolution days, portrays the stresses and strains of the revolutionary period in rich colors, and brings developments leading to the Reform Bill into sharp and clear focus. His technique is genuinely masterful. By what one reader called a "series of dissolving views,"[35] he merges one period into another and gives a sense of continuous growth.

But after 1832, the narrative tends to lose its balanced, many-sided quality and to become a medley of topics, often unconnected by any single thread. Economic analysis was never Trevelyan's strong point and the England of the industrial transformation cries out for economic analysis. Yet after 1832, the interrelations of economic and social and political affairs become blurred and the narrative becomes largely a conventional political account.[36] Finally, the period after 1870 receives little attention and that quite superficial. Yet *Britain in the nineteenth century* became the *vade mecum* of beginning students of history, went through edition after edition, and continues to be reprinted up to the very present. Its success is a tribute, above all, to Trevelyan's brilliance as a literary stylist.

In 1924 Trevelyan traveled to the United States, where he delivered the Lowell lectures at Harvard University. These lectures formed the nucleus of a general survey of English development which took form afterward as a *History of England*.[37] In short order, the general history became his most popular work and has remained, aside from his later *Social history*, the work most widely favored by the public.

The *History of England* has often been compared with

[35] Sidney B. Fay in The Independent, CIX (1922), 140–42.
[36] Review by G. A. Hedger in AHR, XXVIII (1922–23), 114–15.
[37] London, 1926.

47

Green's *Short history*.[38] Like Green, Trevelyan aimed to write a history not of "English kings or English conquests," but of the English people. The result was fortunate. The *History* takes too much for granted to serve as a text for other than English schoolboys, and like *Britain in the nineteenth century* it deteriorates badly as it goes beyond 1870. Trevelyan's excursions into contemporary history were rarely happy ones. But as a stimulating, provocative interpretation of the broad sweep of English development it is incomparable. Living pictures of the early boroughs, country life in Tudor and Stuart times, the impact of the industrial revolution compete with sensitive surveys of language and literature, the common law, parliamentary development. The strength of the *History* is also its weakness. Trevelyan is militantly sure of the superiority of English institutions and character over those of other peoples. His nationalism was not a new characteristic, but its self-consciousness, even its self-satisfaction, is more obvious in a book that stretches over the long reach of English history. And yet the elements which capture his liberal and humanistic imagination are those which make the English story worth telling and worth remembering. Tolerance and compromise, social justice and civil liberty, are today too often in short supply for one to be overly critical of Trevelyan's emphasis on their central place in the English tradition. Like most major works of synthesis, the *History of England* is informed by the positive views of a first-class mind, and this is surely a major work.

Four years after the publication of the *History of England*, the first volume of Trevelyan's Queen Anne trilogy

[38] E. P. Cheyney in *AHR*, XXXII (1926–27), 570–72; Church, p. 79; Plumb, p. 24.

GEORGE MACAULAY TREVELYAN 48

appeared.[39] By now he had become Regius Professor of Modern History at Cambridge and had been honored by the award of the Order of Merit. His academic duties had little evident effect on his prolific pen. *Blenheim* was followed in rapid succession by *Ramillies and the union with Scotland* and by *The peace and the Protestant succession,* the three forming together a detailed picture of *England under Queen Anne.* Like his volume on Wycliffe, the work was accompanied by the publication of a selected group of documents, in this case illustrative of the history of Queen Anne's reign down to 1707.[40]

Trevelyan was at least in part attracted to the period by an almost unconscious desire to take up the story where Macaulay's *History of England* had broken off. In addition, he believed in the "dramatic unity and separateness of the period from 1702–14, lying between the Stuart and Hanoverian eras with a special ethos of its own." He saw the age as one in which Britain "settled her free constitution" and attained her modern place in the world.[41] To most observers, there is little doubt that he placed an artificial strait jacket of unity upon the years of Anne's reign which in reality existed only in the pages of his history.

Of the three volumes, *Blenheim* is easily the best. In four opening chapters reminiscent of Macaulay's famous third chapter, Trevelyan surveys the state of England at the opening of the eighteenth century. His delightful picture of society and institutions is filled with warm detail that brings the period vividly to life. He tends to under-

---

[39] *England under Queen Anne: Blenheim* (London, 1930); *Ramillies and the union with Scotland* (London, 1932); *The peace and the Protestant succession* (London, 1934).

[40] *Select documents for Queen Anne's reign, down to the union with Scotland, 1702–7* (Cambridge, 1929).

[41] *An autobiography,* p. 46.

estimate—or perhaps to view charitably—the brutality and the violence of the age, so that there is an idyllic quality in these pages which hazes over some of its sharp reality. Yet as an evocation of time past, there are few such successful portraits in English historical literature.[42] Once the scene is set, Trevelyan skilfully builds up the tense story until it reaches its climax in the dramatic victory of Marlborough and Eugene of Savoy at Blenheim. The account of the battle is, next to his descriptions of Garibaldi's campaigns, Trevelyan's outstanding military narrative. The scene is etched in sharp detail, the military problems brilliantly explained, and the excitement and importance of the battle made evident.[43] If only for this modest masterpiece of military history, *Blenheim* is likely to be read and reread long after newer interpretations have perhaps altered our picture of the Marlborough wars.

Ramillies and the union with Scotland has fewer high spots than *Blenheim* and much less of its dramatic unity. Yet in several chapters on Scotland in the eighteenth century, Trevelyan copes persuasively with the tangled confusion of Scottish politics against a vivid background of Scottish religion, customs, and traditions.[44] These chapters, it is true, lack the easy at-homeness[45] of his impression of eighteenth-century England. As in that account, Trevelyan is less concerned with the governed than with their superiors, but, more importantly, he is perhaps less effective in conveying the feel of the Scottish environment than of the English. Yet once again his skilful exegesis brings interest to a period that may otherwise lay claim to being among the dullest in English history.

42 *Blenheim*, pp. 1–103.   43 *Ibid.*, pp. 378–95.

44 *Ramillies and the union with Scotland*, pp. 174–219.

45 Review by Violet Barbour in *AHR*, XXXIX (1933–34), 119–20.

The peace and the Protestant succession offers less opportunity for colorful narrative, but the involved unfolding of Whig and Tory policy leading to the peace gives Trevelyan scope to develop an interpretation based, more than most of the Queen Anne study, on fresh new research in the documents. From material discovered in the French archives, he is able to reinterpret the early history of the peace negotiations. He demonstrates particularly that Harley and the Earl of Jersey had more to do with their inception than St. John, to whom earlier historians had given most of the credit.[46] Despite his own Whiggish sympathies, he concludes that the Tory demand for peace had been a wise one and that England had been well served by the replacement of Godolphin's influence by that of Harley and St. John.

The three volumes did much to restore the reputation of Marlborough, even before the publication of Winston Churchill's "work of family piety."[47] Trevelyan was not granted access to the papers at Blenheim Palace, but his assessment of Marlborough agrees in the main with that of Churchill. He takes issue with the devastating portrait sketched by Macaulay. Emphasizing the duke's military genius and pointing up the non-military qualities which were an essential part of his greatness, Trevelyan denies that he was any more venal or corrupt than most men in public life at the time. The intrigues with the Jacobites, so condemned by Macaulay, are portrayed as "insurance" against a possible restoration, a type of hedging indulged in by most of his contemporaries.

One of Trevelyan's most distinguished students has regretted the choice of period for what was evidently de-

[46] *The peace and the Protestant succession*, pp. 176–82.
[47] Trevelyan's phrase in *Blenheim*, p. vi.

signed as his masterwork. J. H. Plumb points out that the tortuous complexity of men and issues in Anne's reign was less appropriate to Trevelyan's historical talents than, for example, the Italy of Garibaldi or the England of the Stuarts. "Backstairs politics," he comments, "the worldliness and cynicism of men seeking power at all costs, twisting and debauching institutions to get it, is not a world in which Trevelyan moves with instinctive ease."[48] In addition, he quite properly notes, Trevelyan's view of the period is distorted by his belief in the historical continuity of the two-party system in English political life.[49] The basic struggle for power in Anne's age was much more a matter of family and territorial connections than of the play of party controversy. Trevelyan's assessment of the issues of the period is therefore much too simple.

All this is true, yet one is still tempted to call *England under Queen Anne* Trevelyan's best work. While specialists have elucidated the weaknesses of his interpretations,[50] its three volumes remain the standard general account of early eighteenth-century England. Above all, its style represents the full fruition of Trevelyan's literary abilities. It is quieter yet firmer in tone than his earlier works, and its polished sentences seem perfectly in tune with the eighteenth-century society it describes. One critic has justly summed up these volumes, in academic language quite unlike that of Trevelyan, as "an epic of English historiography restoring

48 Plumb, pp. 28–30. The Tory historian Sir Charles Petrie makes much the same comment about "the last of the great Whig historians." The age of Anne, he notes in a review of *Blenheim*, "was not an heroic era like that during which the unification of Italy was accomplished, and the historian of the Thousand fails to make Marlborough another Garibaldi" (*Saturday review*, CL [1930], 410).

49 "The two-party system in English political history," *An autobiography and other essays*, pp. 183–99.

50 See, for example, the reviews by W. T. Morgan in *Journal of modern history*, III (1931), 486–88, and VI (1934), 192–94.

the entente between history and literature without severing its alliance with the most modern apparatus of critical research."[51]

While *England under Queen Anne* marked one of the peaks of Trevelyan's historical writing, it was far from his last contribution. In 1932, he published a sketch of the life of his father, Sir George Otto Trevelyan, which gives us a great deal of insight into the author himself. Some years later appeared a life of Viscount Grey.[52] Grey of Fallodon was a subject in whom Trevelyan could delight: statesman, naturalist, scholar, "the last representative of that great Liberal tradition which inherited from the Whigs of the eighteenth century a tradition believing in an aristocracy of intellect based upon an authority of moral order."[53] The book is a warm appreciation of Trevelyan's Northumbrian neighbor, but he so admired the distinguished foreign secretary that he is overly generous on Grey's position during the July crisis. His summation of Grey's career, although it may not be good history, is almost a summation also of all the things he valued in the annals of his own country:

For many troubled years, and at one terrible crisis, he had represented England at her best—her reasonableness, her justice, her desire for peace and friendship between all, and with that her determination not to be frightened into a submission or dazed into a tardiness that would allow one Power time to enslave the world. He was more complex in character than people knew, but in thought he was simple and in purpose direct and firm, and those are qualities which his countrymen usually understand better and value more than versatile cleverness and the artistry of change.[54]

[51] Review by Rev. N. Sykes in *EHR*, L (1935), 152.

[52] *Grey of Fallodon: being the life of Sir Edward Grey afterwards Viscount Grey of Fallodon* (London, 1937).

[53] Church, p. 80.

[54] *Grey of Fallodon*, p. 365.

53

Shortly after the publication of *Grey of Fallodon*, Trevelyan wrote a volume on the English Revolution for the Home University Library. This brief, popular recital was neither so erudite as his *England under Queen Anne* nor so comprehensive as *England under the Stuarts*, but it presented the same essential conclusions. He portrayed the revolution as a "sensible" one, which built the institutional structure upon which later English development rested. As he saw it, the true "glory" of the revolution "lies not in the minimum of violence which was necessary for its success, but in the way of escape from violence which the Revolution found for future generations of Englishmen."[55] Deceptively simple, *The English Revolution* summarizes in a way Trevelyan's lifetime interest in the problems of the seventeenth century.

Finally, 1942 saw the appearance of his *Social history*, which surveyed English life and institutions over a period of six centuries.[56] Because of World War II, Trevelyan was forced to abandon his original plan to begin with Roman times, and lack of paper in England caused the book to be published first in the United States. As a result of these circumstances, it did not receive the final polish of some of his other works, and at times his definition of social history as the history of a people with the politics left out is patently unsatisfactory. Yet as another labor of love the volume is one of Trevelyan's most fascinating. In a sense, the theme of the *Social history* is the rise and fall of rural England.[57] His affection for a pre-industrial society is clear and his most sympathetic descriptions are reserved for a

55 *The English Revolution, 1688–1689* (London, 1938), pp. 7–9.

56 *English social history, a survey of six centuries: Chaucer to Queen Victoria* (New York, 1942).

57 T. C. Mendenhall in *AHR*, XLVIII (1942–43), 776–77.

depiction of rural life. The pages contain less about the common man, about his thoughts and problems, than about the country families, great and humble, whose way of life came to fruition and disappeared during the centuries in question. But in his "series of scenes divided by intervals of time," he makes, amid the horrors of a world in flames, a nostalgic affirmation of the richness and worth of the English experience in the years between Chaucer and Queen Victoria. The book has had an astonishing attraction for Trevelyan's fellow countrymen. Over 400,000 copies have been sold, and its almost bittersweet evocation of their past is likely to appeal to Englishmen for many years to come.

The *Social history* was Trevelyan's last major work. In 1940, Winston Churchill had offered him the Mastership of his beloved Trinity College and here he served until his retirement in 1951. His influence on Cambridge has probably been more marked than on Cambridge historians, but his influence on the general field of English history has been profound. As a member of the scholarly guild he has more than paid the required fee of contributions to knowledge. In using new documents on the Peasants' Rising, in analyzing British policy in the Garibaldi war, in tracing the early peace negotiations toward the end of Anne's reign, he brought to light materials of wide importance to all scholars in the fields in which he chose to labor. But above all, though some would raise the claims of Tawney or Fisher, recent English historiography has produced no one to equal him as a stylist, no one who could make the past come to life so meaningfully and so vividly. He has founded no new school of history, but he has accentuated the merit of an older school. By his commitment and by his example, he has reminded his professional colleagues that history can be read not only as a "discipline" but for pleasure as well. The reception of his works has shown that the educated and intelligent public has learned the lesson well. If Trevelyan towers above other English historians of his time it is because he has had the secret of making all that he has written, in his own words, "a stirring narrative of past events."

GORDON H. MC NEIL

GEORGES LEFEBVRE

1874–1959

Georges Lefebvre was born in Lille, in the Nord Department, in 1874, and here he spent the first half of his life.[1]
His father was a commercial employee, and it was thanks
to a series of scholarships to the newly established Ferry
school system and the University of Lille that the young
Lefebvre received his education. It is interesting to note
that he made his first trip to Paris, less than 150 miles
away, at the age of twenty-four, for the oral examination

Gordon H. McNeil is professor of history at the University of Arkansas.

[1] Biographical details may be found in the following sources: *Annales
historiques de la Révolution française* (hereafter cited as *Annales*), No. 102
(1946), pp. 185–86; No. 106 (1947), pp. 188–90; No. 159 (1960),
passim (this is a memorial issue consisting of articles on Lefebvre by students and colleagues); Georges Lefebvre, *Études sur la Révolution française* (Paris, 1954) (hereafter cited as *Études*), "Notice biographique";
R. R. Palmer, "Georges Lefebvre: the peasants and the French Revolution," *Journal of modern history*, XXXI (1959), 329–42; Marcel Reinhard, "Un historien au XXe siècle: Georges Lefebvre," *Revue historique*
(hereafter cited as *RH*), CCXXIII (1960), 1–12; Beatrice Hyslop,
"Georges Lefebvre, historian," *French historical studies*, I (1960), 265–82.

for the *agrégation*. There then followed a long period, from 1898 to 1924, of teaching in various lycées in the provinces and finally in Paris. It was, as he frankly recorded it, a life of poverty, with both a family and relatives to support. It was also a life of obscurity. Even after he began to teach in Paris, he had no contacts with intellectual circles; and Jaurès, whom he so admired, he never saw except from a distance at a public meeting.

If it was a life of obscurity, and undoubtedly of frustration, it nevertheless was also a life of sober, serious scholarship, which was to continue for the rest of his life. There were the long years spent laboriously gathering the data from hundreds of local archives and writing his impressive thesis, *Les paysans du Nord pendant la Révolution française*,[2] which earned him the doctorate at Paris in 1924 and the notice of his colleagues.[3] The supplementary thesis was his already published *Documents relatifs à l'histoire des subsistances dans le district de Bergues* (1789–an V).[4] In the long introduction to this work he antedated the contributions of Mathiez to the history of the impact of economic regulation during the revolution. He was to return to the subject of the history of the peasants in 1932 with his *Questions agraires au temps de la Terreur*.[5]

On receiving the doctorate at Paris, he held successive appointments at the universities of Clermont, Strasbourg, and Paris; and in 1937, at the age of sixty-three, he followed Sagnac in the chair of the history of the French Revolution at Paris, which he held until, having reached the age of

[2] 2 vols.: Paris, 1924. A one-volume edition, minus the documentation and statistical material, was published in Bari, Italy, in 1959.

[3] For an account of the reception and critical analysis of this book from the perspective of a generation later see the article by Palmer.

[4] 2 vols.: Lille, 1914, 1921.

[5] Strasbourg, 1932; 2d ed., La Roche-sur-Yon, 1954.

sixty-seven in 1941, he was retired. But he continued to lecture, almost without compensation, during the Vichy regime, until his final retirement after the war.

Lefebvre's scholarly activity never ceased. His first interest as a student had been in medieval history and, since early in his career (when he had already shifted his interest to the revolution) he had need of the additional income it offered, he found time to prepare a three-volume translation of Stubbs's *Constitutional history of England*, and he wrote sections of his own for the third volume. This of course was simply a diversion, and his promotion to university lecturing foreshadowed a more consequential field of publication. The first result was his collaboration with Guyot and Sagnac in writing *La Révolution française* for the "Peuples et civilisations" series.[6]

There was also more yet to come on the peasants and the revolution. The year 1932 saw off the presses both his *Questions agraires au temps de la Terreur*, already mentioned, and *La Grande Peur de 1789*,[7] which represents an unprecedented fusing of the author's prior interest in the status of the peasants, as revealed in the local documents, with a newer interest in what may be called social-psychological history. In later years he referred to this as the work with which he was most pleased.[8]

Three years later there appeared his *Napoléon* in the "Peuples et civilisations" series,[9] which was outside the range of his immediate interest, but which was a skilful synthesis of existing knowledge and the insights which he

[6] Vol. XIII, Paris, 1930.   [7] Paris, 1932.

[8] Letter to author, September 10, 1946. See the comments of Reinhard on this (p. 7).

[9] Vol. XIV, Paris, 1935. For a detailed review, which is quite laudatory, see Pieter Geyl, *Napoleon, for and against* (New Haven, 1949), pp. 421–49.

brought to the Napoleonic era from his knowledge of the preceding period. There followed the small volume, *Les Thermidoriens*, in the popular Colin collection,[10] which provided a continuation of the three volumes on the revolution in that series by Mathiez. It in turn was followed after World War II by *Le Directoire*,[11] which completed the series.

Just prior to the outbreak of World War II, for the celebration of the one hundred and fiftieth anniversary of the revolution, Lefebvre contributed—literally, for he accepted no royalties—his *Quatre-vingt-neuf*,[12] a brilliant summary of the events and larger significance of that fateful year, which in the translation by Robert Palmer,[13] widely circulated in a paperback edition,[14] is undoubtedly his best known work in this country. The final volume in the long and distinguished list, which was published in 1951, was a new edition of *La Révolution française*. The work was now his alone, reflecting on the one hand his long years of personal research and extensive reading in the monographic literature, particularly in the social and economic area, and on the other his deeper insight into such subjects as, for example, the psychological origins of the Terror.[15]

In the meantime there had appeared numerous articles and periodic bibliographical essays on the revolutionary and Napoleonic periods in the *Revue historique*, plus a steady stream of book reviews in the *Annales historiques de la Révolution française* (which he edited from 1932 until his

[10] Paris, 1937.   [11] Paris, 1946.   [12] Paris, 1939.

[13] *The coming of the French Revolution* (Princeton, 1947).

[14] New York: Vintage Books, 1957.

[15] See for example the admirable analysis of the European economy and society on the eve of the Revolution (chaps. ii and iii), and the discussion of the origins of the Terror (pp. 401–9: compare pp. 249–53 of the earlier volume).

death), many of which were in the Macaulay tradition, presenting more of Lefebvre's conclusions than of the books themselves.

Lefebvre always conceived of himself as a research scholar who might advance hypotheses and write surveys but whose starting point and solid foundation were always the primary sources, the indispensable documents.[16] For him history must be based on *érudition*—a word he used frequently—and, echoing the aphorism of Seignobos, "No documents, no history," he maintained that "without scholarship, there can be no history."[17] Thus he was bluntly critical of history which was not firmly based on the sources[18] and also of historians who had slighted scholarly research in favor of interpretative writing no matter how well done, even if they were as eminent as Carl Becker.[19]

A more distinctive and personal contribution to the historiography of the revolution was his use of the statistical approach to social and economic history. His thesis had been solidly based on numerous statistical analyses of the sources concerning such matters as landownership and transfer, and class distribution. If in social history one is to study large groups of the population, instead of merely the relatively few who compose the upper classes, as he insisted one should,[20] the statistical method, he maintained, was the only way of arriving at reliable conclusions. "Il faut

[16] For a discussion of Lefebvre's conceptions of historical method, see Jean Suratteau, "Georges Lefebvre, historien politique," *Annales*, No. 159 (1960), pp. 32–46, which is based in part on several articles and lectures which the present author was not able to see.

[17] "Recherche et congrès," *RH*, CCVI (1951), 2.

[18] See for example his review of a book which presumed to present proofs concerning the supposed Masonic conspiracy on the eve of the revolution, in *Annales*, No. 101 (1946), p. 73.

[19] *Ibid.*, No. 117 (1950), 82–85.

[20] "Avenir de l'histoire," *Études*, p. 3.

compter" was a familiar refrain in his discussions of method.[21] Of course he also wrote that all history cannot be recorded in curves on a chart, and that there is always the unique and imponderable; but he repeatedly urged that wherever appropriate the statistical methods of the natural sciences be used.[22]

This certainly applied to the study of social structure, which he realized was the least developed field of history. He was personally aware of the inability of any one person to study more than a single locality and class, and he therefore concluded that significant results could be arrived at only as such methods were used in carefully planned, co-operative efforts.[23] This had been seen at the beginning of the century by Jaurès, who had organized in 1903 a co-operative project for the study of the economic history of the revolution, and Lefebvre contributed to it his study of the food supplies of the district of Bergues already mentioned, as well as his subsequent work on agrarian problems during the Terror. When he assumed the chair of the history of the French Revolution at the Sorbonne he actively encouraged co-operative research. He directed the reorganized Institute for the History of the French Revolution[24] and played a leading part in promoting a co-operative program of research and publication, sponsored by the commission founded by Jaurès, on the French bourgeoisie from the end of the old regime to the Restoration. By the time of his death—twenty years, another world war, and a num-

21 "Un colloque pour l'étude des structures sociales," Annales, No. 147 (1957), pp. 100–101.

22 Remarks of E. Labrousse in Bulletin de la Société d'Histoire Moderne, 12th ser., No. 11, p. 6.

23 "Recherche et congrès," pp. 1–3; Albert Soboul, "Georges Lefebvre, historien de la Révolution française," Annales, No. 159 (1960), pp. 12–13.

24 Annales, No. 102 (1946), pp. 185–86.

ber of national and international conferences later—some progress had been made.[25] At these conferences Lefebvre had discussed methods and problems, he had encouraged any and all co-operative efforts in the columns of the *Annales*, and he had participated in the work himself, having at the time of his death written a few chapters for a pilot study of the bourgeoisie of Orleans.[26]

In any historiographical study one is concerned not only with the methods used by the historian being studied, but also with his particular viewpoint and biases, and his philosophy of history. In the case of Lefebvre, this is no simple matter, for his philosophy and viewpoint can best be called pluralistic or eclectic.[27] There is in his writings and lectures a refreshing absence of dogmatic assertion, for he was no system builder, and he firmly resisted the temptation to simplify when actually writing history. He was critical of oversimplified doctrines of historical causation, and even the much admired Jaurès came in for censure for presenting what Lefebvre considered to be an overly simple explanation of the causes of the revolution.[28] Lefebvre's eclecticism and his lack of dogmatism are neatly illustrated in his conclusion to a review of the various theories concerning the origins of Napoleonic imperialism: "In each of these in-

[25] Reports of progress and future plans, together with extracts from Lefebvre's contributions, appear in *ibid.*, No. 91 (1939), pp. 86–88; No. 94 (1939), p. 374; No. 97 (1940), pp. 56–61; No. 102 (1946), p. 186; No. 105 (1947), pp. 73–82; No. 142 (1956), pp. 104–5; No. 144 (1956), pp. 328–31; No. 147 (1957), pp. 99–105; No. 148 (1957), pp. 278–80; No. 153 (1958), pp. 1–13. See also Marc Bouloiseau, "De Jaurès à Georges Lefebvre: la Commission d'Histoire Économique de la Révolution," *ibid.*, No. 159 (1960), pp. 57–66.

[26] MM. Schneider, Braudel, Labrousse, and Renouvin, "Les orientations de la recherche historique," *RH*, CCXXII (1959), 39.

[27] His approach to these topics was summarized in a series of lectures at the Sorbonne in 1946 on "Notions d'historiographie moderne" and in several additional articles which the author has not seen.

[28] "La Révolution française et les paysans," in *Études*, p. 247.

terpretations, one finds a part of reality, but reality is something more than all of them."[29]

One element of the reality that was Lefebvre was the fact that he was a Frenchman. There was an earnest patriotism which appeared in his lectures and writings, and in 1945 he wrote with old-fashioned bluntness of his having continued to lecture at the Sorbonne during the Vichy period in order to prevent "treason" from placing one of its adherents in his place.[30] One detects the same sense of earnest nationalism two years later when he quoted in a very emotional passage the statement by Robespierre opposing the appointment to the Committee of Public Safety of a man who had participated in the surrender of Valenciennes to the enemy.[31] But his most eloquent statement was the final paragraph in his *Quatre-vingt-neuf*, which was addressed to the youth of France. It invoked the glorious tradition of the revolution and closed with a "Vive la Nation."[32]

This of course is loyalty to the France of the revolutionary tradition, and more specifically for him, to the Jacobin democratic and social republic of 1793–94.[33] On the occasion of the centennial of the revolution of 1848, Lefebvre proudly affirmed that he was a Jacobin, if one wished to call him that, but certainly not the last, for he hoped there were others less old; and he ended the speech with an emotional apotheosis of the republic.[34] It should be noted, and

[29] *Napoléon*, p. 144.   [30] Letter to author, October 11, 1945.

[31] *Annales*, No. 106 (1947), p. 190.

[32] Pp. 246–47. This was omitted from the translation. See also his extremely nationalistic analysis of the "Marseillaise" in his Sorbonne lectures ("La chute du roi," "Les cours de Sorbonne," pp. 88–91).

[33] "Sur la pensée politique de Robespierre," *Études*, pp. 95–98.

[34] "Le 24 février 1848," *1848 et les révolutions du XIXe siècle*, XXXVII (1946), 15–17.

65

it is not unimportant, that this republic meant to him both the equality implied in the ideal of social democracy, and also liberty; and he took the occasion just before his death to remind his readers in the Russian-controlled zone of Germany of the perennial problem of providing institutional safeguards for personal liberty in the face of recurring attempts to deny it.[35]

Lefebvre never wrote a biography, and his preference for groups rather than individuals as the subjects of his study was quite definite.[36] His Napoléon was the history of an era, not of a man; but his treatment of the "great man" par excellence of modern history gives us insight into his conception of the role of the individual in history. His analysis of Napoleon's personality and character is a classic of balanced historical interpretation,[37] the theme of which is that "before all, Napoleon is a tempérament."[38] The basic explanation, although not the complete explanation, for his foreign policy, for example, lies in his ambition, in the irresistible promptings of his character.[39] In the conclusion, Lefebvre presents a carefully weighed analysis which balances the impersonal factors in prior historical developments against this basic tempérament, but he makes no attempt to assess the relative importance of these two forces—simply saying that the man had had considerable influence, but only to the extent that he operated in the mainstream of European history.[40]

Lefebvre was much intrigued throughout his career by

[35] "A la mémoire de Maximilien Robespierre," in Maximilien Robespierre 1758–1794: Beiträge zu seinem 200. Geburtstag, ed. Walter Markov (Berlin, 1958), p. 13. Palmer (p. 334) has called attention to the interesting fact that Lefebvre's essay is the only one of the many written by non-Germans for this volume which was not translated into German.

[36] Suratteau, pp. 43–44.

[37] Pp. 60–66.

[38] P. 62.   [39] P. 145.   [40] P. 565.

the psychological element in history, but it was social-psychological rather than biographical history which was of particular interest to him. In his article, "Foules révolutionnaires," published in 1934,[41] he urged historians to study the collective mentality. This to him was the connecting link between antecedent conditions and resulting events. In the case of the French Revolution, analysis of the mental *contenu* of each class has been recognized as a notable contribution to this scarcely explored field of history. Such of course was his *La Grande Peur*, together with the not very well-known case study entitled "Le meurtre du comte de Dampierre."[42] What interested him particularly, and it is a pity he did not write a general study of the subject, was what he called "le complexe révolutionnaire."[43] By this he meant the specific psychological pattern associated with the "complot aristocratique." It included first a fear of an aristocratic conspiracy against the revolution, a defensive reaction, and then a "volonté punitive" which, he insisted, was one of the keys to the history of the revolution.[44] He makes no attempt to apply some of the newer psychological insights and theories to this pattern, and he has been criticized for this. Having defined the phenomenon, as he saw it in the documents, he simply noted its persistence throughout the revolution until, as he wrote, the "fever" subsided with the military victories of 1794.[45] For Lefebvre this was the basic psychological pattern, and it is a frequent theme in his books, lectures, and reviews.

For one as closely concerned with social and economic history as Lefebvre was, the economic interpretation of events was inevitably a large part of historical reality. But

[41] Reprinted in *Études*, pp. 271–87.

[42] Reprinted in *ibid.*, pp. 288–97.

[43] He referred once to his dossier on this subject in *Annales*, No. 101 (1946), p. 84.

[44] *La Révolution française*, pp. 131–33.   [45] *Ibid.*, p. 409.

as we have seen, it was only part of the total reality in his pluralistic conception of history. He had no sympathy for the doctrinaire economic determinist, yet in his eclectic philosophy of history there was a prominent place assigned to economic factors, and he was constantly alert to see their influence on the political, social, and cultural story, and quick to criticize those who failed, in his opinion, to see their significance.[46]

He acknowledged the influence on his early thinking of French Marxists, notably Jaurès;[47] he took for granted a Marxian "dialectical march of history," for example in the conclusion to *La Révolution française;*[48] and he applied this particular theory to various topics of revolutionary history. Time and again he assumed that the class struggle was a fundamental factor in history, that it was "the principal motive force in history."[49] But in spite of this terminology, he was actually quite free, when describing the course of events and the interplay of multiple causes, from the dogmatism of the extreme Marxist; and in his personal politics he could, so his friends have reported, support the Communist party while not joining it.[50] When one recalls his family background and early life, one can understand his sometimes sharp and acid feelings on the subject of class,[51] as well as such phrases in his writings as the "harsh

[46] See for example his sharp criticism of Herman Wendel's *Danton* on this point in "Sur Danton," *Études,* p. 30.

[47] "Pro Domo," *Annales,* No. 106 (1947), p. 189; Soboul, p. 3.

[48] P. 638.

[49] *Annales,* No. 117 (1950), 81, 85; "À propos d'un centenaire," *RH,* CC (1948), 6–7.

[50] See the interesting analysis in René Garmy, "Georges Lefebvre et l'homme (Souvenirs)," *Annales,* No. 159 (1960), p. 83.

[51] See for example the analysis in his preface to *Die Sansculotten von Paris: Dokumente zur Geschichte der Volksbewegung 1793–1794,* ed. Walter Markov and Albert Soboul (Berlin, 1957), p. ix.

egoism of the bourgeoisie" and the "cascade de mépris."
He sought in this way to characterize the bitter consciousness or sense of class.[52] On occasion he could be quite blunt
on the subject of the interests of the well-to-do—for example, in explaining the lenient treatment of hoarders by
bourgeois jurymen during the Terror. As he put it in one
of his postwar lectures, when hoarding is a current problem,
wolves do not eat one another.[53] He was similarly harsh in
his criticism of Tocqueville for sharing the fear and rancor
of his class.[54] Several years before his death he went so far
as to state that certain reinterpretations of the French and
English Revolutions, such as the suggestions of Professor
Cobban concerning the "myth of the French Revolution,"
reflected the reaction of a dominant class which felt men-
aced by the upsurge of democracy and the Russian Revolution.[55]

Such distortions are not, however, typical. Much more
typical is his cautious and scholarly analysis of social class
structure, and of the role of social class in shaping the
course of events during the revolutionary era. Herein lies
one of his most important contributions to the historiography of the French Revolution. Students of the revolution
in the nineteenth century were aware of the importance of
class considerations. Occasionally they were too aware of
it, and Marx, as every schoolboy at least in Russia knows,
defined all history as the history of class struggles, thus sore-
ly complicating the task of subsequent historians with his
oversimplification of the class structure and its significance.

---

[52] Quatre-vingt-neuf, p. 52; Le Directoire, p. 147.

[53] "Le gouvernement révolutionnaire (2 juin 1793–9 Thermidor II),"
"Cours de l'École Normale Supérieure de Sèvres," p. 140.

[54] "Le 24 février 1848," p. 11; "Introduction" to Alexis de Tocqueville,
L'ancien régime et la Révolution, Œuvres complètes, II (Paris, 1952), 15.

[55] "Le mythe de la Révolution française," Annales, No. 145 (1956), p.
344.

Non-Marxists had other ideas concerning class, but they and the Marxists both lacked the facts which only detailed research could provide.

It was Lefebvre who, brushing aside the verbiage about the "dialectical march of history," and following the lead of Loutchisky and several others, really inaugurated the scholarly study of class structure in the revolutionary period with his research on the peasants. Years of archival work made him particularly alert to the complexities of class structure, the wide variations from region to region, and the fact, often forgotten, that social structures change. His detailed work on the peasants of the Nord Department is a classic case study in complexity and change, even though it is confined to the peasants of a single department in a single decade. In Le Directoire he presented in just a few pages—in sharp contrast to the study of the Nord peasants —a fascinating summary of the class structure at that time, indicating the extreme state of flux which prevailed as a result of the impact on society of the revolution and the many changes which had accompanied it.[56] As a historian he showed little interest in the contributions of sociologists and social anthropologists to an understanding of social class; perhaps he was not aware of the work being done. On the complicated and much discussed subject of the criteria for determining class, his mind was made up. The basic consideration in determining social class, within what had been the third estate, was wealth and income, and therefore the class distribution in a particular community was to be reconstructed from fiscal records concerning income and property.[57] He recognized, however, that a document re-

[56] Le Directoire, pp. 144–47.

[57] Soboul, p. 16. He was continually alert to evidence of this sort. See for example the long review of a brief article based on such documentation for Toulouse in Annales, No. 122 (1951), pp. 198–202.

cording contemporary opinion concerning class status in a particular city might be of value.[58]

His conclusion concerning the rural class structure, in summary, was that the peasant population (leaving aside the non-peasant residents) consisted of a "dominant class" —the "cock of the village" category of well-to-do *fermiers* and *cultivateurs*; a middle class or *petite bourgeoisie paysanne*, which together with the first category comprised the rural bourgeoisie; and at the bottom of the scale the rural proletariat, consisting of *ménagers* and *journaliers*.[59] When he suggested a classification of urban society, he proposed a four-part structure: a dominant class, a middle class, a popular class, and a proletariat of manual laborers.[60] These classifications of the population are a healthy corrective to the oversimplified distinction between bourgeoisie and proletariat which, he repeatedly said, distorted the history of the revolution, and which he found exemplified in two recent works on the period.[61] Conversely it is one of his chief claims to a prominent place in the historiography of the revolution that he analyzed its course in the light of the complexities of class interest, going more deeply than his predecessors had into the actual class considerations which influenced events. When he repeats a familiar theme, such as that of the bourgeois victory of 1789, he does so with a sense of nuance and insight which is a welcome contrast to Jaurès and Mathiez, for example.[62] But the more

[58] *Annales*, No. 138 (1955), pp. 80–82.

[59] *Les paysans du Nord pendant la Révolution française*, pp. 40, 321; *Questions agraires au temps de la Terreur*, p. 69. Cf. "La Révolution française et les paysans," *Études*, pp. 250–51.

[60] "Un colloque pour l'étude des structures sociales," pp. 104–5.

[61] *Annales*, No. 106 (1947), pp. 175, 177; No. 156 (1959), p. 171.

[62] See his discussion of the community of interests, in spite of antagonism on other matters, between aristocracy and bourgeoisie in the capitalistic organization of agriculture ("La Révolution française et les paysans," *Études*, p. 258); and *La Révolution française*, pp. 155–62.

significant contribution is twofold: (1) his identification of the *sans-culotte* group as consisting not only of the urban and rural proletariat but also of the much more politically important popular category of artisans and shopkeepers in the cities and the *petite bourgeoisie* in the villages; and (2) his explanation of how class considerations within this pattern had a definite but limited effect on the course of events.

Once a united third estate in the cities and a "bloc paysan" in the countryside had overthrown the old system of privilege in 1789, there then arose conflict within this victorious "popular front." In the villages, the mass of small proprietors and modest *fermiers* and *métayers* were strongly attached to the traditional communal pattern of collective rights and regulations, with all of the advantages these had for the little man; while the rural bourgeoisie was oriented, by economic interest, toward the modern pattern and legal concepts.[63] The resulting economic conflict was reflected in the political story. The rural, upper bourgeoisie, at outs with the poorer peasants on this and other issues, was uneasy over the threat to its economic dominance,[64] and rightly so, for during the Jacobin republic of the year II the ruling Mountain followed a policy of conciliating the poorer peasants.[65] But then came a reaction which brought the dominant group back into authority in the villages.[66]

A similar conflict developed in the cities over the economic policies made necessary by the impact of revolution

[63] *Les paysans du Nord pendant la Révolution française*, pp. 70–71, 110–11, 254, 425 ff., 906; "La Révolution française et les paysans," *Études*, pp. 250, 263.

[64] *Les paysans du Nord pendant la Révolution française*, pp. 321–24, 798–803.

[65] *Ibid.*, pp. 430, 477–78, 863.

[66] *Ibid.*, pp. 695, 865.

and war, ranging the sans-culottes—the proletariat plus the popular category of artisans and shopkeepers—against the more well-to-do bourgeoisie, or notables. In Lefebvre's opinion numerous controversies of the period stemmed from this conflict, for example the opposition of the sans-culottes in Lyons to the insurrection, which they saw was an upper bourgeois enterprise.[67]

The theme of his books on Thermidor, the Directory, and the Napoleonic period is that the urban and rural upper class reasserted itself, with a heightened consciousness of class as a result of its experiences; and that it did so in a social hierarchy which eventually united the notables, the old upper bourgeoisie, the nouveaux riches of the war years, and the former aristocracy.[68] This was the group which finally completed the bourgeois revolution and took possession of the French government in 1830.[69]

Mention should be made of still another aspect of Lefebvre's scholarly and eclectic approach to the history of social class. While he sees class considerations as affecting such varied decisions as those that fixed the fate of the king and the details of the voting system, he nevertheless disagreed at times with the class interpretation of events. Thus he differed with Mathiez on the economic policies of the year II, and specifically the Ventôse decrees. These, according to Lefebvre, were only a "mesure de circonstance" and not a plan to reorganize society.[70] He contended that the Convention, although a bourgeois body,

[67] Annales, No. 101 (1946), pp. 74, 76.

[68] Les Thermidoriens, pp. 12–13, 54, 107, 198–200, 212–13; La Révolution française, pp. 420–29; Le Directoire, p. 195; Napoléon, pp. 4, 68, 119, 134–38, 408, 412; Les paysans du Nord pendant la Révolution française, pp. 695, 865.

[69] La Révolution française, p. 637.

[70] Ibid., p. 398.

sometimes worked against the interests of its class because its primary concern was not to defend those interests but to win the war.[71]

May one, less than a year and a half after Lefebvre's death, attempt an assessment of his place in the historiography of the French Revolution? Such an evaluation at this early date is risky. Yet certain conclusions seem to be evident.

Lefebvre was the leader in the twentieth-century movement in the direction of the scholarly study of the social and economic history of the French Revolution, and of the peasants in particular; and by both example and exhortation throughout his long career as scholar, professor, and editor he gave a strong stimulus to the careful, professional, and analytical work which so clearly distinguishes his own writing (and that of those who have followed his example) from earlier attempts to describe social and economic developments during the revolution. Yet he had no idea that he had achieved a definitive understanding of French society during that period, and the theme of tentativeness—that more work must be done, that new insights and hypotheses would and should appear—runs through all his work. Hence also the cordial reception he accorded to the recent studies of writers in the area of social history who further refined his work on class.[72]

Belonging to an older generation, he himself made very little use of the insights of the various social sciences which were developing during his lifetime. He thought that perhaps psychoanalysis would some day make a contribution to historical understanding, but he felt that that day had not

[71] Ibid., pp. 546–49.

[72] See for example his reviews of recent books by Soboul and Rudé in Annales, No. 156 (1959), pp. 164–73, 174–77.

yet arrived.[73] His own characterization of Napoleon as a *tempérament* was a first step, in his opinion, in the direction of a sort of biological-psychological approach to history, but he was careful to say that this was just a hypothesis.[74] His work on the Great Fear and his emphasis on the "complot aristocratique" during the revolution, as well as his studies of class structure, took him to the borders of social psychology and sociology, and also, when he studied the peasant village, to the borders of social anthropology as well. He affirmed that history in the future should join forces with these related disciplines,[75] but he himself was cautious. He was reluctant to stray very far from his documents, and he avoided easy formulas.

Lefebvre united the caution of the research scholar, ever aware of his dependence on his documents, with a willingness at least to consider new methods, whether they be statistical or psychoanalytical. This combined approach he applied both to economic and social history on the one hand, and to a newer category of social-psychological history on the other. Herein lies his significance in the historiography of the French Revolution.

[73] *Ibid.*, No. 120 (1950), p. 392.

[74] *Ibid.*, No. 136 (1954), p. 268. See also his comments on this in "Quelques réflexions sur l'histoire des civilisations," *ibid.*, pp. 102–3.

[75] "Avenir de l'histoire," *Études*, p. 6.

HAROLD T. PARKER

HERBERT
BUTTERFIELD

1900—

The pursuit of knowledge in some subjects, such as political science, lends itself easily to immediate helpfulness. The
pursuit of other studies, such as history, contributes to wisdom. To the mature historian the chief value of his investigation is not its ultimate achievement, the delicate, pre-
carious definition of historical truth, but rather the by-
product which gradually accrues, the growing understanding
of human affairs. The chief problem of the historian is how
to communicate that deeper understanding which he believes he has attained to readers or listeners who have not
passed through the same process of investigation and reflection that he has. Among contemporary British authors
Professor Herbert Butterfield of Cambridge University has
probably been most successful in communicating a historian's wisdom, not only in his volumes of essays but also in
his narrative histories which at their best exemplify with

Harold T. Parker is professor of history at Duke University.

remarkable fidelity the theory of historiography to which he is devoted.[1]

"The genesis of historical events," in Butterfield's opinion, "lies in human beings. If we take all the individuals of France at a given moment in 1789, they represent so many separate wells of life, so many sources of decision and action. The bustling activity of these people, the thoughts of their brains, their desires and self-assertiveness, their constant adjustments to situations" are the subject matter of history.[2] The historian tries to enter into these personalities, to describe and explain their thoughts and actions, and the interweavings among the individuals. He acquires a certain feeling for the subtlety and texture of historical events. He comes to sense the elasticity of history. He becomes aware that human beings, never entirely good, never entirely evil, are frequently caught in predicaments for which no single individual or group is to blame.

Thus, before World War I, foreign ministers, chancellors, and military chiefs of staff, responsible for national security, naturally felt that their country should be armed with military power superior to that of any potential rival. They increased its armament. The rival, actuated by apprehension, responded with an augmentation of his force. The original

[1] In the preparation of the essay I am indebted to the South Atlantic quarterly for permission to reprint three paragraphs from my review of Herbert Butterfield's History and human relations and to the members of my graduate seminar in Modern European History for kindly reading and discussing Butterfield's books with me. The members of the seminar included Richard Brashares, Mary Cubbison, John Cunningham, Tyler Deierhoi, William Halloran, Glenn Harper, Alf Heggoy, Marshall Jarrett, Edward Jones, Leland Lengel, John Moore, Joseph Morrison, Henry Porter, Larry Richman, Patrick Sowle, and Vernon Stumpf. I am profoundly grateful also to two of my colleagues, Professors John Fisher and William T. Laprade, for reading the essay in manuscript and offering numerous suggestions. No one but myself, however, is responsible for the errors remaining.

[2] History and human relations (London, 1951), p. 66. All footnote references are to books or articles by Butterfield unless another author is indicated.

country, for additional protection, then formed an alliance with a third power. The rival, in retaliation, tried to arrange a counteralliance. And so on, back and forth in a mounting spiral of anxiety which culminated in war. Or again, in the parliamentary crisis of 1779–80 there was something to be said for George III and Lord North and against their opponents, the Rockinghamites. On both sides there was "the play of vested interests, the sheer struggle for places, profits, and power," and on both sides there were honest men.[3] And, as in the background of World War I, out of the clash of wills arose a situation which no one had willed.

The historian absorbed in describing the delicate intricacy of this process of historical change is repelled by the crudeness and rigidity of single-line interpretations such as the Marxian, however suggestive their details may be. Nor does he desire to pass moral judgment on individuals who, like himself, are a mixture of human frailties. To raise the question of right and wrong arrests the historian just as his inquiry may be leading to deeper levels of understanding. Moreover, the historian is not equipped by his training or apparatus to decide ethical issues. He may describe and explain a massacre; he can give evidence that Napoleon lied or that Pope Alexander VI poisoned people; he may term a man a coward, a fanatic, or a drunkard, but for the historian to condemn or exonerate is to overstep the bounds of his competence and to distort the angle of his description.

This type of academic history which seeks the subtle comprehension of the past is consonant, Butterfield holds, with Christian belief. The historian is interested in the drama of human personalities; Christianity, likewise, finds each "individual soul of eternal moment."[4] Even as the historian

[3] George III, Lord North, and the people, 1779–80 (London, 1949), p. viii.

[4] Christianity and history (New York, 1949), p. 28.

declines to pass judgment on fellow human beings, so the Christian, feeling that all are sinners, all are poor in the sight of God, hesitates to condemn others. The historian approaches the problems of evidence and explanation with intellectual humility and flexibility of mind. He tries to empty himself of personal views and valuations. Christianity also encourages elasticity of thought. The Christian "can be prepared for any surprises" in history, for "he need put no limits to the Creator's versatility." Devotion to God, furthermore, rescues the Christian from devotion to the nation, to a secular cause, or to an abstract noun, to those fanaticisms which often twist the modern historian's account. A confident reliance upon God frees the historian to discover and describe flexibly "complication and change," "the web spun out of the play of time and circumstance,"[5] and thus to lead himself and his readers toward the enlarged thinking so necessary to an understanding of the past and present.

Butterfield had reached these essential ideas about history and its study before he was thirty-one years old. He was born in 1900, and they were expressed for the most part in his second major book, The Whig interpretation of history, published in 1931. They have formed the basis of all his articles and books ever since. Eventually, when his diaries and letters and the successive drafts of his printed works become available, it may be possible to trace the origin and inner development of his views. Meanwhile, it is possible to do something just as important: to describe the application of his essential ideas to five fields of historical knowledge and theory, indicate the special insights he has reached in each of these fields, and appraise the quality of his general and specialized understanding.

[5] The Whig interpretation of history (London, 1950 ed.), pp. 65–66.

Butterfield frequently admonishes the reader to walk alongside a historical character, put on the character's thinking cap, and see the situation and problems as he viewed them. Perhaps it would not be unfair to apply the same approach to Butterfield. If we did, we should have to spend imaginatively most of our time at Cambridge University, for he has been associated with that institution in one connection or another for over forty years, as Scholar of Peterhouse College in his youth, as Fellow of Peterhouse from 1923 to 1955, as Master of Peterhouse since 1955, as University Professor of Modern History since 1944, and most recently as Vice-Chancellor.

His first book, *The historical novel*, which was awarded the Le Bas Prize for 1923 at Cambridge, revealed his youthful preconceptions about the writing of history. The historian, in his opinion, "loves the past for its own sake and tries to live in it, tries to live over again the lost life of yesterday."[6] He uses the accumulated traces from the past "to recapture a bygone age and turn it into something that is at once a picture and a story."[7] He recovers the adventure of the lives of his historical characters, and forgets what came after. "To the men of 1807 the year 1808 was a mystery,"[8] and with them the historian does not see what lies around the next turn of the road. At the same time that Butterfield was having these ideas he was being trained by a master historian of diplomacy, Harold Temperley, in the tradition of writing diplomatic history "of high and complicated texture."[9]

With the conception of history as both resurrection and story and with the ideal of diplomatic history as a high and

[6] *The historical novel* (Cambridge, 1924), p. 8.
[7] *Ibid.*   [8] *Ibid.*, p. 23.
[9] "The Teach yourself history library," *History*, N.S., XXXIII (October 1948), 202.

noble art, Butterfield undertook the task of describing the diplomatic interchanges which accompanied the campaigns of Napoleon against the fourth coalition, from the Prussian collapse at Jena to the end of the negotiations by which Russia, Prussia, and Austria, after Tilsit, tried to persuade England to treat with France. Butterfield's youthful ideals about history-writing tended to determine both his problems and his solutions. If he was to see Napoleon, Hardenberg, Alexander I, Stadion, or Canning in the actual process of thinking, he had to seek the evidence that most closely mirrored their thoughts. He had to visit the Public Record Office in London, the Archives of the Ministry of Foreign Affairs in Paris, the Court and State Archives in Vienna, and the libraries containing the printed correspondence drawn from the Prussian and Russian archives, and he had to peruse the reports from ambassadors, ministers, and spies which came to the leading statesmen by day and their replies which went out by night. Also, if the account were to resurrect personalities and events once alive, the young Butterfield's narrative had to be as vivid as he could make it.

The result of his efforts was a 375-page volume, *The peace tactics of Napoleon, 1806–8* (1929), a work of high achievement. To be sure, the book has its faults. The title is something of a misnomer, since Butterfield spends as much time in the camps of Napoleon's antagonists as he does in that of Napoleon. The author, furthermore, might have consulted the folios of the French National Archives, to thicken his presentation of French policy. And a scholar who has read the Russian documents on Tilsit may be permitted to question whether Alexander ratified the new system "with his heart."[10] In the light of the evidence, a plausible alternative interpretation is that Alexander, in or-

[10] *The Peace tactics of Napoleon, 1806–8* (Cambridge, 1929), p. 303.

der to test and exploit the possibilities of the new arrangements with Napoleon, may well have entered into them wholeheartedly but not with his heart, which would have been a very different matter. Nevertheless, when all reservations have been stated, the volume remains a superb achievement. What might have been a blow-by-blow, that is a summary-of-dispatch by summary-of-dispatch, chronicle became in Butterfield's hands a creative narrative, characterized by skilful exploitation of the documents, telling character sketches, the recapture of shifting moods and atmosphere, a dense vocabulary reflecting richness of thought and images, and acute awareness of "the strange tangle, the hidden undercurrents and the clash of personalities that lay behind a Napoleonic war"[11]—in brief, a vivid exposition of complexity. Unforgettable and distinctive is the portrait of Napoleon as a genius who could, like Einstein, perceive the implications of a new circumstance for the overturn of a currently held theory or policy, reshuffle his universe of policy in accord with the implications of the new circumstance, and then push the implications of the new theory or policy to their utmost practical conclusions.

The success of the *Peace tactics* prompted the publishers, Gerald Duckworth and Company, to invite Butterfield to contribute a brief life of Napoleon to their Great Lives series. Through his work on the *Peace tactics*, Butterfield had become aware of "the complexity of human change and the unpredictable character of the ultimate consequences of any given act or decision of men."[12] He had come to believe that a history, even a short account, should attempt to communicate the texture of that complexity. In addition, by the time he wrote the volume for the Great Lives series, he had acquired theories about how history moves—way-

[11] *Ibid.*, p. vii.
[12] *The Whig interpretation of history*, p. 21.

wardly and through the interacting adaptations of individuals to problems; about how reform should be accomplished —gradually and tactfully, with a feeling for how consequences proceed out of actions in the historical process; and about how Providence operates—mysteriously, deflecting men's labors to unpredictable results. Complexity, waywardness, unpredictability, and mystery in history are more easily communicated in a detailed narrative of many words than in a short biography.

In the *Peace tactics*, Butterfield had been at ease. He had had approximately 130,000 words to describe a single aspect of Napoleon's activity during a period of only six months, from October 1807 to April 1808. For the Great Lives series Butterfield was apparently allotted only 30,000 words to recount the entire life of this many-sided genius, Napoleon, the key figure in the entire Western world when complicated Europe reached a peak of complication as it passed through revolution into a new era. In a few thousand words how could Butterfield state the bare, indispensable facts about Napoleon and his times, and still communicate to a popular audience the complexity of historical change? Butterfield's solution in part was to tell a narrative of indispensable information, and to form the narrative in such a way that it had the qualities of complexity, unpredictability, and waywardness that he believed the movement of history possessed. The narrative is, in a sense, a symbolic construct. It does not re-present the past, but it represents Butterfield's conception of its movement. The solution has true narative and expositional economy. Each word, in effect, buys two objects: a story of what happened and a theory about the way things happen. Also, the narrative permitted Butterfield to comment on the proper conduct of diplomacy, the accomplishment of reform, and the ways of Providence. One need compare only the early pages of

Herbert Fisher's *Napoleon* with those of Butterfield to appreciate the superior sophistication and density of the latter's account.

From the early 1930's until recently Butterfield has been pursuing several lines of investigation concurrently. Even while composing his brief *Napoleon*, published in 1939, he embarked on a large-scale biography of the eighteenth-century Whig, Charles James Fox. Fragments and by-products of this enterprise appeared in two articles in the *Cambridge historical journal*, "Lord North and Mr. Robinson, 1779" (1937), and "Charles James Fox and the Whig Opposition in 1792" (1949), and in two books, *George III, Lord North and the people, 1779–1780* (1949), and *George III and the historians* (1957). In 1947 a committee was formed "to establish the teaching of the history of science on a regular footing at Cambridge University," and Butterfield was appointed chairman. To inaugurate the new program he delivered a series of lectures which were published in 1949 as *The origins of modern science, 1300–1800*. The study begins at the Middle Ages, when men took their picture of the workings of the world largely from Aristotle, and it traces the gradual emergence of new views in dynamics (the University of Padua and Galileo), celestial mechanics (Copernicus, Kepler, and Newton), anatomy and physiology (Vesalius and Harvey), and methodological theory (Bacon and Descartes). It closes with lectures on "The place of the scientific revolution in Western civilisation" ("it outshines everything since the rise of Christianity and reduces the Renaissance and Reformation to the rank of mere episodes"),[13] on the delayed revolution in chemistry (Lavoisier), and on eighteenth-century adumbrations of evolutionary ideas.

Meanwhile, as Butterfield wrote history, he became self-

13 *The origins of modern science, 1300–1800* (London, 1949), p. vii.

conscious about his activity. He pondered the ways of great historians, the successive phases of the historiography of a controversial subject, the nature of everyday historical occurrences, and the relation of such occurrences to spiritual interpretations of the universe. His reflections appeared, most notably, in two articles in *History*, "The *Teach yourself history* library" (1948) and "The role of the individual in history" (1955); in four books, *The Whig interpretation of history* (1931), *The Englishman and his history* (1944), *Christianity and history* (1949), and *Man on his past* (1955); and in a collection of essays, *History and human relations* (1951). The publication of three major works, *The origins of modern science; George III, Lord North, and the people;* and *Christianity and history*, mark 1949 as a year of fruition for Butterfield.

It is a *tour de force* for a general historian to attempt a history of science, for the inner logic of scientific discovery and the decisive mathematical and technological considerations in a scientist's mind may elude him. Butterfield brought to the attempt a belief long ago expressed in *The historical novel* that a historian should steep himself in the past and live over its thoughts; an ability, exhibited in his portrayals of the moods and ideas of Alexander I and Napoleon, to describe imaginatively subtle and delicate transpositions of mind; a theory, alluded to in *Napoleon*, that momentum in history derives from individuals solving problems; and a zeal for transmuting and translating technical history for the non-student world. In brief, he brought to the history of science an approach which involved for the historical investigator a self-emptying of current preconceptions, an imaginative walking alongside historical characters and seeing the world as they viewed it from time to time, and, finally, a focusing on the particular intellectual problems which puzzled a historical generation and whose solu-

tion involved a change in men's ideas about the world. Butterfield was interested in portraying the moving transposi-
tion of ideas taking place in the minds of his scientists.

Where monographic investigation provided the material
for the exercise of this approach and for Butterfield's gift of
imaginative sympathy, and where scientific change had proceeded largely through the alteration of men's ideas about
physical circumstance, the lectures have marvelous insight
and appeal. The lectures on the theory of impetus, on Copernicus, and on Newton are models of narrative explication of subtle changes in mood and atmosphere in transi-
tional centuries. An occasional lecture is less satisfactory. In
some instances, the detailed monographic preparation, indispensable to Butterfield's approach, is wanting. In two
cases, the discussions of Galileo and of the chemical revolution, Butterfield unaccountably abandons his approach of
walking alongside the historical characters and offers not a
description but a commentary which baffles the uninitiated.
In addition, the nature of Butterfield's own education leads
him to stress the ideational aspect of the growth of science
and to neglect the role of experiment. He even seems to
confuse observation of nature with experiment, that is with
observation under controlled conditions. One would never
guess from his discussion that men of science spent a good
deal of time in the laboratory. Probably as a result, he is not
as fortunate in describing scientific change that proceeded
less from the alteration of men's ideas about old data than
from the irruption of new experimental facts. These occasional lapses derived not from a defect in Butterfield's approach but from a failure to be consequent in its application. Whether from lack of monographic preparation or
from haste in getting up the lectures, or from an intellectual's constitutional antipathy to manual labor, Butterfield
sometimes fails to walk alongside the scientist as he en-

tered the laboratory, to stand beside him as he worked with his hands, and to share his excitement as new evidence spouted up before his eyes. When the approach was applied, however, as it was in most of the lectures, the result was a depth and subtlety of insight never before reached in a published work on the origins of modern science.

It should not astonish anyone that two books (*Origins of modern science* and *George III, Lord North, and the people*) published by the same author in the same year should exhibit the same virtues and defects. In both works the virtues derive from the soundness of the basic approach and from Butterfield's flair for imaginative understanding of historical characters, and the shortcomings from his failure to apply his own principles rigorously. One can surmise how *George III* came to be written. In the process of investigating the life of Charles James Fox, Butterfield noticed that Fox's participation in the extra-parliamentary agitation of 1779–80 at the impressionable age of thirty was the most important political experience "which went to the shaping of his mind"[14] and shaped his activity through the rest of his life. Also Butterfield concluded that the political activity of these years (actually, eighteen months from January 1779 to July 1780) formed "an important chapter in the political education of the British people"[15] and began the national movement for parliamentary reform. He explored these months and began to compose a narrative, which in his view ran as follows.

The American war was going against Great Britain. Burgoyne had surrendered in 1777, and in the spring of 1778 Clinton withdrew from Philadelphia to New York. France and Spain entered the conflict, and in August 1779 the combined Franco-Spanish fleet rode unchallenged outside of

[14] *George III, Lord North, and the people*, p. 224.
[15] *Ibid.*, p. 219.

defenseless Plymouth and withdrew only by reason of disease and disorganization in its own ranks. An invasion of England or Ireland seemed to be threatening. The Irish leaders, reacting to a stagnation in Irish agriculture and manufacture aggravated by the restrictive British commercial policy, were forming committees of correspondence and bands of armed volunteers and entering into non-importation agreements. The chief minister, Lord North, although charming, good-humored, and adept in debate in the House of Commons and hence useful to George III, was at best a poor executive. Now, dejected and despairing, he drifted into inaction and allowed appointments, military and naval preparations, and negotiations with the Irish to slip into chaos. George, not the tyrant of Whig imagining but an anxious ruler struggling to save an empire, tried privately to toughen North's policy through intrigues with North's intimate advisers, John Robinson and Charles Jenkinson. Almost inadvertently and in response to immediate need, George thus increased his participation and influence in the government. The British were distressed by the military and naval reverses and by the inadequacy of the ministers and were feeling the burden of war taxes and of commercial dislocations.

In this situation Wilkes revived in a Middlesex by-election the cry of violation of freedom of election, and promised to move in the House of Commons an inquiry into the true cause of British misfortunes. According to Butterfield, a Yorkshire clergyman, the Reverend Christopher Wyvill, organized in December 1779 a meeting of Yorkshire landowners and persuaded them both to petition parliament for the elimination of waste in public expenditures and to form a committee of correspondence to promote the objects of the petition. In January and February, other counties and the city of Westminster drafted similar petitions and established committees of correspondence. Wyvill and other leaders envisaged the consolidation of these committees of representative property-owners into a national body which would demand constitutional reform: the annual election of parliament and the addition of one hundred county members to the House of Commons. The Rockingham faction of Whigs, which was in opposition to North and the king, attempted to take the petitioning movement under its wing by having Burke propose in Commons economical reform, that is, the abolition of useless offices in the king's appointment. The measure would serve to reduce both expenditures and that portion of the king's influence derived from patronage. Charles James Fox put himself at the head of the agitation in Westminster, and in the role of tribune of the people soon found himself declaiming that if parliament did not respond to the petitions, parliament would be reformed. The House of Commons would become representative of the people and be elected annually.

However, the storm of agitation soon dissipated. News of Admiral Rodney's victory over a Spanish squadron reached London in late February and helped to allay dissatisfaction. North was adept in managing the debate in the House of Commons. The independent members were willing to vote in principle for economic reform and the reduction of royal influence, but they refused to abolish specific offices in the king's household. The opposition divided between those who wanted only economical reform and those who desired reform of parliament as well. The king's firmness in handling the Gordon Riots restored much of his prestige. The news of Clinton's capture of Charleston revived hopes for a successful issue to the American war. Parliament adjourned on July 9, 1780, without enacting any significant reform legislation. Nevertheless, out of clash and co-operation of wills and plans arose situations and consequences which no one had willed or planned. Fox was caught for the cause of parliamentary reform and learned that role of tribune of the people to which he periodically returned. The agitation contributed to the gradual transformation of the Whigs from an assemblage of "family connections" to a group with a program. The reformers of the Yorkshire movement, such as Cartwright and Jebb, learned they could not win parliametary reform with a rush; they formed a Society of Constitutional Information and settled down to persevering agitation. None of these consequences had been foreseen or intended by the reformers when they started their agitation in the autumn of 1779. The reformers, actually, had intended different consequences; their intentions had made a difference, but not the difference they had intended.

Butterfield's narrative has the supreme virtue of communicating a scholar's mellow wisdom about the movement of history, that is, about the movement of life. The book has several secondary virtues besides: George III and North have never been better portrayed; "the role of James Burgh in gathering the material and formulating the shibboleths used in the movement for parliamentary reform" is recognized;[16] the steady attention paid to the influence of London on political events is welcome. Nevertheless, the volume is open to criticism on Butterfield's own principles. If the historian is to resurrect the past, he must attempt to give each individual, event, and institution the importance it had in its time. However, in this book Butterfield adopts another criterion of selection and emphasis: the importance of an event for a later age, for the later career of Fox and the later political development of Great Britain. On this ground, he gives undue emphasis and space to the extraparliamentary agitation, and underplays parliament where

[16] Review of *George III, Lord North, and the people* by W. T. Laprade, *American historical review*, LVI (1950–51), 340.

the crucial decisions were ultimately rendered. Summarizing swiftly the parliamentary debates, he never probes the interplay of factional feeling, of self-interest, and of the attitude toward the king that helped explain the debates and the balloting. As a consequence, he remains in the congenial world of rational intentions and ideational programs that he describes so well and neglects the meaner aspects of political maneuvering in the Commons. He thus distorts the past and misses the opportunity to explore the shadowy interrelations between reason, aspiration, principles, faiths, and ideals on the one hand and simpler impulses and interests on the other. Perhaps because he came to the subject indirectly, he did not pick it up at the right end, and his book, for all its wisdom, never came out quite right.[17]

As we have observed, while he wrote history, Butterfield was also publishing essays and books on the history of the writing of history, the nature of the historical process, and its relation to spiritual concerns. These volumes possess the same qualities of imaginative sympathy, the same sense of human complication, and the same emphasis on ideational issues that distinguish his narrative histories, and they broaden the theoretical, philosophical, and spiritual context in which these narrative histories are sustained. In his

[17] The book also suffers from several secondary defects. For example, the meaning of the word "people" is never exactly defined. Does it denote everyone in England or only the politically conscious freeholders? One is never certain. On page 181 "the country itself rises up," but on pages 196–98 the Yorkshire movement turns out to be one of freeholders and gentlemen. There are several inconsistencies of argument. On page 8, for instance, "liberty" is saved by the conflict between the king and aristocracy, but if (p. 41) the king had no "lust for despotic power," one wonders whether liberty was really endangered. In one sentence on page 53 the interior of the country was unconcerned during the invasion scare of August 1779, while in a succeeding sentence "the country was indeed astir." The evidence (p. 59) adduced to prove that there was an invasion "scare" is contradictory. Nor is proof offered that the invasion crisis affected a single vote in parliament, a single rioter, or a single member of the Yorkshire Association.

91

essays Butterfield shows how the history of historiography may be carried into regions of fresh discovery. In his Whig interpretation of history he notes that the tendency to study history with direct reference to a present need, ideal, or situation distorts the account. In the seventeenth century, for example, historically minded lawyers and politically minded antiquarians, seeking precedents to use against the Stuart monarchs, interpreted Magna Carta as a great statement of historic English liberties and saw the barons of Runnymede as champions of liberty against monarchical encroachment. Later "Whig" historians of the seventeenth, eighteenth, and nineteenth centuries interpreted all English history as a struggle between the children of light (the champions of liberty and parliament) and the children of darkness (the champions of royal prerogative), and imagined the British constitution as "coming down by virtue of the work of long generations of whigs and in spite of the obstructions of a long line of tyrants and tories."[18]

Such a thesis is anathema to Butterfield as a historian. It fails to see the past from inside the past. It tends to make the alleged partisans of liberty seem more modern than they actually were. It overlooks the fact that the complex present is the complicated product of a very complex past. The British constitution, the embodiment of balances, compromises, and adjustments, is the result not of the victory of one group of wills over another but of the interplay of many wills. If we do not perceive this complex interplay of wills, we cannot see ourselves as part of the historical process and operate most effectively in it. Nevertheless, Butterfield concluded in his Englishman and his history that though the activity of "Whig" lawyers and historians had produced bad history, the search for "liberal" precedents and the misconstruing of the Middle Ages had been good

18 The Whig interpretation of history, p. 41.

statesmanship. It had reconciled change with continuity, and fostered in Englishmen "an affection for tradition, a desire for gradualness, an adherence to ancient liberties."[19] Factual error had turned out to be pragmatic truth.

A research student investigating a controversial subject which has been studied for centuries may benefit, Butterfield also argues, from an examination of its historiography. A student of Martin Luther, for example, may discover that as generations pass, "a solid core of scholarly conclusions ... which is above the play of wind and weather" has been built.[20] He may recover insights and appreciations which have been forgotten. Though he can never remove the subjective element "from his narratives and expositions," he may neutralize it somewhat by seeing how other historians have been conditioned.[21] He may unravel the controversial issues, become more alive to the nature of his methods, and see what should be the next step in the inquiry. With these purposes in mind, Butterfield traces in his *George III and the historians* what historians have written about the opening years of that monarch's reign. His account is not a flat chronological survey of what successive historians have said about George, but an active utilization of the controversies among the historians to clarify the issues with respect to the king's intention at the moment of accession, the structure of eighteenth-century British politics, the nature of party, the importance of extra-parliamentary opinion, and the roles of self-interest and rational intention in political activity. Clarification of the issues, Butterfield believes, may prepare the way for a more sophisticated solution.

While not following him into the intricacies of his pres-

[19] The Englishman and his history (Cambridge, 1944), p. 72.
[20] Man on his past: the study of the history of historical scholarship (Cambridge, 1955), p. 26.
[21] Ibid., p. 23.

entation, we may note one line of his argument. The earliest serious historical reconstruction of the first decade of George III's reign was published in 1802 by John Adolphus, a Tory historian. In his preface, Adolphus remarked that "I have generally found in the state of party connexions, and the legitimate objects of honourable ambition, sufficient means of accounting for the actions of men either possessed of, or struggling for power, without feigning, as a cause of their conduct, an excess of mental depravity or political turpitude."[22] The Whig historians of the mid-nineteenth century, taking their cue from the recently published papers of George's opponents, endowed the latter with ideals and a program: the defense of the British constitution against an ambitious, arbitrary king. In the twentieth century, however, historians have returned to the earlier interpretation of British politics of the period in terms of struggle for gain. Butterfield, while welcoming this trend, believes that in the hands of Lewis Namier and his disciples it has gone too far. Men, even politicians, are not simply manipulative creatures and repositories of self-interest. They sometimes have rational intentions and purposes which affect their conduct. It is ideas and varied attitudes which distinguish one individual or one century from another. To focus on men only as repositories of self-interest and manipulation is to reduce all individuals and centuries to the same dull level. A scholar with this philosophy will be apt to forget "that when one confronts a different age of history or a different country from one's own, there are transpositions to be made in the mind, there is something that has to be done with one's personality."[23] Namier and his disciples might have learned from earlier historians of George III something of the importance of ideas. In any

[22] George III and the historians (rev. ed.; New York, 1959), p. 62.
[23] History and human relations, p. 242.

case, once other historians become aware of the issue revealed by a study of the historiography, self-interest versus self-interest and rational intention, they will be better able to render a more sophisticated appraisal of any political situation in George's reign.[24]

Butterfield's conception of the historical process—that out of the clash of wills arise events and situations no one has willed—might be held by an individual who believed that history is "a tale told by an idiot, full of sound and fury, signifying nothing." Or, to phrase the thought less poetically, history might be viewed as "just one damned thing after another." However, Butterfield is a Christian, and for him what arises out of a clash of human wills may be God's will. That such is the case, he observes, cannot be proved by the evidence and apparatus available to the technical historian. The methods of the historian—the assembly of data, the critical scrutiny of evidence for authenticity and accuracy, the search for secular relationships among individuals—do not equip him to handle the problems of the Incarnation, Crucifixion, and Resurrection or of ultimate meaning in history. At the same time, the apparent capriciousness of events—the wicked sometimes prosper and

[24] *George III and the historians* is a double-barreled treatise: it traces the historiography about George III and it presents an extensive and astonishingly bitter indictment of the work of Lewis Namier and his disciples. Butterfield criticizes the Namier "school" on the grounds that they prefer an analysis of the structure of politics to a narrative of political events; they ignore the work of their predecessors, and thus make their contribution seem more novel and original than it is; they lock themselves up in the factional struggles in parliament and thus neglect the influence of extra-parliamentary events and especially the role of London; they portray politicians simply as repositories of self-interest, and hence misinterpret the Chatham Ministry of 1766, the Rockingham Whigs, and the nature of party. Except the first one, Butterfield's main charges seem well founded. If a general historian must first offer a cross-section of social forces at a given date and then make it move, it was natural for Namier to offer an analysis of British politics in 1760 before proceeding to a narrative. Namier is a master of narrative when he chooses to employ it.

thrive while the righteous fall in disaster—seems to defy any providential explanation. But for Butterfield, believing is seeing. He believes in a God who is Lord of History, and his faith leads him to perceive the ways of Providence in historical events.

He is interested in Providence less as provision and sustenance than as judgment and grace. Every individual sins, Butterfield thinks, through pride and indestructible egoism. But human sin "does not carry man out from under the Providence of God; it only holds him under Providence in the form of judgment."[25] Some individuals, such as Napoleon and Hitler, sinned grievously in their human presumption, and their actions provoked retaliatory power which destroyed them. Other men, Frederick the Great and Bismarck, for example, sinned in pride but were moderate in action. Retribution came later, when the Prussian system they founded was carried to excess by Hitler. Even systems such as ancient Rome and the British Empire, founded on brigandage but softened to a degree of order and justice, ultimately decayed from the inadequacy of human nature. In all these instances, sin brought its own ruin. Man, Butterfield holds, is operating in a divine historical order so arranged that judgment falls if not on individuals then on systems based on pride.

Providence also appears in history as grace, the capacity of the superintending spirit to bring good out of evil. The fire of London cleared the city of ugliness and permitted a superior reconstruction. The mistake of provoking the American colonists to rebel led England to invent a new conception of empire. Even the picture of undeserved suffering, such as Israel or Christ, may call people to penitence. Even a catastrophe which overwhelms the righteous

[25] Waldo Beach, "The pattern of Providence," Theology today, XVI (July 1959), 238.

and unrighteous alike may stimulate a contemplative mind to profound reflection on the role of disaster in history. Besides, "it is hard to rid oneself of the impression that in general the highest vision and the rarest creative achievements of the mind must come from great internal pressure and are born of a high degree of distress."[26] If the process and end of history are the manufacture, education, and refinement of human souls, then distress and disaster are essential elements in the story. In the light of these two concepts—a judgment which broods over all of us, especially over the presumptuous and those who condemn others for presumption, and a grace which brings good out of evil— Butterfield can explain to his own satisfaction events that give many believers in Providence trouble.

He does not, to be sure, clarify how he reconciles God's sovereignty with man's freedom. At one point he resorts to metaphor. History can be compared to a symphony written by a divine improviser. Human beings in the orchestra, in freedom and in sin, strike right and wrong notes, and the divine "composer himself is only composing the music inch by inch as the orchestra is playing it,"[27] taking into account the notes that have been struck. One cannot resist remarking that Butterfield's Deity, like his historical characters, seems to be solving problems as they arise. Other statements seem, like this metaphor, to suggest that Butterfield believes in a limited Providence. He once observed: "The industrial revolution and the rise of the capitalistic system are the best that Providence can do with human cupidity at certain stages of the story."[28] However, unlike human beings, Providence retains ultimate mastery. "It is this Providence which in fact has the last word to say about the results."[29] Butterfield does not describe the means by which

[26] Christianity and history, p. 76.   [28] Ibid., pp. 34–35.
[27] Ibid., p. 95.   [29] Ibid., p. 100.

Providence reached and affected human beings. Again he offers figures of speech. "Perhaps a better picture of our situation would be that of a child who played her piece very badly when she was alone, but when the music-teacher sat at her side played it passably well, though the music-teacher never touched her, never said anything, but operated by pure sympathetic attraction and by just being there. Perhaps history is a thing that would stop happening if God held His breath, or could be imagined as turning away to think of something else."[30] However, we may be sure that "God works upon our lives in detail" and "touches men in things which are most intimate."[31]

It should be apparent by now that Butterfield's theology and his philosophy about history cohere and harmoniously reinforce one another. Both the historian and the Christian theologian are interested in the spectacle of happenings in time. For both, human personalities are central. History "deals with the drama of human life as the affair of individual personalities";[32] to Christian theology human souls are the purpose and end of the story. Also in both fields of study each individual as well as each generation is equidistant from eternity. The historian studies each generation in and for itself; the theologian thinks of each generation as related directly to God and existing for His glory. Yet both disciplines take a low view of human nature and of its capabilities for mastering itself or events. History uncovers human cupidity and self-righteousness. Theology dwells on the universal human sins of pride and egoism from which men can be saved only by God's grace. In a world divided by selfishness, Christianity can seek to bind the human race together by love while the historian attempts to reconcile

---

[30] Ibid., p. 111.
[31] Ibid., p. 59; also Man on his past, p. 140.
[32] Christianity and history, p. 26.

individuals through teaching mutual comprehension. So interrelated are Butterfield's historical philosophy and his theology that he believes that in tracing the interconnections of mundane events he is "studying the ways of Providence."[33] Presumably, that faith has lent a singular sweetness and delight to his historical work.

Future generations may not remember Butterfield as a great scholar. His activity has been too diversified to permit him to produce a multivolumed *magnum opus* or even a large corpus of solid scholarly volumes. To a professor, society seems to be composed of conspiracies to interrupt him, of invitations to turn away from the main line of his research and be immediately useful by giving lectures, by serving on committees, and by performing administrative functions. Betrayed by his facility and versatility, and probably also by his perception of opportunities to do good and his desire to do it, Butterfield has hearkened to the seductive voices. Besides his teaching and administrative duties at Cambridge, he lectured in Germany in 1938, 1948, 1949, and 1950; delivered the Riddell Memorial Lectures at Durham University in 1951, the David Murray Lecture at Glasgow University, the Wiles Trust Lectures at the Queen's University of Belfast; was editor of the *Cambridge historical journal* from 1938 to 1952; and so on. Also, he has strayed from his projected biography of Charles James Fox to write on many themes. As a consequence, the thoroughness of his scholarship has suffered. Except in the *Peace tactics* and the interpretive essays on historiography, one can never be sure that Butterfield has not missed a pivotal bit of evidence which might overturn his whole reconstruction. Perhaps in scholarship it is well to be more single-

[33] "The Christian and history," *Spectator*, CXCIV (April 29, 1955), 545.

minded, to have, like Francis Parkman, only one idea, and to develop it through a lifetime of effort and publication.

Later generations may also question the low estimate Butterfield places on the capacity of able men to achieve some of their intentions. Prior to World War I it was fashionable to be optimistic about human nature and to portray, for example, Edward I, Cavour, and Bismarck as master strategists who from design respectively formed parliament, unified Italy, and united Germany in accord with a master plan. Postwar generations have been more pessimistic with regard to human capabilities, and historians have tended to portray the same men as resourceful devisers of expedients who merely solved problems as they arose. While the reaction against naive optimism is welcome, one wonders whether the pendulum has not swung back too far. True, no one can ever know the ultimate consequences of his acts, no one can ever know completely what he does to himself or to others. But some capable men have been able to slant events in the direction they wished them to go. Cavour intended to unite Italy under a parliamentary government and Lenin-Stalin to have a society in which the government owned the means of production. While opportunistic and flexible in their means, each was steadfast in his aims and achieved their realization in institutions. Perhaps this is an instance in which historical revisionism needs to be revised, and the older trends in historiography combined with the new.

It may be wondered as well whether Butterfield's Christian interpretation of history does not sometimes impair the flexibility of his historical imagination and the accuracy of his account. To write history correctly is one of the most difficult of human enterprises, because to do it the historian must divest himself of his personal assumptions and of his knowledge of what came after the event he is describing.

Try as he may to empty himself, he tends to bring something of himself to his investigation. As Butterfield observed in his *Whig interpretation of history*, the effect of this personal intrusion is both to enrich and to distort the account. In his portrayals of individual historical characters engaged in concrete happenings, Butterfield appears marvelously free of personal bias. But in his reflections on general history, he violates his precept of self-emptying and smuggles into his account those Christian emphases he wishes to extract. Likewise, in the realm of moral judgment he is self-contradictory. In his detailed narratives he loyally observes his maxim to refrain from passing sentence on individuals. But in his general reflections he stresses those instances where Providence has passed judgment on individuals and systems. One is reminded of the celebrated story about the great French medievalist, Fustel de Coulanges. Once when an admiring audience broke into his lecture with applause, he held up his hand and said: "Do not applaud. 'Tis not I who speak, but History which speaks through me." Is not Butterfield subject to a similar self-deception? Is he not saying: " 'Tis not I who judge, but Providence, whose judgments I merely note and record"? Perhaps, after all, the best historian, not necessarily the greatest, is apt to be an individual who was once a Christian but no longer is, who absorbed the general values of imaginative sympathy and compassion but is no longer swayed by particular beliefs, who is conscious of his presuppositions insofar as anyone can be, and whose only passion is the desire to understand.

However, despite his self-contradictions or perhaps in part because of them, Butterfield has served as a source of ideas and illumination to readers of his own generation. In describing another writer an author will sometimes drop a remark which seems to be self-descriptive. In *George III and the historians* Butterfield observes that "the case of Harold Temperley or of Laprade will tend to show that a man of some insight may pierce into the essentials of a political situation without any vast apparatus of erudition."[34] And he concludes an essay on the origins of the Seven Years' War by noting that "even with a more limited range of materials, Ranke has the genius to seize the main truths. His 'hunches' are one of the interesting features of the story. In the last resort, sheer insight is the greatest asset of them all."[35] This asset Butterfield possesses, and he has manifested it in every field of history he has entered and every book he has written. One has only to compare the *Peace tactics of Napoleon* with its immediate predecessor, Édouard Driault's *Tilsit*, the brief *Napoleon* with the similar volume by Herbert Fisher, the *Origins of modern science* with the standard *A history of science* by W. C. Dampier, the essays on historiography and historical method with G. P. Gooch's *History and historians of the nineteenth century*—one has only to make these comparisons to realize that in every subject Butterfield has essayed he has set a new standard of philosophical narrative by his technique of walking alongside each historical character, by his imaginative sympathy, and by his insight and wisdom. To read his books is, for the professional historian, to raise one's conception of achievement and to renew the springs of one's aspiration.

[34] *George III and the historians*, p. 201.
[35] *Man on his past*, p. 170.

RICHARD H. BAUER

VEIT
VALENTIN

1885–1947

Veit Valentin was both a distinguished historian and an outspoken liberal.[1] As a historian, he will be remembered primarily for his monumental and authoritative studies on the revolution of 1848 in Germany, some of which, perhaps, will never be superseded. In addition, he was the author of many books, pamphlets, essays, and articles on modern Germany, including a history of the German peo-

Richard H. Bauer is professor of history at the University of Maryland.

[1] For their generous aid in the preparation of this essay, the author is indebted to Mrs. Scott Elledge, the former Mrs. Veit Valentin, of Northfield, Minnesota; Dr. Ludwig Bergsträsser and Dr. Gerhard Ritter of Germany; Dr. Hans Wehberg of Geneva, Switzerland; Dr. George P. Gooch, Dr. Fritz Demuth, Miss Winifred Taffs, and Miss C. V. Wedgwood of England; Dr. Sergius Yakobson and Dr. Fritz Epstein of the Library of Congress; the late Dr. Ernst Jäckh of Columbia University, Dr. Dieter Cunz of Ohio State University, Dr. Carl Wittke of Western Reserve University, Dr. Adolf Zucker of the University of Maryland, Dr. Fritz Karl Mann of American University, and Dr. George F. Hallgarten of Washington, D.C.; and to Mr. Lucian W. Kempner of the U.S. Forces, Frankfurt a.M., Germany.

ple. Indeed, this gifted, versatile, and prolific historian found time to write a two-volume *Weltgeschichte*, which reflected his broad cultural interests and humanistic outlook.

As a liberal, he was one of the few German historians who supported the Weimar republic. Politically, he found himself very close to the democrats of the revolution of 1848, whom he regarded as the real heroes of the movement. For his political convictions, however, he suffered much abuse, loss of academic position, and, eventually, exile. The main attacks on him came from various nationalistic and pan-German groups, which included, to his sorrow, a number of prominent historians.

Valentin's career as a historian readily divides itself into three stages. The reign of William II embraced the formative period of his life, during which he began his studies on the revolution of 1848. The period of the Weimar republic was, in some respects, the most creative, since it witnessed the completion, among numerous other publications, of his *magnum opus* on the revolution. During the third and last period of his life—from the establishment of the Third Reich to the end of World War II—he was an exile in Britain and the United States, where he continued to produce additional important books and essays.

Of Huguenot ancestry, Rudolf Johann Maximilian Veit Valentin was born on March 25, 1885 in Frankfurt-am-Main.[2] His father, who bore the same name, was principal of the Wöhlerschule, a *Realgymnasium* in Frankfurt. A recognized and productive scholar with a broad cultural and liberal outlook, he was deeply interested in art and the history of art, with emphasis on the Renaissance, and car-

[2] A sketch of Valentin's life appears in *Kürschners deutscher Gelehrten-Kalender* (Berlin and Leipzig, 1931), pp. 3083 ff.

ried on research into the life and works of Goethe.[3] Of Austrian background, Valentin's mother was a gifted musician whose skill in playing the piano was far above average. In addition, she ventured into the field of musicology and succeeded in publishing two noteworthy books.[4]

Reared in an atmosphere of culture, the young Valentin early developed an interest in history. The challenging intellectual environment of his home, which was enriched by contacts with distinguished visitors, produced in him a broad cultural and humanistic outlook. After receiving his elementary education at the preparatory school of the Wöhlerschule, he attended the Kaiser Friedrich Gymnasium in Frankfurt, where he excelled in all subjects and was graduated *summa cum laude* in 1903. In the next four years he attended the universities of Heidelberg, Berlin, and Munich, taking his major work in the fields of medieval and modern history, economics, and political science. He was very fortunate in having among his professors some of Germany's foremost historians, including Erich Marcks, Max Lenz, Dietrich Schäfer, Eduard Meyer, and Gustav von Schmoller. Heidelberg awarded him a doctoral degree in 1906, after which he went on an extended trip, for purposes of research, to Italy, France, and Britain.

It was Marcks, the distinguished historian and biographer of Bismarck, to whom Valentin was attracted. Valentin described Marcks as the "teacher and guide" of his university years and as his "permanent counsellor and

[3] A few of his more important publications were *Über Kunst, Künstler und Kunstwerke* (Frankfurt a.M., 1889), *Ästhetische Schriften* (Berlin, 1894), *Erläuterungen zu Goethes Faust* (Dresden, 1897), and *Die klassische Walpurgisnacht* (Leipzig, 1901).

[4] Karoline Valentin, *Geschichte der Musik in Frankfurt-am-Main vom Anfange des XIV. bis zum Anfange des XVIII. Jahrhunderts* (Frankfurt a.M., 1906) and *Theater und Musik am fürstlich leiningischen Hofe* (Würzburg, 1921).

friend."[5] When the young student expressed his desire to write his doctoral dissertation on some aspect of the revolution of 1848, Marcks suggested that he might examine the political, economic, and intellectual conditions in Frankfurt prior to the revolution, with the object of comparing them with contemporary developments in Germany.[6] In following this suggestion, Valentin began his research on a topic that finally led him to undertake the ambitious project of writing a history of the revolution of 1848 in Germany. Ever since his student days, he commented in 1930, he had regarded the preparation of such a comprehensive work as "an important scholarly and patriotic task."[7]

In his dissertation, *Politisches, geistiges, und wirtschaftliches Leben in Frankfurt-am-Main vor dem Beginn der Revolution 1848–49*,[8] he surveyed the basic developments in the city from 1815 to 1848. He carefully examined every aspect of the city's life—its significance as a commercial, trading, and banking center, its relation to the neighboring states and to the Bund, its social structure and classes, its cultural institutions, and, most important of all, the forces that were at work in effecting fundamental changes. This thesis, which he published at the age of twenty-two, reflected considerable historical insight and graphic powers of description. His vivid portrayal of contemporary people— the lowly as well as the important—was noteworthy.

From describing life in Frankfurt before the revolution, Valentin proceeded to do further research on the role of the city both during and after the upheaval. He shortly published his *Frankfurt-am-Main und die Revolution von*

[5] *Fürst Karl Leiningen und das deutsche Einheitsproblem* (Stuttgart and Berlin, 1910), p. v.

[6] *Ibid.*

[7] *Geschichte der deutschen Revolution von 1848–49* (Berlin, 1930–31), I, vii.

[8] Stuttgart, 1907.

1848–49,[9] into which he incorporated his dissertation as the introductory chapter. Writing from the liberal point of view, he evaluated, on the one hand, the influence of Frankfurt, as the main theater of the revolution, on the general course of the German revolutionary movement, and, on the other, the impact of the revolution on the internal life of the city. Here again he brought to life, through his powers of description, the numerous people who had participated in the events—the high and lowly, the statesmen and politicians, the educators, the poets, miscellaneous writers and journalists—and related them to the basic issues, conflicts, and currents of the time.

The book received much favorable criticism and enhanced Valentin's reputation as a promising young historian. Professor G. Kaufmann of Breslau referred to it as a "finished performance," and praised its judicious use of sources, its comprehensive treatment of all participating groups, its calm approach to controversial political matters, and its character sketches of leaders like Heinrich von Gagern, Joseph von Radowitz, Prince Felix Lichnowsky, Robert Blum, and others.[10] Even more laudatory was the review in the *Historische Zeitschrift*, where Gustav Mayer stated that Valentin, in publishing the book, "had introduced himself into the realm of historical scholarship in a very promising and—in this instance, one can say—in a brilliant manner."[11] Less enthusiastic was the review by F. Frensdorff of Göttingen who, while conceding that Valentin had written "a very readable presentation," insisted that the author had not exploited the sources to fullest

[9] Stuttgart, 1908.
[10] *Historische Vierteljahrschrift*, XIII (1910), 114–16.
[11] CV (1910), 387.

advantage and that the book tended to exaggerate the role of Frankfurt, both in German affairs and in the revolution.[12]

As he penetrated more deeply into the revolution of 1848, Valentin became interested in the career of Prince Karl Leiningen, whom the Frankfurt parliament had selected as the first president of the cabinet of ministers under Archduke John, the imperial administrator. He was intrigued by the family connections, complex character, and advanced liberal views of the prince, who was a half-brother of Queen Victoria of Britain and a cousin of the Prince-Consort Albert of Coburg, and whose ancestral lands—originally on the left bank of the Rhine—had been mediatized in 1803 and thereafter lay mainly in Baden, but partly in Bavaria and Hesse. On the basis of extensive research in the Leiningen archives in Amorbach and the archives of the royal house in Windsor Castle, Valentin published *Fürst Karl Leiningen und das deutsche Einheitsproblem*,[13] which he dedicated to Marcks. In this book he characterized Leiningen as "a prince and a private individual; a large landed proprietor and a liberal; a parliamentarian and a minister; a born ruler and the irresponsible correspondent of crowned heads; a cavalier and a father of his petty people; a courtier and a patriot."[14] He was greatly impressed by the prince, not only because of the latter's liberal ideas, his bold intellect, and his unusual political talent, but primarily because Leiningen, some years before the revolution, had advocated a united and liberal Germany under the leadership of Prussia.

This book, too, received favorable comments in various

[12] *Göttingische gelehrten Anzeigen*, CLXXIII (1911), 27–39.
[13] See note 5.
[14] *Fürst Karl Leiningen und das deutsche Einheitsproblem*, p. v.

historical journals.[15] Indeed, it led to his appointment in 1910 as Privatdozent at the University of Freiburg. Here he joined a distinguished group of historians, among whom was Friedrich Meinecke, who in 1914 accepted an offer from the University of Berlin. The most influential personality at this time, however, was Georg von Below, who had come to Freiburg from Tübingen in 1905, served as dean during his first year, and in 1916 was elevated to the office of rector of the university. As a scholar, he had achieved distinction for his contributions to medieval constitutional history, for some of which, indeed, he had gained recognition among historians in other countries. Respected by many German historians, he had been selected as chairman of the Verband deutscher Historiker, and, among other honors, he had been elected to the board of the Leopold von Ranke Verein, which had been founded in 1906.[16]

But there was another side to Below—one that had most fateful consequences for Valentin. As a member of the board of the Alldeutscher Verein, Below was affiliated with various pan-German organizations and was a frequent contributor to their newspapers and journals. He was a warm friend and admirer of Admiral Tirpitz. Together with H. Stewart Chamberlain, he founded in April 1917 *Deutschlands Erneuerung*,[17] an outspoken pan-German periodical with strong antidemocratic, anti-Semitic, and militaristic overtones. In fact, many of its articles bear a striking similarity to later Nazi publications.

[15] See, for example, *Historische Zeitschrift* (hereafter cited as *HZ*), CVII (1911), 595.

[16] *Kürschners deutscher Gelehrten-Kalender* (Berlin, 1926), pp. 98 ff. A eulogistic summary of Below's life was written by his widow, Minnie von Below: *Georg v. Below: ein Lebensbild für seine Freunde* (Stuttgart, 1930).

[17] Subtitled *Monatsheft für das deutsche Volk*, it was published in Munich.

Valentin's first few years at Freiburg were relatively peaceful and productive. He lectured on such topics as the revolution of 1848, German history since 1871, the origins of political parties in Germany, colonial history, and, occasionally, the Renaissance and Frederick the Great.[18] To enable him to continue his research on the revolution of 1848, the faculty granted him a leave of absence from 1912 to 1914.[19] With generous support from the Freiburger Wissenschaftliche Gesellschaft, he examined and evaluated more archival material.[20] During the summer of 1914, he was working in Munich, when the war suddenly forced him to postpone his research.

Valentin was found to be unsuited for service in the armed forces, but declared available for other assignments.[21] At first he was employed by the postal censorship, and after August 1915 by the press agency subject to General Gaede's command.[22] He also rendered local garrison duty for shorter periods of time. In 1916, with the warm support of the faculty, he was promoted to an assistant professorship at Freiburg.[23] As the war entered its third year, however, he became involved in a prolonged and bitter conflict with the pan-Germans, with dire consequences for his future.

Of Valentin's miscellaneous publications during the war, two of them—Bismarck und seine Zeit[24] and Kolonial-geschichte der Neuzeit[25]—had been in preparation before the outbreak of hostilities. In the short biography of Bismarck, he leaned heavily on Marcks's lectures and studies

[18] Gerhard Ritter to author, June 26, 1959.

[19] Geschichte der deutschen Revolution von 1848–49, I, vii.

[20] Ibid., II, vii.

[21] Der Vortrupp. Deutsche Zeitschrift für das Menschentum unserer Zeit, VIII (1919), 387.

[22] Ibid.   [24] Berlin, 1915.

[23] See note 18.   [25] Tübingen, 1915.

on the chancellor. He appraised Bismarck as a political genius who was responsible for "the greatest things which the German people had experienced in centuries."[26] He admired the chancellor as a diplomat who "had secured the external position of Germany" and had succeeded in becoming "the arbiter of Europe."[27] But he was sharply critical of the statesman's internal policies, which he described as "aberrations on as grand a scale as his creative deeds."[28] In particular, the chancellor's *Kulturkampf* and his persecution of the socialists were tragic blunders with fateful consequences for the future. He failed in "the pacification of the entire nation," and his domestic policies resulted "not only in the enrichment of the internal life of the Reich, but also in making it more confused and rendering it more difficult."[29] The critics, in general, reacted favorably to this little volume, which rapidly passed through four editions.

Valentin's *Kolonialgeschichte der Neuzeit* was an outline of a series of lectures which he had delivered at the university. His purpose was to introduce students, teachers, and wider historical circles into a new area of modern history which hitherto had been neglected in Germany. In a sense, then, he was a pioneer, although others—Alfred Zimmermann and Gustav Roloff, for example—had previously published some noteworthy books in this field. Antoine Guilland called the book "a good résumé of all the colonial enterprises of modern peoples. . . . Professor Valentin seeks to show that the German nation has something to learn from each, especially from the English, whose experience seems to him decisive."[30] Zimmermann, who had

[26] *Bismarck und seine Zeit*, p. 109.   [28] *Ibid.*, p. 108.
[27] *Ibid.*   [29] *Ibid.*, pp. 109 ff.
[30] *American historical review* (hereafter cited as *AHR*), XXV (1919–20), 652.

been instrumental in collecting books and data on colonial matters for the foreign office, stated that Valentin's book gave the reader "a picture, in concise form, of the colonial development of the world to the present."[31] But Karl Hadank, a severe critic, concluded that, while Valentin had a fascinating style and superior powers of description, the book was superficial, full of unsupported statements, various misconceptions, and definitely inferior to Roloff's book on colonization.[32]

Hardly had the war started when Valentin, who had always manifested a keen interest in current German developments, began to participate in various controversies relating to the problems of war and peace. Deeply patriotic, he opposed the extreme nationalistic views of such historians as Schäfer and Below, who favored annexationist policies. In his first pamphlet, *Die Mächte des Dreiverbandes*,[33] which was published a few weeks after Britain's entry into the war, he set forth the reasons why the Triple Entente had decided to fight the Central powers. He regretted the clash between Britain and Germany, all the more so because influential groups in both countries had been striving for a peaceful settlement of their differences.[34] In another essay, "Das englische Gesicht," he reminded his readers that Britain, despite her aid to Belgium, must not be regarded as a friend of small nations; on the contrary, her policies were solely determined by self-interest, as a brief survey of her relations with Portugal, Ireland, and the Boers would indicate.[35] The foregoing publications were none too

[31] *Weltwirtschaftliche Archiv*, VII (July–October, 1916), 476–79.

[32] *Deutsche Literaturzeitung*, XXXVII (1916), 149–54.

[33] Munich and Berlin, 1914.

[34] *Die Mächte des Dreiverbandes*, pp. 1–22.

[35] M. Frischeisen-Koehler, J. Jastrow, Eduard Freiherr von der Goltz, Gustav Roloff, Veit Valentin, Franz von Liszt, *Das englische Gesicht* (Berlin, 1915), pp. 205–21.

controversial, but his next one, *Belgien und die grosse Politik der Neuzeit,*[36] aroused the wrath of the pan-German elements. Influenced by the writings of Henri Pirenne, the noted Belgian historian, he insisted that Belgian independence must be restored at the end of the war:

Belgium is the form of state for which the southern Netherlands have striven for centuries; there exists a historically founded and justifiable Belgian independence movement, there is a Belgian history and a Belgian political idea. The great powers, Spain, Austria, and France, who wanted to occupy Belgium, have shattered on them.[37]

Valentin's advocacy of Belgian independence was most unacceptable to pan-German reviewers, who attacked his ideas as unrealistic, and, in one case, as hostile to German interests. Bitterly opposed, too, was his academic superior, Below, who was a vociferous supporter of Flemish separatism.[38] However, influential groups in the foreign office, who were convinced that the extreme statements by annexationists were harmful to the German war effort and jeopardized Germany's chance to negotiate a moderate peace, were favorably impressed by his outlook. Ernst Jäckh, consultant to the foreign office, decided to enlist his services:

I invited him to come to Berlin to discuss with me a possible publication in the series of "Flugschriften" I was editing during the war. He came and we had a thorough conversation about his Freiburg situation. He complained about the difficulties he was having with the influential historian Georg v. Below at Freiburg University. Below was a rabid pan-German in contrast with Valentin's anti-pan-German convictions. Below being the leading historian in Freiburg, he would not have any chance

---

36 Munich, 1915.

37 *Belgien und die grosse Politik der Neuzeit,* p. 25.

38 Georg von Below, *Kriegs und Friedensfragen* (Dresden, 1917) and "Was bedeutet der Fall Valentin?" *Deutschlands Erneuerung,* V (1921), 83 ff.

of an academic career there, Valentin said. I offered to try to
find for him a way to Berlin and suggested first that he should
write a "Flugschrift" about Belgium, and then another monograph concerning "Bismarcks Friedensschluesse." Both should
aim to educate governmental and public opinion for peacemaking along the moderate lines of Bismarck, particularly in his
dealings with Austria. Valentin agreed and did it in such a
masterful way that it impressed my friends in the foreign office,
particularly the Secretary of State v. Jagow. . . .[39]

But this association with the foreign office, like his connection with Freiburg, was soon to be terminated as a result of the increasingly vehement attack on him by various
nationalistic groups and their spokesmen. Of all these on-
slaughts, the two most damaging ones, as far as his academic career was concerned, took place shortly after his
promotion to an assistant professorship. They were made
by two like-minded historians—Below, the new rector of
the university, and Paul N. Cossmann, editor of the Süd-
deutsche Monatshefte, both of whom attempted to silence
him and, if necessary, to discredit him.

It was Valentin's devastating review of Count Reventlow's third edition of Deutschlands auswärtige Politik 1888–
1904, which he had published in the Preussische Jahrbücher, that gave rise to another bitter clash with Below.[40]
Reventlow, a prolific pan-German writer, enjoyed enormous
popularity among the nationalistic elements in Germany.[41]
In this lengthy review, which had the approval of Hans
Delbrück, the editor, Valentin compared the new edition
of the book with the first, pointing out that Reventlow had
made important additions and deletions solely in the in-

[39] Ernst Jäckh to author, June 11, 1959.

[40] Graf Reventlow als Geschichtsschreiber. Sonderdruck aus den Preus-
sischen Jahrbüchern, Augustheft 1916, mit der Antwort des Grafen Reventlow und einem Schlusswort (Berlin, 1916).

[41] Lothar Persius, Graf Ernst zu Reventlow (Berlin, 1918).

terest of furthering pan-German propaganda. He vigorously rejected the count's allegation that Britain, before 1914, "had organized the world for years . . . in order to conduct a war of annihilation against Germany."[42] In short, he questioned Reventlow's historical methodology, and denounced the book as "a crass example of historical demagoguery."[43] Below at once came to the defense of Reventlow. He tersely informed Valentin that the latter's attacks on the count "did not redound to his honor"—a statement that was interpreted by the young professor as being both offensive and insulting.[44] As the controversy between the two men intensified, it became apparent to Valentin that his position at the university was endangered. In fact, the faculty, with the support of the rector, began to consider measures whereby Valentin might be induced to resign.[45]

Meanwhile Valentin's controversy with Cossmann, the other rabid pan-German historian, only aggravated the situation for him. During the summer of 1916, while on his way to Berlin, where he had an assignment with the foreign office, he stopped in Munich on July 20 to visit Marcks.[46] He also decided to call on Cossmann, an old acquaintance who had been one of his father's students. On the following morning he met Cossmann in the latter's editorial office, where he was introduced to Theodor Heuss, a business friend of the editor, and, like him, an ardent supporter of Tirpitz.[47] In the bitter exchange of words that followed, Valentin assumed that his remarks to the editor were strict-

[42] *Graf Reventlow als Geschichtsschreiber*, p. 6.

[43] *Ibid.*, p. 13.

[44] Felix Rachfahl, *Der Fall Valentin: Die amtlichen Urkunden. Im Auftrag der Philosophischen Fakultät zu Freiburg i. Br.* (Leipzig, 1920), p. 1.

[45] *Ibid.*, pp. 6 ff.

[46] *Der Vortrupp*, VIII (1919), 387 ff.

[47] *Ibid.*, pp. 389–91.

ly confidential; he was not aware that Heuss, who over-
heard him, carefully recorded the conversation, particularly
his severe denunciation of Tirpitz. A few days later Cossmann and Heuss sent a copy of the recorded conversation
to the admiralty, which thereupon requested the foreign
office to dismiss Valentin immediately.[48] To discredit his
political foe still more, Cossmann addressed a letter, dated
October 24, 1916, to the Bavarian minister of war, com-
plaining that Valentin, as an emissary of the foreign office,
had tried to influence him.[49] Valentin's dismissal from his
Berlin assignment came as a cruel and unexpected blow;
he was shocked and indignant over Cossmann's under-
handed betrayal. Even Marcks, in a letter to Valentin dated
August 24, 1916, expressed his disgust at the fanaticism and
recklessness of the editor.[50] Valentin, in a moment of in-
discretion, dispatched on September 19, 1916 a sharp letter
of rebuke to Cossmann. It was couched in strong terms and
contained some uncomplimentary references. Cossmann, in
turn, considered the letter libelous—something Valentin
should have foreseen—and instituted a lawsuit on September 26 against its author.[51] In the trial that was held in
Munich on November 30, 1916, Valentin was outmaneuvered by Cossmann and had to withdraw his charges against
the editor.[52]

The outcome of the trial had a disastrous effect on Valentin's academic career. He realized that, with Below's hand
strengthened, his future at Freiburg was hopeless. When
the faculty increased its pressure on him to resign—and

[48] Ibid., p. 391.
[49] Ibid.
[50] Ibid., p. 394.
[51] Ibid., pp. 398 ff. See also notes 38 and 44 above for accounts by v.
Below and Rachfahl.
[52] Der Vortrupp, VIII (1919), 406.

with Below "leaking" a highly important decision of the
ministry of education of Baden to the press—he declined
to do so at once, hoping to move to another university.[53]
Failing in this, he finally submitted his "voluntary" resignation, under protest, on May 13, 1917.[54] But he was not
without friends. Delbrück, who had feuded with Below for
some time, reminded the faculty that Valentin's failings, if
any, were far less serious than the harm which the belligerent rector, through his intemperate and abusive attacks,
had done.[55] Later, various liberal publications, such as the
Frankfurter Zeitung, the *Berliner Tageblatt*, and *Das neue
Deutschland*, concluded that the university had removed
Valentin solely for his outspoken democratic views.[56] Even
sharper was the attack by Hermann Poppert, the editor of
the liberal *Vortrupp*, who examined the basic documents
and decided that Valentin had been unjustly dismissed. To
answer these criticisms, the university published its own
version of the affair. According to the historian Felix Rachfahl, the editor of this account, the faculty had not been
motivated by political considerations. Rather, it had acted
only after Valentin had rudely offended his older colleague
and head of the university by his public activities.[57] True,
the arguments in support of his resignation, according to
Gerhard Ritter, were not, in the form in which they appeared, political; but undoubtedly the majority of Valentin's colleagues, like Below himself, regarded his political
outlook and activities as "unpatriotic."[58]

[53] Rachfahl, pp. 101 ff.
[54] *Ibid.*, pp. 118 ff.
[55] *Preussische Jahrbücher*, CLXXII (1918), 126–29; CLXXIII (1918), 116–18.
[56] *Deutschlands Erneuerung*, V (1921), 88–90.
[57] Rachfahl, p. 83.
[58] Ritter to author, June 26, 1959.

In spite of this ordeal, Valentin succeeded in publishing another monograph on the war, *Entente und Neutralität*.[59] Its purpose was to disprove certain Allied allegations, which had been circulated among the small neutral nations, that Germany alone, since the invasion of Belgium, was a threat to their neutrality. He pointed out that the Allies themselves had been guilty of frequent interference through military, economic, and political measures and concluded that the small neutral countries would find less sympathy among them than among the Central powers.

Fortunately, Valentin's tragic experiences during the war did not interrupt his historical activities for long. Thanks to his courage in facing adversity as well as to the changing political climate, he was able to make a fresh start. The more congenial atmosphere of the Weimar republic, combined with a renewal of interest in the origins of German democratic ideas, stimulated his own research on the revolution of 1848. He lectured regularly at the Handelshochschule in Berlin, mostly on modern German history, and at the Hochschule für Politik, the founder and president of which was Jäckh, his close friend.[60] In 1920 he secured a position as a member of the research department of the Reichsarchiv in Potsdam. While faithfully discharging his administrative duties, he found time to carry on extensive research on topics that attracted him—a circumstance that helps to explain his enormous literary output during this period. His main task at the archives, as assigned to him by the minister of interior in 1923, was the completion of his unfinished study of the revolution of 1848.[61] From time to time he visited other German archives in search of material, and in the fall of 1928 he worked in the central

[59] Leipzig, 1917.
[60] Jäckh to author, June 11, 1959.
[61] *Geschichte der deutschen Revolution von 1848–49*, I, vii.

archives of Moscow, where he discovered new sources on the March revolution in Berlin.[62] As a result of this official assignment, some of his unfriendly critics referred to him as "a spokesman" for the Weimar regime.

Though not an official spokesman, he was an ardent and loyal supporter of the republic. As a member of the Democratic party and as an adherent of its left wing, he attempted, through his writings, to defend the republic and to strengthen the democratic elements and forces in German society. He steadfastly advocated a solution of domestic problems by means of democratic reform. Deeply concerned with contemporary developments, he never hesitated to discuss issues and policies which, in his opinion, vitally affected the future of the nation. His political writings were primarily directed against various nationalistic groups which were attributing the German military collapse of 1918, as well as the humiliating terms of the Treaty of Versailles, to the republican leadership. He repeatedly rejected the "stab-in-the-back" explanation for Germany's defeat, and severely criticized Ludendorff's political and diplomatic maneuvers during the conflict. In fact, he singled out Ludendorff "as having been most responsible" for the German catastrophe.[63] Even among his colleagues in the Reichsarchiv, who were engaged in the writing of the history of the war, there were reactionary groups, particularly in the military section of the research staff, who deliberately attempted to exonerate Ludendorff and other military leaders. Together with Ludwig Bergsträsser, who like himself was attached to the civilian staff, Valentin vigorously protested against these attempts to exempt the high command from responsibility for the final defeat. He supported

[62] Ibid.

[63] See Valentin's article, "Die Vorgeschichte des Waffenstillstandes 1918," HZ, CXXXIV (1926), 56–66.

Bergsträsser in insisting that, in judging the factors that explain the collapse, it was not enough to study the reports of the commanding officers. The attitudes and complaints of the common soldier during the last months of the war must also be carefully examined.[64]

As an active member of the Völkerbundsliga, he advocated Germany's entry into the League of Nations. In his monograph, Die 48er Demokratie und der Völkerbundsgedanke,[65] he pointed out that Arnold Ruge, a democratic leader of the Frankfurt assembly, had urged the creation of a democratically elected congress of nations "for the purpose of realizing European disarmament"; he reminded his readers that the International Peace Society held one of its early sessions in Frankfurt August 22–24, 1850. The purpose of his book, Geschichte des Völkerbundsgedankens in Deutschland,[66] was to indicate that the idea of a league of nations was deeply rooted in German history; he surveyed the contributions of leading German philosophers, notably Kant, to the concept of world peace, and pointed out how, unfortunately, the universalism of the eighteenth century gave way, from Hegel to Bismarck, to the demands of the omnipotent state.

Besides supporting the league, Valentin was also very active in various peace organizations. From 1926 to 1932 he was co-editor with Hans Wehberg of Die Friedenswarte. Founded in 1899 by Alfred H. Fried, this journal was dedicated to international understanding and organization.[67] Valentin contributed numerous articles and book reviews, and conducted a featured column entitled "Politische

[64] Ludwig Bergsträsser to author, May 27, 1959.
[65] (Berlin, 1919), pp. 6, 9–18, 19–31.
[66] Berlin, 1920.
[67] Die Friedenswarte. Blätter für internationale zwischenstaatliche Organisation (Zurich: Polygraphischer Verlag). Vols. XXVI–XXXII (1926–32).

Glossarum," in which he commented on significant events. For his activities in support of various peace organizations he was sometimes called a pacifist. But this designation is not correct, in spite of his abhorrence for war. He himself rejected the term throughout his life and considered himself, if anything, an "anti-militarist."[68]

During the "flag controversy" (*Flaggenstreit*) that erupted shortly after the establishment of the Weimar republic, Valentin came to the defense of the official republican colors of "black-red-gold." For a growing number of nationalistic Germans these colors symbolized treachery, defeat, despair, and socialism; they preferred the old imperial colors of "black-white-red," with which they associated honor, glory, and victory. Valentin engaged in a bitter debate with Egmont Zechlin, a nationalist historian who maintained that the republican flag had been tainted by defeat and humiliation.[69] As an outgrowth of this debate Valentin, in collaboration with Ottfried Neubecker, published *Die deutschen Farben*;[70] the former contributed the historical essay, and the latter, an expert in heraldry, was responsible for the bibliography, the tables, and pertinent documents. The republican colors, concluded Valentin, were most honorable ones; they were associated with the wars of liberation and the revolution of 1848; in general, they represented the best democratic traditions of Germany.[71]

Various pro-monarchist and nationalistic groups admiringly turned to Frederick the Great as the type of ruler whom Germany needed in her hour of degradation. On the

[68] Mrs. Scott Elledge to author, May 11, 1959.

[69] *Archiv für Politik und Geschichte*, V (1925), 354–67; VI (1926), 176–97, 616–20. Egmont Zechlin, *Schwarz rot gold und Schwarz weiss rot in Geschichte und Gegenwart* (Berlin, 1926).

[70] Leipzig, 1929.   [71] *Die deutschen Farben*, pp. 1–68.

other hand, leftist writers like Kurt Kersten portrayed the
king as a brutal oppressor of the poor, and Werner Hegemann characterized him as a liar, traitor, glutton, idler,
chatterbox, exploiter, and perverted genius.[72] According to
Valentin, neither of these extreme presentations revealed
the true significance of the Prussian king. To correct these
distortions, he presented his own interpretation in *Friedrich
der Grosse*.[73] Stripping Frederick of all glamor and legend-
ry, he portrayed the king, against the background of the
eighteenth century, as an exceptional ruler and, to some
extent, as a man of genius.

Not all of his publications during the Weimar period
were inspired by his lively interest in current problems. He
also dealt extensively with other topics, primarily in diplomatic history. He published a long essay on the history of
German political parties, a pamphlet on Bismarck's foreign
policy from 1871 to 1890, a study on the background of the
Reinsurance Treaty, two penetrating reviews of *Die grosse
Politik*, and an article on the diplomatic history of World
War I.[74] He likewise produced *Deutschlands Aussenpolitik
von Bismarcks Abgang bis zum Ende des Weltkrieges*,[75]
which was largely based on his research in the foreign office during the war and, to some extent, on the Kautsky
documents. In tracing German diplomatic history from

[72] Kurt Kersten, *Fridericus und sein Werk* (Berlin, 1925); Werner
Hegemann, *Fridericus Rex, oder, Das Königsopfer* (Hellerau, 1926).

[73] Berlin, 1927.

[74] Miscellaneous articles by Valentin include: "Die politischen Parteien
Deutschlands" in *Teubners Handbuch der Staats- und Wirtschaftskunde*
(Leipzig and Berlin, 1924), II, 24–47; *Bismarcks Aussenpolitik 1871–1890*
(Berlin, 1921); "Neues über die Vorgeschichte des Rückversicherungsver-
trages," in F. Lampe and G. H. Franke (eds.), *Staatsbürgerliche Erziehung*
(Breslau, 1924), pp. 302–13; "Diplomatische Geschichte des Weltkrieges,"
in Karl Strupp (ed.), *Wörterbuch des Völkerrechts und der Diplomatie*
(Berlin and Leipzig, 1929), III, 433–43.

[75] Berlin, 1921.

123

Bismarck's fall to the collapse of the German empire, he described, first of all, the deterioration of Germany's international position under Bismarck's successors; next, he gave a graphic account of the July crisis in 1914; finally, he appraised German diplomacy during the war by underscoring the political and diplomatic blunders of Ludendorff. In assessing the responsibility for the war, he put the major blame on Austria and Russia, and then on Germany, which shared it equally with France and Britain. Reviews of the book were quite favorable. Sidney B. Fay stated that it was written "with imagination, lucidity, and with a warmth of style which have given the book a deservedly wide reading in Germany."[76]

His main historical interest, however, continued to be centered in the revolution of 1848. In the same year that the Weimar assembly drafted a new constitution, he published *Die erste deutsche Nationalversammlung.*[77] Aware of the renewed interest in the revolution of 1848 and its democratic ideas, he pointed out that the Frankfurt assembly, which had been discredited by Prussian national historians, deserved much greater attention; in fact, its members, he maintained, had dealt with many of the same problems, such as the fundamental rights of citizens, that confronted the framers of the Weimar constitution. In this book he gave a vivid description of the members, leaders, parliamentary procedure, constitutional debates, and miscellaneous problems of the assembly. His sympathies, of course, lay with the party of the left—the so-called "party of youth" —whose leaders he praised as the true and noblest representatives of the German people. Reviews of the book, to a considerable extent, reflected the political bias of the reviewers. Even the harsher critics, who attacked it for its

[76] *AHR*, XXX (1924–25), 141–43.
[77] Munich and Berlin, 1919.

overemphasis on the left and its failure to stress foreign
affairs, admired Valentin's remarkable style in portraying
the leaders of the assembly.[78]

In probing into German conditions before 1848, Valentin often had to reckon with the pro-Prussian interpretations of Treitschke, whose *Deutsche Geschichte im neunzehnten Jahrhundert* outlined German developments to
the eve of the revolution. While he did not accept many
of Treitschke's biased and one-sided views, he was impressed by the latter's literary ability, his fighting personality, and his influence as a popular historian and publicist.
As a result of his growing familiarity with Treitschke's
writings, he published an abridged edition of the *Deutsche
Geschichte im neunzehnten Jahrhundert*, in which he reproduced sixteen selections from this important work.[79] In
an introductory biographical sketch, he wrote: "Treitschke
was the last historian who spoke to the entire German nation: he was unique. His work was and remains more important than his person, which has fallen prey to the
ravages of time."[80] As another by-product of his researches
into the background of the revolution, Valentin published,
in collaboration with several other scholars, a new edition
of Heinrich Heine's works.[81] He edited those sections which
included the poet's political writings. As an admirer of
Heine, he regarded the poet as the most outspoken herald

[78] The review by Antoine Guilland in the AHR, XXV (1919–20), 648,
is most favorable. More critical are the reviews by Adolf Rapp in the HZ,
CXXIV (1921), 306–11, and F. Frensdorff in *Göttingische gelehrten Anzeigen*, CLXXXII (1920), 226–37.

[79] Heinrich von Treitschke, *Deutsche Geschichte im neunzehnten Jahrhundert*. Ausgewählt von Veit Valentin (2 vols.; Berlin, 1927).

[80] *Ibid.*, I, xx.

[81] *Heines Werke*, in "Goldene Klassiker-Bibliothek." Herausgegeben mit
Einleitungen und Anmerkungen versehen von Hermann Friedemann, He-
lene Hermann, Erwin Kalischer, Raimund Pissin und Veit Valentin (Berlin, Leipzig, Vienna, Stuttgart, 1927).

of the revolution, who united in his person, more so than any other, the national, liberal, and humanistic ideals of the revolutionary movement.

Valentin's monumental study, *Geschichte der deutschen Revolution von 1848–49*,[82] on which he had worked for two decades, appeared during the final years of the Weimar republic. Intended for the general reader as well as for the historian, it was the first exhaustive treatment of the revolution, and, in a sense, marked the culmination of a long period of research on various aspects of this movement by other German scholars. Indeed, the author had familiarized himself with the previous literature, ranging all the way from the earlier disparaging accounts of the Frankfurt assembly that were published during the Bismarck era to the more sympathetic studies that were composed after World War I. He appended a helpful historiographical essay in which he gave a critical survey of the sources, earlier interpretations of the revolution, and the current state of research on it. His comprehensive bibliography, which included an astonishing amount of unpublished material that he had found in the archives of Vienna, Moscow, Munich, Darmstadt, Stuttgart, and Frankfurt, is invaluable to the student of the revolution.

In the first volume the author described the preliminaries that led to the stirring events of 1848; he contended that the revolutionary activities of that year were deeply rooted in German conditions, and that they were not merely a superficial reaction to French developments; in fact, he in-

[82] Vol. I, *Bis zum Zusammentritt des Frankfurter Parlamentes;* Vol. II, *Bis zum Ende der Volksbewegung von 1849* (Berlin, 1930, 1931). An abridged translation appears under the title of *1848: chapters of German history,* translated by Ethel Talbot Scheffauer (London, 1940). This translation has been criticized both for its poor editorial work and for its omission of important sections in favor of more popular passages. See *AHR,* LV (1949–50), 362–64, and *New statesman and nation,* XIX (1940), 730.

sisted that the old political framework of Germany, as characterized by the Metternich system and the ineffective Bund, could no longer contain the dynamic economic, social, liberal, and nationalistic forces that encompassed the German people. In the second volume he traced the dramatic but tragic course of the revolution throughout Germany to its ultimate collapse. He related how the revolutionaries, in their attempts to create a united Germany on a liberal basis, became involved in a growing number of complex and troublesome issues, both internal and external, which contributed to their final failure. Among the more important of these issues were the constitutional problem, the relations between the large German states and the viceregency, the threat from radical democratic and social revolutionary elements, the problem of national minorities, the Schleswig-Holstein controversy, the September crisis, the counter-revolution in Austria, the Prussian coup d'état, the survival of particularism, and the civil war over the imperial constitution. In the concluding chapter the author made a final appraisal of the historical significance of the revolution.

Valentin's principal views and interpretations might be briefly summarized as follows: (1) Unlike Treitschke and other adherents of the Prussian school of historians, he approached the revolution from an all-German viewpoint; he was sharply critical, not only of the Prussian Junkers, but also of the personality and policies of King Frederick William IV, whom he regarded as an unworthy recipient of the German crown; he referred to Prussia as an adventurous upstart among nations and as the executioner of the revolution. (2) He was one of the first historians to examine the underlying social causes of the revolution, without neglecting to include the influence of nationalism, liberalism, and other intellectual currents. German society, he insisted, was undergoing a basic social transformation, which resulted in growing dissatisfaction with existing conditions. He pointed out how the three-class system of society in Germany—the feudal nobility, the large middle class of town and country, and the impoverished lower class—was thrown out of balance by the formation of a new social class—"the patriciate of titles and money," whose members had risen from the middle class; as a result, the middle class suffered severe losses, while its less fortunate members, particularly the craftsmen and petty traders, were confronted with the danger of sinking into the lower class. (3) Valentin was the first historian to stress the struggle of democracy as a most important aspect of the revolution, with the strongest support for the idea coming from the middle and lower classes, including "the little man." He believed that the democrats had the best solution for Germany—the creation of a national state on a democratic basis; unfortunately, various social revolutionary tendencies, with which he was not in sympathy, identified themselves with the democratic idea and thereby discredited it. (4) Of the nine chapters in the second volume, only two are devoted to a consideration of the membership, parties, and problems of the Frankfurt assembly. Valentin had no intention of minimizing its role—in fact, he often indicated a warm appreciation for its work—but he regarded the revolutionary currents throughout Germany as relatively more important. (5) He placed much greater weight on the historical significance of the revolution than did preceding historians, many of whom, he insisted, deliberately belittled its importance. For him it remained the great German movement for democracy and freedom, which stood between Stein and Bismarck. Though ruthlessly trampled upon by the forces of the counterrevolution, it continued as a living force in German history; it was "the undying ally in all future struggles of the German nation."[83]

More than any of Valentin's previous works, the publication of this exhaustive study, which was greeted by numerous reviewers as a significant contribution, established his reputation.[84] He was commended for the thorough examination of the sources, including his extensive use of diplomatic documents in his evaluation of external factors, the comprehensive survey of the revolution in all parts of Germany, the emphasis on neglected aspects and people of the movement, the effective literary style, and the graphic portrayal of the leaders—the lesser known as well as the more prominent. Axel von Harnack stated that the author "could look with pride on his completed work," and that "his name would be enduringly associated with an important epoch of German history."[85] On the negative side, several of his reviewers—including some who found many admirable qualities in his book—felt that he, as an unofficial spokesman for the Weimar republic, overemphasized the democratic element in the revolution. Some believed that he dealt too harshly with Prussia and the role of King Frederick William IV. Then too there was considerable disagreement with the author's treatment of the influence of the foreign powers on the course of the revolution. Whereas Valentin contended that Prussia, in the absence of strong leadership, failed to exploit the differences among the great powers in the interest of German unification, his critics maintained that such a course would have been disastrous, since Britain, France, and Russia were firmly

[83] Geschichte der deutschen Revolution von 1848–49, II, 593.

[84] One of the best evaluations of Valentin's contribution is to be found in Kurt Schwerin, "The revolution of 1848 and the German historian" (Ph.D. diss., Columbia University, 1955), pp. 372–407. This thesis is available in microfilm.

[85] HZ, XLVII (1932), 178.

united in their opposition to German unity. A few reviewers characterized the work as being somewhat weak in organization and synthesis.[86]

As a by-product of his comprehensive study on the revolution, he published *Das Hambacher National Fest*[87]; like numerous other articles and books that appeared on this topic in 1932, it was a centennial publication, commemorating the historic demonstration of 25,000 Germans at Hambach a century before. The significance of this festival had been subject to varying interpretations; some writers had minimized it, while others had regarded it as important for its liberal, nationalistic, and socialistic strivings, depending on the outlook of the author; some even insisted that it had heralded the idea of the Weimar republic. For Valentin it was an extraordinary event, particularly in its relation to the revolution of 1848; it "was the first German political assembly on a grand style," and "stood between the Wartburg festival and the Frankfurt parliament."[88] It was definitely more important than the Wartburg affair; whereas the latter reflected the views of the academic youth, the gathering at Hambach represented the various social classes of the German people. Some of the ideas that had been expressed on this occasion "led directly to the Frankfurt *Paulskirche*; others, which peered into the future, reflected a European and humanitarian outlook."[89]

Ironically enough, Valentin's *magnum opus* on the revo-

[86] For further comments on Valentin's appraisal of the revolution of 1848 see Paul Wentzcke, *Die unvollendete deutsche Revolution 1848* (Munich, 1938), pp. ix ff.; *Jahresberichte für deutsche Geschichte*, VI (1930), 207–8; Erich Marcks, "Die europäische Mächte und die 48er Revolution," *HZ*, CXLVIII (1933), 98 ff.; H. Oncken, *Das deutsche Reich und die Vorgeschichte des Weltkrieges* (Leipzig, 1933), I, 60 ff.; Hans Rothfels, "1848—one hundred years later," *Journal of modern history* (hereafter cited as *JMH*), XX (1948), 301 n.; Koppel Pinson, *Modern Germany* (New York, 1954), p. 583.

[87] Berlin, 1932. [88] *Ibid.*, p. 81. [89] *Ibid.*

lution of 1848, which reflected the democratic spirit of the Weimar republic, appeared at a time when all liberal ideas were ruthlessly stifled by a growing reactionary nationalism. But the author himself, even after the Nazis had seized power, steadfastly refused to be intimidated; he continued to give expression to his liberal views. Failing to silence him, the Nazi minister of the interior, Wilhelm Frick, on June 22, 1933 dismissed him from his position at the archives and deprived him of his status as a civil servant.[90] With the loss of his position, he was also denied the right to publish any of his works in Germany. Preferring freedom to tyranny, he decided to go into exile.

While traveling in Italy in the summer of 1933, Valentin accepted an invitation from the University of London to lecture on German history as a guest of University College. This temporary lectureship was created and financed by a group of English scholars led by such eminent historians as George P. Gooch and George M. Trevelyan, who felt the need for the establishment of a permanent chair of German history. Gooch wrote that ". . . incredible as it may sound, there was no provision in the University of London, the largest of the British Commonwealth, for the teaching of German history, and it was left to a group of scholars, among them George Trevelyan and myself, to finance a temporary lectureship."[91]

From 1933 to 1939, when Valentin was naturalized as a British subject, he was associated with University College as "Special Lecturer in German History and Institutions." Here, in the land of academic freedom, away from the stifling atmosphere of the Hitler dictatorship, he started life anew. According to Gooch,

He fitted easily into our tolerant way of life, and proved an inspiring teacher to advanced and research students. During these

[90] Valentin, Weltgeschichte, II, "Nachwort," 711.
[91] G. P. Gooch to author, Apr. 7, 1959.

years I saw a good deal of him, and his visits were always a pleasure. He was such a 'live wire' that it was impossible to be dull in his company. His bubbling vitality was Gallic rather than Teutonic, for the French strain in his blood had survived two centuries of transplantation.[92]

In addition to lecturing, he conducted postgraduate seminars at the Institute of Historical Research. They were attended not only by English students but by political exiles with varied backgrounds. Under Valentin's stimulating guidance, they proved to be enriching experiences to both professor and students. Winifred Taffs, the author of a biography of Lord Odo Russell, attended one of his seminars. She writes in retrospect:

Among those who sat around the table on Wednesday evenings, five were exiles from their homeland, some of whom afterwards went to America, and one, Miss Horowitz, to Israel, where she is now playing her part in building up the Jewish national home. One of our English members was Miss Wedgwood, now eminent as a historian. Most professors have their own method of conducting their seminars, and Professor Valentin's was to ask each member in turn to be prepared to open the session with a paper or talk on some aspect of his own particular subject. Discussion then followed, during which he was active in giving helpful criticism and that valuable advice which is the fruit of wide and learned experience. . . .[93]

As a member of the seminar, Miss C. V. Wedgwood too recalls with pleasure her association with Valentin:

. . . At the time I was working on my book on the Thirty Years War. As a free-lance working rather outside the usual academic orbit I depended a great deal on the generosity of scholars like Professor Valentin to help me in my earlier years. Professor Valentin gave me most helpful advice about sources, especially for Wallenstein on whom he had of course written himself. Apart from this, he was at the time much interested in English poetry and sometimes asked me—I was at that time a rather

---

[92] *Ibid.*   [93] Miss Winifred Taffs to author, Mar. 25, 1959.

earnest young highbrow—to read aloud and discuss poems with him. In return he helped me with my education in philosophy which had been much neglected, and I remember he most kindly went all through Kant's *On Perpetual Peace* with me. The English poet he liked best was A. E. Housman, I remember. What chiefly impressed me about him was his unfailing courage and the irrepressible good-humor and high spirits with which he faced the difficulties of a life in exile. . . .[94]

Together with Fritz Demuth, chairman of the Emergency Community of German Scholars in Foreign Countries, Valentin rendered valuable assistance and counsel to an increasing number of German scholars in exile. He served for a time as a member of the board of this organization. In 1937 he organized the German Scientific Society, which brought together noted scholars in exile for the purpose of sponsoring both social and intellectual activities. According to Demuth, Valentin

. . . succeeded in assembling 40–50 scholars and in arranging programs in English private homes, where lectures were given and sociable teas were enjoyed. Thus his endeavors appeared in a humanly attractive form; the lectures, which took place from two to three times each month, became valuable centers, especially for young scholars, preferably historians, economists, sociologists, and psychologists. I remember with pleasure the lectures by Valentin, F. Hertz, Karl Mannheim, also those by younger people. . . .[95]

In Britain Valentin continued to be a prolific writer; he completed numerous articles and two books during his stay of six years. He contributed a series of essays on German history, for the benefit of his English readers, to the *Contemporary review*.[96] Noteworthy too was the publication of

[94] Miss C. V. Wedgwood to author, Nov. 26, 1959.
[95] Demuth to author, July 3, 1959.
[96] The following articles by Valentin are noteworthy: "Leading factors of German history," CXL (1936), 67–73; "Joseph II," CLI (1937), 572–76; "Bismarck's political technique," CLIV (1938), 60–68; "Political Catholicism in Germany," CLXVIII (1945), 38–42.

his paper, "Bismarck and England in the earlier part of his career,"[97] which he had read to the Royal Historical Society on October 8, 1936; its purpose was to emphasize that Bismarck's attitude toward Britain, in spite of several irritations, was basically friendly from 1848 to 1871.

In *Bismarcks Reichsgründung im Urteil englischer Diplomaten*,[98] Valentin traced the official relations of British diplomats with the leaders of the nationalist movement in Germany. It was an outgrowth of his studies on the revolution of 1848, for which he utilized the diplomatic reports of Lord Cowley, who had been the British representative to the federal diet in Frankfurt until 1852. By examining in the Public Record Office the unpublished dispatches from other British agents in Frankfurt, Berlin, Munich, Dresden, and Hannover over a period of two decades, he was able to assess the official British reactions to Bismarck's policy of unification. The book contained no startling revelations, but the confidential conversations between German leaders and British diplomats helped to clarify many aspects of Anglo-German relations.

Even more important was the publication, shortly before the outbreak of World War II, of his two-volume *Weltgeschichte*,[99] on which he had begun preparation some thirty years before. He wrote it primarily for the benefit of educated laymen, preferably for those who had a desire for more learning; he hoped that it might stimulate them to do further reading on topics of special interest to them. For him the main theme of *Weltgeschichte* was

[97] *Transactions of the Royal Historical Society*, 4th ser. (London, 1937), XX, 13–30.

[98] Amsterdam, 1937.

[99] Amsterdam, 1939. A new edition has appeared under the title *Knaurs Weltgeschichte*. Fortgeführt bis zur Gegenwart von Albert Wucher (Munich, 1959).

the struggle for four of life's greatest possessions: religion, art, science, and government. The goal and meaning of Welt- geschichte is to allow a great—and ever greater—part of man- kind to participate independently, under tolerable moral and economic conditions, in these four great possessions.[100]

He observed that Weltgeschichte taught no lessons, and that it destroyed many illusions. He denied the existence of basic laws, economic or others, that explained the rise and fall of civilizations. He did not believe that there was a similarity between the history of a people and the life cycle of an organism, since the former possesses an almost mi- raculous power of transformation and renewal. If anything, Weltgeschichte gave one courage to face the problems of the present, and it strengthened one's faith in the future of mankind.

As the best example of his versatility, this book reflected Valentin's remarkable familiarity with a wide variety of topics in philosophy, religion, art, and literature. It also revealed his aesthetic appreciation of man's great cultural achievements. In his description of nations and cultures, he was fair and sympathetic, always rising above petty na- tionalisms and prejudices. According to Gooch, the Welt- geschichte is "as good a summary as we possess. It deserved its success and its translation into Spanish for South Ameri- can readers."[101] Hugo Fischer, in the Contemporary review, stated that

. . . the writing and characterization is wonderfully timeless, that is, free from any taint of party feeling. A cheerful wisdom pervades the whole; the hard spade-work of the learned mole

[100] Ibid., I, 9.

[101] Gooch to author, April 7, 1959. The Spanish version is entitled Hi- storia universal, los pueblos, los hombres (2d ed.; 3 vols.; Buenos Aires, 1944–45). There is also a Portuguese edition: Historia universal, os povos, os homens (3 vols.; São Paulo, 1947–48).

is never visible. We participate in the untiring freshness and delight with which he beholds the panorama.[102]

With the approach of the war, Valentin faced still another crisis in his life. The plan to establish a chair of German history at University College, which had been under consideration since his arrival in 1933, had to be abandoned; public sentiment, understandably enough, did not favor such an idea at a time when tension between Britain and Germany was mounting. To make matters worse, funds which he had received from various private sources, such as the Society for the Protection of Science and Learning, began to fail. For the third time—first at the end of World War I and then in 1933—his future seemed insecure and uncertain. Again he was denied continuity and stability. There was no further course open to him but to seek and explore other avenues of opportunity.

Fortunately, an opportunity came from the United States, where his reputation as an authority on the revolution of 1848 had preceded him. The Institute of International Education of New York invited him to conduct a lecture tour, under its auspices, at various colleges and universities.[103] He accepted this invitation and embarked for the United States, arriving there shortly after the outbreak of World War II. At once he set out on his lecture tour and spoke to college audiences on such topics as "National Socialism from the point of view of an exile," "Causes of the present European war," "Frederick the Great," and others relating to German history.

During the winter of 1940–41, he produced a manuscript, which is still unpublished, on the life of Eduard Lasker, the noted German liberal who opposed Bismarck in

[102] CLV (1939), 634.
[103] Letter of Institute of International Education to author, Mar. 19, 1959.

the Reichstag; sources for this study were made available
to him by some of Lasker's relatives who had migrated to
the United States.[104] Most significant was Valentin's discovery, during the year 1943–44, of the papers of Gerson
Bleichröder, the well-known Berlin banker and Bismarck's
man of business, in the home of Mr. F. H. Bruner of New
York City, who is the heir of the Bleichröder firm; on the
basis of these papers, he began the preparation of a manuscript, "Bismarck-Bleichröder-Rothschild, interrelations between *haute finance* and politics in the Bismarck era"; it
was never published, since it did not go beyond the first
draft and still required extensive revisions.[105] During the
winter of 1944–45 he undertook another project, "The
Central European emigration to the United States around
1848," on which he did preliminary research at the Library
of Congress; the data which he collected dealt largely with
the European background of the emigrants, with which he
was thoroughly familiar; this study, like the one on Bleichröder, was never completed.[106]

His book, *The German people*,[107] which appeared both
in German and English editions, was his most noteworthy
publication in the United States. Based primarily on his
lectures at the University College, this survey of German
civilization was designed to serve both the needs of the
college student and the general reader. Aside from its merits
and deficiencies as a textbook, its real significance lay in
the fact that it contained Valentin's final appraisal and
judgments of Germany. In guiding the reader through the
complexities of German history, he avoided all extremist

104 Mrs. Scott Elledge to author, May 11, 1959.
105 *Ibid.*
106 Carl Wittke to author, March 5, 1959.
107 New York, 1946. The German edition is entitled *Geschichte der
Deutschen* (2 vols.; Berlin, 1947).

interpretations, preferring to point out the negative and positive forces in each period. He praised the cultural and humanistic achievements, but condemned the militaristic and oppressive tendencies. Following the pattern which he had established in his studies on the revolution of 1848, he wove the basic German developments around leading personalities; indeed, his graphic biographical sketches formed the distinctive feature of the book. His portrayal, for example, of the six heroes of German history—Luther, Frederick the Great, Kant, Goethe, Stein, and Bismarck—indicated both their shortcomings and strength; none of them, he insisted, had anything in common with Hitler, "the genius among German demagogues."[108] In the last half of the book, which dealt with the nineteenth and twentieth centuries, he traced, as one of his themes, the tragic course of German liberalism. The revolution of 1848, of course, loomed large in his account; he was proud of the gallant efforts of the liberals to create a nation-state on a constitutional basis and regarded their defeat as a great tragedy not only for Germany but for the whole world. No blind admirer of Bismarck, he approved the chancellor's policies of moderation in foreign affairs, but characterized the latter's internal measures as mistaken and disastrous. While very critical of German leadership under William II, he maintained that neither the emperor nor his collaborators wanted to dominate the world. He expressed warm sympathy for the Weimar republic, to which he referred as a great disappointment but no disgrace; its leaders, he believed, were men of character and decision. National Socialism, in his opinion, "recapitulated the entire gamut of German history"; he characterized this movement as anti-liberal, anti-Semitic, anti-Christian, and anti-Marxian.[109]

[108] The German people, p. 635.   [109] Ibid., p. 631.

In the closing paragraphs of the book, which he composed after he had returned from a trip to Europe in 1945, he made a rather severe indictment of the German national character, which had been molded by various geographical, historical, racial, and social factors. Among the negative traits of Germans, he listed their "petty self-seeking," their "envy, touchiness, jealousy, ambition without generosity," their "respect for power, for the authority of the uniform, the title, the office, the inside information," their "chronic distrust of, skeptical disbelief in, the efficacy of the central and supreme authority—the Emperor of the Holy Roman Empire, the Imperial High Court, or later, the federal diet at Frankfurt"—their "ludicrous emphasis on social differences," their "exaggerated professionalism," and their "tendency to extremes."[110]

Yet Valentin refused to despair, and looked forward to the time when Germany, after a period of self-examination, reorientation, and regeneration, would return to her best cultural and humanistic traditions. "No inward regeneration is possible without a ruthless analysis of German national character. This will be accomplished best by the Germans themselves."[111] He concluded:

There is upon Germany something amounting to a blight, a curse. The best Germans have deplored it, and no enemy could say harsher things about the country than some Germans themselves have said. They said these things, of course, not for destructive but creative purposes. To see, now, a whole nation put in the position of a defendant at the bar is a new thing in history. It is in the best interests of the German nation itself that the truly guilty be punished, in order that the nation may survive and overcome this terrible crisis and inaugurate a new historical life in conformity with the world conscience, as well as with the most illustrious qualities of the elder Germany herself.[112]

110 Ibid., pp. 675 ff.   111 Ibid., p. 685.   112 Ibid.

139

On January 12, 1947, a few months after the publication of his history of Germany, Valentin died in Washington, D.C. at the age of sixty-one. His passing "at the height of his powers was a tragedy for his friends in both hemispheres and a grave loss to the world of historical scholarship, for he combined erudition with insight, imagination and judgment."[113]

From the foregoing survey of Valentin's historical career and analysis of his most important works, it is clear that he stood completely outside the conservative Prussian tradition. While he admired the constructive contributions of some Prussian statesmen, such as Stein, he made no attempt to glorify Prussian institutions and leaders. He had no sympathy for the arrogance and military spirit of the Junkers. Nor did he seek refuge in the Austrian camp of historians, since he believed that "Austria was by no means the innocent lamb that had been attacked by the wolf of Berlin."[114] Unlike the majority of German historians—particularly pan-Germans like Below and Schäfer—whose coordination into the Nazi Reich was easily accomplished, he rejected the Nazi ideology as a degradation of the human spirit, a denial of Christianity and civilization, and a negation of Germany's best cultural traditions, as represented by Kant, Lessing, Goethe, and Wilhelm von Humboldt. Meinecke, too, came to the same conclusion, but much later.

After the second World War Meinecke appealed to his countrymen to follow his example by turning their eyes from the Iron Chancellor to Goethe. While his conversion occurred in his old age, Valentin was a liberal from the very beginning, never at any moment intoxicated by military glory or grandiose material achievements.[115]

[113] Gooch to author, April 7, 1959.　　[114] *Ibid.*　　[115] *Ibid.*

As a historian with strong democratic traditions, who manifested a warm and human interest in the common people—the "man in the street"—Valentin belonged to a small group of liberal historians which included, among others, such men as Walter Goetz, Johannes Ziekursch, and Hermann Kantorowicz.[116] All his basic works reflected his deep interest in the course of German democracy.

If his writings were mainly characterized by an uncompromising liberalism and a devotion to democracy, they also revealed a remarkable versatility, a superior literary ability, and a pronounced humanistic outlook. They ranged all the way from German colonial history, in which field he might be regarded as a pioneer, to a comprehensive *Weltgeschichte*, which bears testimony to his wide cultural interests. They often dealt with diplomatic, political, and biographical topics, and, as in the case of his studies on the revolution of 1848, he emphasized social history, preferring the latter to an economic approach. Thanks to his effective literary style, his books, as a rule, are very readable—a rather rare achievement among German historians. Even his hostile critics paid tribute to his literary gifts, his facility of expression, and his skill in portraiture. Out of the dusty documents in the archives he was able to re-create living people, both the high and the lowly. Aided by these powers of description, he often succeeded in imparting to his readers a sense of the living reality of the past. He believed that ". . . an important task of historical research is to enlarge its realm of truth; and it will always be one of the higher functions of historical writing to people this realm with living characters."[117]

Since many of Valentin's publications were intimately

[116] Oscar J. Hammen, "German historians and the advent of the National Socialist State," *JMH*, XIII (1941), 162 ff.

[117] *Fürst Karl Leiningen und das deutsche Einheitsproblem*, p. 1.

related to the heated political issues of his day—such as the controversies over pan-Germanism, the League of Nations, pacifism, and the national colors—they have lost much of their appeal, except for the historian who is interested in the course of German liberalism. However, his studies on the revolution of 1848 in Germany, which culminated in his comprehensive history of this movement, continue to be of paramount importance to the historian. While they are not definitive—no historical work, for that matter, remains so for long—they are not likely to be superseded in the near future. In any case, they will serve as a basic reference work for future scholars who wish to delve more deeply into the revolution, suggesting to them valuable clues and insights.

Valentin's tragic but heroic career was in a sense symbolic of the fate of German liberalism. Like the forty-eighters who preferred exile to oppression, he too sought refuge in other lands. Yet, wherever he went, he carried within him the best liberal and humanistic traditions of Germany, without abandoning the hope for their ultimate survival and triumph in his native land. In her tribute to him, Miss Taffs stated that ". . . he stood for a Germany that may some day become as great a power for good as Hitler's *Reich* was for evil."[118]

---

[118] Miss Taffs to author, March 25, 1959.

S. WILLIAM HALPERIN

PIERRE
RENOUVIN
1893—

The career of Pierre Renouvin, professor at the Sorbonne
and member of the Institut, has been one of the most brilliant in the recent annals of French historical scholarship.
He first vaulted to fame with the publication of *Les origines immédiates de la guerre (28 juin–4 août 1914)*,[1] when
he was thirty-two years old. Since then, thanks to a succession of outstanding works, his reputation has continued to
grow. Today he is regarded as one of the foremost diplomatic historians of our time. Diplomatic history is of course
an area in which Frenchmen have traditionally excelled.
Renouvin thus represents one of the latest in a long chain
of illustrious names that have given his country so eminent
a place in this domain. He has received many marks of rec-

S. William Halperin is professor of modern history at the University of
Chicago.

[1] Paris, 1925. In this essay no effort is made to discuss all of Renouvin's
writings. Only the most important ones are dealt with.

ognition. One of these is honorary foreign membership in the American Historical Association. Since the death of Georges Lefebvre in August 1959, Renouvin has been the only Frenchman to enjoy this distinction.

Not by his writings alone has Renouvin served the cause of historical scholarship. In 1928 he was named one of two secretaries assigned to a newly appointed national commission headed by the well-known historian Sébastien Charléty. The task of this commission was to arrange and supervise the publication of a monumental series which has since become famous the world over as the *Documents diplomatiques français, 1871–1914.* In addition to his secretarial duties, Renouvin shared with his friend Charles Appuhn responsibility for the preparation of the eleven volumes covering the period from 1911 to 1914.[2] This assignment, which of course called for careful selection and editing, he completed in 1939.[3] Six years later, following the return to a normal rhythm in scholarly activity as in everything else, Renouvin was appointed to fill the vacancy created some time before by the death of Charléty.[4] While serving as president of the commission, he directed the preparation of the volumes for the years 1894–1900 and 1907–11.[5] In 1959 he had the satisfaction of seeing the last instalment of the series go to press. Thus a project of incalculable value to scholars everywhere was finally brought to completion. Should the French government undertake a sequel to it by publishing the diplomatic correspondence for the period between the two world wars, Renouvin will in all likelihood be invited to direct such an enterprise.

Despite the claims of research, writing, and teaching, Renouvin has accepted heavy editorial responsibilities. From

2 Renouvin to author, May 2, 1960.

3 *Ibid.*   4 *Ibid.*   5 *Ibid.*

1923 to 1939 he served as *rédacteur en chef* of the *Revue d'histoire de la Guerre mondiale*. Throughout the greater part of this period he also handled the documentary section of the *Esprit international*, a periodical published in Paris under the auspices of the European Center of the Carnegie Endowment for International Peace. In 1941 he took over the direction of France's leading historical journal, the *Revue historique*. This enabled him to play a central role in the scholarly life of his country.

Renouvin has likewise been active in the field of educational administration. From 1955 to 1958, without giving up any part of his teaching duties at the Sorbonne and at the Institut d'Études Politiques, where he lectures on the history of international relations, he served as dean of the Faculty of Letters of the University of Paris. In this capacity he devoted his efforts mainly to organizing the so-called "third cycle" of higher education.[6] Although the task took much of his time and energy, it did not interrupt or slow the rhythm of his productivity as a historian. On the contrary, it coincided with an accelerated tempo of publication and the appearance of his best work.

Renouvin was born and educated in Paris. He attended the Lycée Louis le Grand. His professors were impressed with his interest in history and urged him to go into teaching. At the Sorbonne he followed their advice. Under the direction of Alphonse Aulard, the celebrated historian of the French Revolution, he did his first bit of original research. The subject chosen was one aspect of the work of the French provincial assemblies of 1787. In 1912, before he was twenty, he successfully passed the examination for the *agrégation* in history. However, he began to feel that the

[6] *Ibid.* For the genesis of the "third cycle" see Renouvin's article, "Le troisième cycle de l'enseignement supérieur des lettres," in *Revue de l'enseignment supérieur*, No. 3 (1959), pp. 113–29.

life of a lycée professor might not be entirely to his taste. He turned to the study of law and won his licentiate in 1913.

At this point he experienced another change of heart and reverted single-mindedly to his interest in history. Resuming his research under the direction of Aulard, Renouvin planned a comprehensive study of the origins, development, and accomplishments of the provincial assemblies of 1787. The outbreak of hostilities in the summer of 1914 interrupted these labors. Renouvin served as an infantry officer. He was severely wounded in 1917. Unable to discharge his military duties because of the handicapping injuries he had sustained, he returned in 1918 to the project on the provincial assemblies. Three years later the work was completed and published as a doctoral dissertation.[7] Based on a tremendous amount of archival research and betraying the author's thorough familiarity with the printed sources, it constituted a well-nigh definitive treatment of the subject. In preparing it Renouvin had received advice and encouragement not only from Aulard but from two other distinguished scholars: Camille Bloch and Marcel Marion. He treasured their help; they welcomed him into their well-tilled field. But already the eighteenth century had ceased to monopolize his attention. He forsook it for a new and absorbing interest: the history of the recent war. He never regretted this shift. It paved the way for his debut as a diplomatic historian.[8]

[7] *Les assemblées provinciales de 1787: origines, développement, résultats* (Paris, 1921).

[8] It also resulted in his being asked to write *Les formes du gouvernement de guerre* (Paris, 1925.) This excellent monograph formed part of a monumental series on the history of the recent war sponsored by the Carnegie Endowment for International Peace. Renouvin's contribution was an analysis of the operation of France's wartime government. It began with a sketch of the regime on the eve of the struggle and concluded with a résumé of the new trends that had sprung from the war.

The change of direction came about as a consequence of the French government's decision in 1921 to create at the University of Paris a program of study focusing on the critical examination of sources pertaining to the years 1914–18. The Sorbonne wished to entrust this program to an *agrégé* in history who was a war veteran and who had earned the *doctorat ès lettres*. It chose Renouvin, and he promptly inaugurated the program with a seminar on the sources for a study of the crisis of July 1914. He repeated this seminar during the next few years. In devoting his attention to the origins of the war, Renouvin was expressing not only a new and genuine professional interest. He was also, like so many other young Frenchmen who had spent years in the trenches, seeking for purely personal reasons to learn more about the conflict which had so profoundly affected the course of their lives.[9]

This professional and personal concern, together with encouragement from many of his colleagues, led Renouvin to prepare a monograph on a delicate, thorny, but extremely popular subject. Controversy over the question of responsibility for the outbreak of war in 1914 had raged without interruption ever since the early days of the struggle. Germany's enemies pointed an accusing finger at her. She denied the charge and accused her accusers. In the course of the dispute a great many diplomatic documents were published. To be sure, they shed light on the convolutions of the July crisis. But the story they were made to tell by the interested parties who pieced the evidence together was never quite the same; it tended to vary with the nationality of the narrator. Thus the controversy remained not only unresolved but more heated than ever. Scholars had entered the fray. As a consequence it developed into an erudite free-

9 Renouvin to author, August 2, 1960.

for-all, a battle fought with the paraphernalia of learning in
which the object more often was to defend or attack rather
than to ascertain the truth for its own sake and to follow it
wherever it might lead.

To this controversy Renouvin brought a refreshing degree of judiciousness and *sangfroid*. In his introduction to
Les origines immédiates de la guerre, which he completed
in March 1925, he faced up to the problem of trying to be
objective about so touchy a subject. Having noted the rabid
partisanship that still dominated the discussion, he declared
his intent to proceed differently. But even if it were true
that the methods of the research historian could be applied
to a subject of this kind, how could anyone be certain, Renouvin wondered, that he was in fact approaching it in the
proper frame of mind? During the war, of course, impartiality had been out of the question. The interests and prestige of the belligerent powers had been too much involved.
But even now, almost eleven years after the start of the war,
it seemed quite impossible to carry on research without taking sides. Yet the attempt had to be made. This, Renouvin
explained, he had tried to do. He had sought, before reaching any conclusions, to study the facts in an entirely critical
spirit.[10]

But even with the best of intentions, did not the investigator make himself vulnerable by looking for the truth at a
time when the available evidence was still incomplete and,
worse yet, open to suspicion? To be sure, as Renouvin
pointed out, the documents published since 1919 by the republican governments of Austria and Germany had greatly
facilitated the task of the researcher. Helpful too, if used
with the utmost caution, were the memoirs of statesmen
and ambassadors and the reams of testimony—sworn affi-

[10] *Les origines immédiates de la guerre*, pp. vi–vii.

149

davits—gathered by a committee acting at the behest of the German national assembly. Needless to say, the historian would have to rely mainly on the diplomatic correspondence; but the rub here was that France and England had not yet followed the example of Austria and Germany. So far the two Western powers had merely announced their intention of doing so. However, the lacuna was really not too serious: the Russian correspondence revealed a good deal about the attitude of Paris and London. But there was still another difficulty, and it constituted the principal reason for anxiety: even the invaluable official publications could not be trusted unreservedly. Important or useful documents might have been left out of them. Renouvin cited in this connection the case of the German collection assembled by Karl Kautsky. Renouvin was satisfied that Kautsky, an ardent foe of William II, had omitted nothing that was damaging to the imperial regime. But he called attention to sworn testimony indicating that some compromising documents might have been destroyed before Kautsky was given access to the files of the Wilhelmstrasse. While thus making the point that the published correspondence did not merit absolute confidence, Renouvin also warned against exaggerated distrust. The important thing, given the incomplete and uncertain character of the available evidence, was to assume that any conclusions reached would have to be tentative. Yet this was scarcely a reason for avoiding the subject. Most of the actors and witnesses were still alive. So long as they were, a historical inquiry into the July crisis would not prove fruitless. But it must be undertaken at once, not deferred until some later date.[11]

In keeping with the self-imposed attitude of the historian who sought to explain rather than to argue or judge, Re-

11 *Ibid.*, pp. vii, viii–x, xi–xii.

nouvin drew no invidious distinctions between the powers when he assessed the underlying origins of the war. All of them without exception were caught in a web of cause and effect from which they could not or would not break out. Thus Renouvin noted that after 1871, when Germany established her hegemony in Europe, a prolonged counterreaction set in which eventually produced the Entente Cordiale of 1904, the Anglo-Russian rapprochement of 1907, and the Anglo-French conventions of 1912. The Germans saw in this a threat of "encirclement." The two Moroccan crises of 1905 and 1911 rekindled the long-standing animosity which France and Germany felt toward one another and led both of them to intensify their military preparations. The Balkan crisis of 1912–13, following that of 1908–9, brought the interests of Austria and Russia to the point of direct confrontation. Because the Treaty of Bucharest of August 10, 1913 represented a setback for them, the Austrians were determined not to accept the resultant situation. The Germans had refrained from egging Vienna on while the crisis was in progress. However, they came away feeling that they had lost ground. Russia, in the meanwhile, had expanded her armaments and tightened her military ties with the French. In the latter she sensed a new firmness.

The idea that war was inevitable tended to spread. The circumstances of European politics, the armaments race, the growing rivalry between the two groups of powers, seemed unavoidably to lead to this idea. The conflict was expected; when the statesman arrived at this conviction, he reasoned and acted as if the trend were invincible. He would have to be able to prepare for the struggle without believing in it; how could he escape from this fatality?

Such was the moral situation that dominated the decisions of the statesmen in July 1914 and explained the evolution of the crisis.[12]

12 *Ibid.*, p. xiii.

151

All this was impartial enough. But when Renouvin began his microscopic examination of the July crisis, he lost little time taking a stand. Without departing from the fair-minded, judicious approach he had promised to adopt, he made no bones about the fact that, according to his reading of the evidence, the Germans, together with the Austrians, were largely responsible for the transformation of the original Austro-Serb quarrel into a European struggle. His reconstruction of what happened naturally centered on the first days of July, when Austria queried the Germans. Powerful elements in Vienna wanted to make war on the Serbs in retaliation for the assassination of Archduke Francis Ferdinand at Sarajevo. But first they had to know the attitude of Germany. There were influential people in the Dual Monarchy who wished to defer the settling of accounts with Serbia. Germany, by the stand she took, would decide. Did she advise caution, restraint, or delay? On the contrary, she decided to utilize the Austro-Serb crisis to bolster the prestige of her ally. This was to be achieved by immediate Austrian action against Serbia. The Germans, to be sure, wished to keep the hostilities confined to those two countries—which of course would have meant throwing tiny Serbia to the Austrian wolves. The trouble might not spread. The Germans had no desire to attack or involve Russia. Neither they nor the Austrians wanted a general war. But they knowingly and willingly accepted that risk:[13] this was the crucial, decisive point. By the 27th of July, the Germans, in concert with the Austrians, had created the "conditions" of a conflict that was to engulf the great powers.[14]

While by no means blind to the considerations that could be adduced in defense or extenuation of Germany's

13 *Ibid.*, p. 27.　　　　14 *Ibid.*, p. 256.

behavior—notably the fear of alienating her only remaining ally and thus finding herself completely isolated vis-à-vis the "encircling" powers of the Triple Entente—Renouvin saw little merit in the line taken by some of her apologists. Indeed, but still in the spirit of the truth-seeker rather than the polemicist, he even went so far as to accuse them of distorting the meaning of certain facts. Thus they sought to draw attention to the secret intentions of the powers in order to suggest that if Germany had been clumsy, the Entente had been too adroit. Renouvin objected that an approach of this kind would not contribute to a clarification of the main problem.[15] He readily acknowledged, in discussing the general, underlying causes of the conflict, that mutual distrust and the system of alliances affected the diplomacy of all the powers. He also pointed out that the already drafted plans of the military exercised an even greater influence on the course of the July crisis and that they played a role in Russia as well as in Germany.[16] But he insisted that the question of responsibility could be properly understood only by assessing the conduct of the powers at the very beginning of the crisis, when they were still in a position to decide freely what they proposed to do. Later their freedom would be gone. From the available data on the initial phase of the drama, it was reasonably clear to him that the Central powers betrayed an aggressive intent by refusing any solution other than force in dealing with the Serbs. Germany and Austria took this stand with their eyes wide open, after coolly envisaging all the possible consequences. "Within the context of the *immediate* origins of the conflict," Renouvin concluded, the position they assumed proved to be the predominant factor.[17]

As he moved through the successive phases of his analy-

[15] *Ibid.*, p. 265.   [16] *Ibid.*, pp. 266–68.   [17] *Ibid.*, p. 268.

153

sis, Renouvin continued to maintain the detachment of a scientific historian even though by his judgments he identified himself with the anti-German camp. In addition, he handled the evidence, which of course admitted of more than one interpretation, with extraordinary skill and finesse. Not the conclusion, which obviously contained nothing new, but the nuanced, fair-minded, masterly way in which it had been reached, made *Les origines immédiates de la guerre* a landmark in the historiography of July 1914. To be sure, it had its flaws. One of these, and it was undoubtedly serious, was the relative paucity of attention given to the much disputed subject of Franco-Russian relations during the crisis. But in comparison with all preceding studies, the book represented a giant step forward.

The long-awaited British documents on July 1914 were published in 1926. Renouvin, who had been planning to bring out a second edition of his book, wisely waited until the new collection was available. Leaning heavily on it, he went over the ground again and wrote a considerably augmented version.[18] He was able to clarify several important points, but the general lines of the original treatment remained unchanged. Other writers took note of what he had done when they proceeded to construct accounts of their own. Although his own interest shifted toward subjects of larger chronological scope, he followed with close attention the fantastic growth of the literature on July 1914 and occasionally composed an article on it. He was of course familiar with such distinguished works as *The origins of the World War* by Sidney B. Fay, *The coming of the war: 1914* by Bernadotte E. Schmitt, *Der Ausbruch des Weltkrieges* by Alfred von Wegerer, and *Le origini della guerra*

[18] It was published in Paris in 1927 under the original title. Shortly afterward an English translation appeared: *The immediate origins of the war* (New Haven, 1928).

del 1914 by Luigi Albertini. In subsequent books he himself returned, but only briefly, to the events of the crisis. Each time he reaffirmed in substance the position he had taken in 1925. *Les origines immédiates de la guerre* received widespread acclaim. In the United States, where the question of war guilt had precipitated a lively controversy among diplomatic historians, leading experts were at one in paying tribute to the signal nature of Renouvin's contribution. Schmitt described Renouvin as a "fair-minded" man who, like certain writers in other lands, was "animated by an honest desire to ascertain the truth" and to state his case "dispassionately."[19] Furthermore, Renouvin neglected "none of the nuances"[20] and maintained "excellent proportions" in the construction of his narrative.[21] For the developments that followed Germany's "blank check" to Austria, Renouvin's treatment, because of its superior organization which enabled the reader to follow the chronological sequence without difficulty, surpassed even so splendid an account as Fay's.[22] Charles Seymour also gave it high praise. In the preface to the English translation of Renouvin's book, he eulogized the Frenchman as belonging to the select company of "objective scholars" who had succeeded in freeing themselves from the thrall of "national prejudice" and "wartime emotion" and who were consequently able "to approach the task of investigation in a scientific frame of mind."[23] Renouvin's research was marked by "strict adherence to the canons of historical scholarship,"[24] and his conclusions were "framed with judicial care."[25] Very appropri-

[19] Bernadotte E. Schmitt, "The origins of the war," *Journal of modern history,* I (1929), 112, 119.
[20] *Ibid.,* p. 113.   [21] *Ibid.,* p. 116.   [22] *Ibid.*
[23] *The immediate origins of the war,* p. xiii.
[24] *Ibid.*   [25] *Ibid.,* p. xiv.

ately Seymour added: "It is notable that the critics of his work, whether among the advocates of the cause of the Entente, or those of the cause of Germany, have confined their objections to details and have acknowledged their confidence in his capacity for handling diplomatic documents and in his desire to evaluate the evidence impartially."[26]

This allusion to the unanimous applause which greeted *Les origines immédiates de la guerre* found partial confirmation in the reaction of Fay. Both Schmitt and Seymour belonged to the circle of scholars who held that Germany was mainly responsible for the outbreak of the war. Fay, on the other hand, was a leading "revisionist" who claimed that at least some of the charges leveled against Germany in connection with the question of war guilt were either baseless or exaggerated. Consequently, particular interest attached to his judgment of Renouvin's work, which presented a balanced but nonetheless critical estimate of Germany's role. In his review of the first edition, Fay showed himself to be second to no one in extolling its merits. He wrote:

M. Renouvin is a cautious objective scholar. He has sifted carefully all the evidence on the diplomatic crisis which followed the assassination of the Archduke at Sarajevo. He has written by far the best account of the immediate causes of the war which has appeared from the hand of a Frenchman. He establishes, day by day and hour by hour, the exact sequence of actions. This is the kind of book which makes a real advance toward the truth. He sweeps away most of the legends which have fed upon prejudice, propaganda, and ignorance, and which led the Versailles Peace Commission presided over by Mr. Lansing to make the untrue charge that Germany and her allies deliberately plotted the war.[27]

Thus, while praising the book, Fay was careful to stress the impossibility of squaring Renouvin's account with the

26 *Ibid.*
27 American historical review, XXXI (1925–26), 354–55.

extreme Allied position on war guilt. However, the fact remained, as Fay himself hastened to note, that "even after clearing away the falsifications and legends which have too long passed current in the Entente countries, M. Renouvin still has serious charges against the Central Powers which throw on them a large share of the responsibility."[28] Not all of these accusations were sound, Fay insisted. Furthermore, Renouvin's treatment of certain points was too brief. But he predicted that historians would indorse Renouvin's conclusion that the general as distinguished from the immediate causes of the war "were at work more or less in all countries in Europe."[29] The American scholar thus gave a boost to his own contention that special responsibility could not be ascribed to any one power or combination of powers.

A few years later Fay reviewed the English translation of the second edition. This time, while again expressing disagreement with Renouvin on a number of points, he went even further than before in praising the book. He declared that "one can not fail to admire the clarity, grasp, and judiciousness with which M. Renouvin has sifted the mass of documentary evidence, punctured and discarded untenable legends, and written what seems to the reviewer quite the best comprehensive treatment in any language which he has read on this difficult and thorny subject."[30] No finer tribute could have been paid to the quality of *Les origines immédiates de la guerre.*

During the three and a half decades that have elapsed since his debut as a diplomatic historian, Renouvin enhanced his reputation in a variety of ways. But more than anything else historical synthesis proved to be his forte. Here he performed impressively, so much so that he stood out even in a land where the art of synthesis boasts many

[28] *Ibid.*, p. 355.　　　　　　　[29] *Ibid.*
[30] *Ibid.*, XXXIII (1927–28), 878.

consummate practitioners. Although he by no means stopped conducting original investigations, he threw himself increasingly into this broader type of endeavor.

Renouvin's skill in fusing and elucidating the findings of recent research was demonstrated in the pages of his *La crise européenne et la grande guerre* (1904–1918).[31] Published in 1934, it promptly won recognition as a major pioneering effort. Although more than one fourth of the book dealt with developments that antedated August 1914, its significance lay in the fact that it represented the first serious attempt to write a truly comprehensive history of the war years. Renouvin had become interested in the subject when he commenced his critical investigations into the sources on the July crisis. For him the origins of the struggle were quite inseparable from its entire course during the following four and a quarter years. Indeed, from 1922 to 1931, when he was awarded a professorship at the Sorbonne, the historiography of the war remained his single most consistent preoccupation.[32] The work which he finally published in 1934 thus meant something very special to him.

The best of the previously published general histories of the conflict stressed the military aspect. Renouvin's approach was far broader. To each of the disparate but interrelated facets of the struggle—military, naval, diplomatic, economic, social, and psychological—he gave a nicely proportioned share of his attention. Moreover, he treated not only Europe but the Far East, the United States, and Latin America. His discussion of conditions and happenings in these faraway regions betrayed an expertise that reflected the depth as well as the range of his scholarship.

[31] Paris, 1934. This volume appeared as part of the "Peuples et civilisations" series edited jointly by Louis Halphen and Philippe Sagnac.

[32] Renouvin to author, August 2, 1960.

Grappling with an immense amount of material, Renouvin performed prodigies of compression and condensation. Yet he retained enough detail to convey the authentic flavor, even the dramatic, exciting quality of the period. He brought his own recapitulatory conclusions into the narrative without appreciably impairing its smooth, natural flow. The problem of organization, always difficult in an undertaking of this type, he resolved by skilfully blending the topical and chronological approaches and by trusting to his own sense of proportion. A lucid style, a high degree of factual accuracy, and an objective or at least reasoned treatment of controversial issues served to underscore the general excellence of the volume. As one reviewer remarked, what Renouvin had achieved was "synthesis in the finest French manner."[33]

In some respects such a judgment was even more applicable to La question d'Extrême-Orient, 1840–1940,[34] which appeared a dozen years later. In this work, which Renouvin chose to write because it fitted so perfectly into his expanding purview as a diplomatic historian, he again exhibited his flair for synthesis, but he did so with a narrative and analytical brilliance that signalized the full maturation of the talent first disclosed in Les origines immédiates de la guerre. La question d'Extrême-Orient traced with superb accuracy, clarity and compactness the successive phases of international relations in the Far East and the Pacific during a hundred years of spectacular and momentous change. Renouvin's description of the motives and moves of the great powers, which was grounded in the best available knowledge, represented one of the finest expositions of its kind in any language. To provide the necessary background for an under-

[33] Charles Seymour in his discussion of the book in American historical review, XL (1934–35), 742.
[34] Paris, 1946.

standing of this diplomatic story, Renouvin summarized
the important developments that took place within China
and Japan. He also recapitulated the relevant happenings in
Indo-China, Siam, Burma, and the Pacific Islands. He was
of course no Orientalist, and this he was careful to emphasize.[35] Yet, in depicting the peoples and institutions of the
Far East, he displayed a comprehension of the subject that
would have brought no discredit even on the most knowl-
edgeable specialist in the history of the area.

The bibliographies appended to each of the chapters disclosed how far-flung had been Renouvin's quest for up-to-
date and dependable information. But considerably more
impressive was the craftsmanship with which he wove these
data together. Trenchant in content and beautifully proportioned in form, the work was highly lauded even by those
who did not find it flawless. Thus John K. Fairbank, after
calling attention to some inadequacies in Renouvin's treatment of the Asiatic background, explained that he had
raised "these minor points only because M. Renouvin's
high standing in the field of diplomatic history makes it
unnecessary to dilate upon his masterly grasp of the subject
of this book and the great precision and finesse of his presentation of it."[36]

In the years directly following the publication of Les origines immédiates de la guerre, Renouvin had collaborated
with several other distinguished scholars to produce, under
the editorship of Henri Hauser, a diplomatic history of Europe from 1871 to 1914.[37] Shortly afterward he had published, with the European Center of the Carnegie Endowment for International Peace acting as sponsor, an incisive

[35] See La question d'Extrême-Orient, 1840–1940, p. 1 n.

[36] American historical review, LIII (1947–48), 340.

[37] Histoire diplomatique de l'Europe (1871–1914) (2 vols.; Paris, 1929).

survey of European diplomacy from 1815 to 1914.[38] Then, just before the outbreak of World War II, he had co-authored a work entitled *La paix armée et la grande guerre* (*1871–1919*).[39] These studies, together with *La crise européenne et la grande guerre* and *La question d'Extrême-Orient*, represented leisurely stages in Renouvin's progress toward the culminal four-volume history of international relations from 1815 to 1945 which he published in the 1950's. His teaching program at the Institut d'Études Politiques dovetailed nicely with the task of completing this ambitious undertaking. Another magnificent example of historical synthesis, the work assembled an enormous amount of material and welded it into a limpid, gracefully written, skilfully compressed and closely reasoned exposition. The bibliographies showed that Renouvin had overlooked relatively little in the way of important articles, monographs, and general works. Publications in several languages other than French—Russian, Polish, and Swedish as well as English, German, Italian, and Spanish—figured in this vast array of sources. Having kept abreast of recent research, Renouvin was able to maintain a high level of both up-to-dateness and accuracy throughout the many phases and ramifications of his narrative.

No one was more aware than he that despite the proliferation of documentary publications, there were still innumerable gaps or thinly covered spots in the evidence. Consequently, a host of significant questions could be answered not at all or only in the most tentative and guarded fashion. While duly noting these lacunae and indicating the meth-

[38] *Histoire diplomatique* (*1815–1914*) (Paris, 1930). This was a verbatim transcription of a course of lectures Renouvin had given in the academic year 1928–29 at the Institut des Hautes Études Internationales.

[39] Paris, 1939. Renouvin's collaborators were Edmond Préclin and Georges Hardy.

odological problems they raised, Renouvin squeezed what he could out of the data at his disposal and even ventured some shrewd hypotheses along the way. In the process he compiled an excellent summation of the best available knowledge.

The marvelous lucidity and compactness of his treatment, which evoked universal admiration, matched the almost Olympian detachment, the combination of steadfast judiciousness and cool objectivity, with which he viewed each of the episodes and individuals he discussed. His methods varied, but he relied mainly on an alternation of the topical and chronological, the analytical and narrative approaches. He displayed keen perspective in appraising the meaning of what transpired amidst the kaleidoscopic succession of events. Cutting through much of the underbrush, he made the large trees and the contour of the forest stand out in bold relief. Frequent summaries stressed saliences and interrelationships, thereby enhancing the cogency of the exposition. To be sure, the distribution of emphasis left something to be desired. Renouvin gave the periods 1815–1914 and 1914–45 an equal amount of space. But such a lopsided division hardly detracted from the achievement as a whole. As a general yet pithy and searching recapitulation of the principal happenings in the world's diplomatic arena during the vast era under review, it represented a veritable tour de force, surpassing all previous works of comparable scope. True, although some fresh details were introduced, the interpretations contained nothing really original or startlingly new. But several of them were extraordinarily suggestive. Every now and then flashes of insight illumined or clarified the reconstruction of events, the description of actors and their motives. The familiar thus acquired a richness of dimension which made it more meaningful than it had been before.

The four volumes formed the second half of a series which Renouvin himself had planned and edited and which covered the history of international relations since the Middle Ages.[40] At the very outset the reader's attention was drawn to the forces that shaped or influenced the course of international affairs. These forces Renouvin identified as political, socio-psychological, ideological, and economic in character. The first three overlapped a good deal and were at times quite indistinguishable. To be sure, all of them were constantly operative, but with varying degrees of intensity and effectiveness in different periods and circumstances. It was therefore impossible, Renouvin concluded, to establish any definite hierarchy among them; the fluctuating nature of their roles ruled out any rigid classification on the basis of relative importance. In any case, so far as he was concerned, the purpose of the study of international relations was neither to establish "historical laws" nor to provide lessons. Rather, it was to try to comprehend the complex interaction of those "causes" that had produced the world's "great transformations."[41]

Although Renouvin thus declined to accept any theoretical, hard-and-fast rating of the forces at work in the sphere of diplomacy, he tended in practice to ascribe a primary role to one or another of the non-economic categories. This was quite evident, for example, in his treatment of the period from 1815 to 1871, his analysis of the origins of World War I, and his reconstruction of the troubled years that preceded the coming of the second holocaust. Exponents of

[40] Pierre Renouvin (ed.), Histoire des relations internationales (8 vols.; Paris, 1953–58). The volumes written by Renouvin are Le XIXᵉ siècle. I. De 1815 à 1871: l'Europe des nationalités et l'éveil de nouveaux mondes (Paris, 1954); Le XIXᵉ siècle. II. De 1871 à 1914: l'apogée de l'Europe (Paris, 1955); Les crises du XXᵉ siècle. I. De 1914 à 1929 (Paris, 1957); Les crises du XXᵉ siècle. II. De 1929 à 1945 (Paris, 1958).

[41] Le XIXᵉ siècle. I. De 1815 à 1871, p. 404.

the economic interpretation of history were bound to de-
mur, but the evidence which Renouvin marshaled seemed
to be against them. Although admittedly no economic or
any other kind of determinist, he was in actuality far from
blind to the importance of the role played by economic interests in the international domain as well as in the realm
of domestic affairs. Indeed, he maintained that they figured
so significantly as motives or pretexts that it was imperative
for the diplomatic historian not to lose sight of them.[42] He
himself never failed to bring them into his analysis, if only
to show that although they were influential, they were not
necessarily decisive. He conceded that at certain moments
they did predominate, but he concluded quite correctly that
at least in the succession of periods with which he was concerned, such moments were comparatively rare.

One of the instances in which they exerted a controlling
influence was the subjection of the Far East to European
penetration.[43] They played a significant although in the last
analysis an essentially contributory role in the growth of the
national movements that presented European diplomacy
with some of its severest tests. The socio-psychological impact generated by the currents of national sentiment proved
the decisive factor.[44] On the other hand, in the case of the
revolts which felled Spanish and Portuguese rule in Latin
America, economic interests were preponderant.[45] But this
had few parallels elsewhere. Although commercial considerations exerted a powerful and palpable influence on the
behavior of the European nations before 1914, the outbreak
of World War I could hardly be explained in terms of
trade rivalry.[46] To be sure, the Franco-German and Russo-

[42] *Les crises du XXe siècle. I. De 1914 à 1929*, p. 218.
[43] *Le XIXe siècle. I. De 1815 à 1871*, pp. 400–401, 403.
[44] *Ibid.*, pp. 401–2.   [45] *Ibid.*, p. 402.
[46] *Le XIXe siècle. II. De 1871 à 1914*, p. 382.

German difficulties that cropped up during this period were related to a conflict of economic interests, but the latter apparently played only a secondary role in producing these complications.[47] Even in the oft-cited case of Anglo-German commercial rivalry after 1890, the available evidence did not support the thesis that British businessmen favored a resort to arms to eliminate German competition. In fact, they showed themselves hostile to the idea of military intervention of any kind in July 1914. As for the leaders of German industry, there was no proof that they wanted war. The pith of the matter was that although economic rivalry did affect the psychology of nations, it tended mainly to reinforce already existing suspicions and to strengthen the "desire for power." Thereby it increased the chances of a general war, but it was not the direct cause.[48]

Admittedly the state of international relations would have been decidedly different in 1914 if profound changes had not taken place in the economic sphere during the preceding half-century. But surely, Renouvin contended, it could not be argued that the conflict was the inevitable result of clashing material interests. Actually, the war did not break out until competing political designs came into violent collision. True, economic considerations figured in these designs. But it was not thoughts of material gain that determined the behavior of governments and peoples. The explanation for their conduct was to be found in the impact upon them of national feeling and passion.[49] Here Renouvin placed himself on apparently unassailable ground. Nothing in the voluminous data he had sifted conflicted with the thesis that the first great struggle of the twentieth century sprang from non-economic causes.

Turning to more recent developments, Renouvin con-

[47] Ibid.   [48] Ibid.
[49] Ibid., p. 384.

tinued his appraisal of the underlying forces in international relations. In this context he scrutinized the repercussions of the world-wide depression that started in 1929. He noted that the ferment it produced assumed divergent forms in the various countries and concluded from his examination of the evidence that the reason for this was political: the existence of long-standing attitudinal differences between the nations.[50] Adverting to the central fact of international affairs from 1933 onward, the bellicosity of Germany, Renouvin rejected as completely unproved the contention that economic pressures forced the Nazis to embark upon a policy of conquest.[51] Was such a policy really imposed by the need for economic expansion, as argued by certain writers, or was it at bottom the result of something else? Addressing himself to this question, Renouvin pointed out that economic necessities were never invoked at the conferences in which Hitler divulged to his subordinates the motives and goals of his foreign policy. Moreover, it was quite plain that Germany could have satisfied her need for economic expansion without resorting to arms. It was therefore possible to maintain that the foreign policy of the Nazis, far from having been determined by economic preoccupations, stemmed instead from an essentially different source: the craving for political and military preponderance.[52] Did economic considerations push the Western powers into the series of disastrous blunders they committed on the eve of World War II? Renouvin did not think so. He was inclined to ascribe the behavior of England and France mainly to "the currents of collective psychology,"[53] by which he meant the political attitudes then prevalent in those two countries, as distinguished from purely material concerns. Given

[50] See *Les crises du XXᵉ siècle. II. De 1929 à 1945*, p. 21.
[51] *Ibid.*, pp. 195–96.
[52] *Ibid.*, pp. 196–97.   [53] *Ibid.*, p. 199.

the present state of our knowledge, the distinction thus made by Renouvin and the thesis he rested on it seemed plausible enough. While economic interests obviously helped to fashion the Anglo-French image of what was right, desirable, and necessary, they apparently failed to produce nearly as much effect as the imperatives of national security and prestige.

The last major topic treated by Renouvin was the world in 1945, immediately after the cessation of hostilities. In assessing the already emerging rivalry between the United States and the Soviet Union, he analyzed the American decision, reached toward the end of the year, to extend loans to the countries of Western Europe. Although he noted the economic considerations that undoubtedly helped to produce this decision, he correctly insisted that political preoccupations were uppermost in Washington: the stated aim of the American program, which foreshadowed the Marshall Plan, was to preserve "a civilization of free men and free institutions."[54] As for the Russians, although Renouvin did not say so, it was clear that the mainsprings of their behavior, their motives and aims, were likewise political in character.

In addition to the forces that determined or influenced the direction of international relations, there were of course the actors who occupied the center of the stage, the men who held positions of authority in the various countries, particularly those states in Europe and outside it that had long been or were in the process of becoming great powers. In this connection, it should be noted that the governments of such extra-European countries as the United States and Japan, to which Renouvin paid heed as soon as they began to loom on the international horizon, received increasing

[54] *Ibid.*, p. 397.

attention as the chronicle unfolded. When he had reached the end of World War I, Renouvin appropriately titled his next chapter "The decline of Europe."[55] He was obviously interested in the rulers, statesmen, and diplomats from all the lands that figured to a greater or lesser degree in successive alignments and alliances, in the tale of adventures, crises, and wars. Almost at the very beginning of his first volume, where he sketched some of the larger contours of the story he proposed to tell, he cautioned against slighting the personal factor. How, he queried, could one neglect the actor's temperament, his conception of the national destiny, his understanding or misapprehension of the underlying forces?[56] With the period 1815–71 in mind, he went on to elaborate this point as follows:

[Any] . . . explanation [of the course of international relations] . . . would remain incomplete and deceptive if it failed to consider the behavior and initiatives of the statesmen. No one can doubt this in the case of Cavour, Bismarck, or Napoleon III. But how many other instances, at first glance less obvious, ought to come to mind! How, for example, can one fail to see the personal role of Canning in the dissolution of the Holy Alliance, or the influence of Palmerston's temperament in the prodromes of the revolutions of 1848? How can one forget that the France of 1830, under a sovereign other than Louis Philippe, could have become once again the agent of a great upheaval, or that the provisional government of 1848 was unwilling to give armed support to the Italian and German unitary movements? And when Russia, in 1853, by rekindling the Ottoman crisis, opened the way for transformations in Central Europe, did she not do so as a consequence of the personal wishes of the tsar? Analogous statements of fact are suggested by the Egypt of Mehemet Ali, the Japan of Okubo, the Spanish America of San Martín and Bolívar. To be sure, the initiatives of the statesmen were successful only insofar as the way had

55 Les crises du XXᵉ siècle. I. De 1914 à 1929, chap. v, pp. 130–53.

56 Le XIXᵉ siècle. I. De 1815 à 1871, p. 28.

been prepared for them by the operation of the underlying forces; but when these forces did not find a man capable of directing them, they came to nought: this was true of the German unitary movement in 1848. Undoubtedly one can argue with some plausibility that Italian unity would ultimately have been achieved even without Cavour and Napoleon III, or German unity without Bismarck. But when? If they had been delayed for thirty years, would not the consequences for the life of Europe and the world have been entirely different?[57]

Proceeding with his analysis, Renouvin cited the years from 1871 to 1890 as an example of how important at times the role of the personal factor could be despite the constant and pervasive impact of the underlying forces. Throughout those years Bismarck, invested with the office of German chancellor, bestrode the international scene like a colossus. In this rather unusual situation, the man became indistinguishable from something called "Bismarckianism," which was a socio-psychological reality.[58] But very different, according to Renouvin, was the interval from Bismarck's fall to 1914. This period he characterized as one in which the statesmen played a comparatively insignificant role. Their actions appeared to be dominated by conditions which they themselves perhaps failed to see clearly but which in any case they felt powerless to master. There were a few exceptions, but they occurred outside Europe: in Japan and in the United States of Theodore Roosevelt.[59] After World War I, Europe too had its exceptions. One of these was Hitler. The personal element in his career could hardly be underestimated, even though he acted out a collective desire for power and domination.[60]

Renouvin not only recounted what the statesmen did;

[57] Ibid., pp. 403–4.
[58] Le XIXe siècle. II. De 1871 à 1914, p. 378.
[59] Ibid., p. 379.
[60] See Les crises du XXe siècle. II. De 1929 à 1945, p. 193.

he also sought to indicate what they were like. In so doing, he showed remarkable perceptiveness. The portrayal of Napoleon III stood out as perhaps the finest in the entire work. Penetrating too were the vignettes of Alexander I, Metternich, Palmerston, Frederick William IV, Cavour, Bismarck and Hitler. These sketches related character traits to aims and policies. They added so much in the way of depth and pattern that it was regrettable Renouvin did not compose more of them. He missed many excellent opportunities, especially for the period 1914–45. As a consequence, in this respect the last two volumes did not equal the first and second.

Despite his flair for depicting the occasionally decisive, frequently important, but never negligible role of the personal factor, Renouvin showed no inclination to pursue this aspect of diplomatic history when he completed his four-volume work in 1958. Instead, he pushed on in the opposite direction. Anxious to do something about the lacunae he considered most serious, he decided to amass as much new data as possible on the forces that shaped the course of international relations from 1848, the year of revolutions, to the end of World War II. According to Renouvin's own description of the project, it would embrace among other things "demographic, economic, and financial influences and the role of religious questions and national sentiment."[61] The value of this project is self-evident. So is Renouvin's unique fitness to undertake it. The results of his research will be eagerly awaited.

Needless to say, what Renouvin may yet accomplish will have to be taken into account before any final estimate can be made of his place in the historiography of the twentieth century. However, his writings are already considerable, and

[61] Renouvin to author, May 2, 1960.

they bear the stamp of a true blend of science and art. To be sure, he is not primarily an innovator; he has done relatively little to push back the frontiers of knowledge. But he stands out as one of the most judicious and lucid historians of our generation. He is also eminently rewarding. Within his chosen domain, he has assembled virtually everything we know, tested, refined, and fused it, and made it more luminous.

JOHN EDWIN FAGG

SIR CHARLES
WEBSTER

1886—

In September 1959 a newspaper account of the conference
of the International Council for Philosophy and Humanistic Studies at Ann Arbor, Michigan, featured the remarks
of Sir Charles Webster.[1] This former president of the
British Academy discussed the failure of scientists to appreciate the contributions of ancient civilizations but also
chided humanists for their ignorance of science, for not
attempting to understand, among other things, the second
law of thermodynamics. The last point caught the fancy
of a number of readers, and Sir Charles enjoyed the brief
publicity provoked by his observation. His role as a free-
ranging commentator on intellectual matters is not new.

John Edwin Fagg is associate professor of history at New York University.

[1] New York Times, September 24, 1959, p. 39. Many statements in this
essay are based on the author's recollections of conversations with Sir
Charles at Princeton in November 1952, at London in April and May of
1959, and at New York in October 1959.

During the past forty years he has lectured in many countries at more institutions of learning than he remembers. He participates in the Congress of Historical Sciences and in UNESCO activities. As a friend of the great in several nations he has been influential in promoting international co-operation and the opening of archives. A senior historian, retired since 1953 as a professor, he still guides his students and warns, advises, and stimulates the profession. And he is heeded, for he has much to say. Furthermore, a multivolume history of the British strategic bombing offensive against Germany, which he wrote with Noble Frankland, is about to be published, an event awaited eagerly by military historians of World War II.

Webster's voice is one of infectious optimism, of the triumph of hope over fear even in a nuclear age. This historian of diplomacy and wars of the past century and a half truly believes humanity is improving. It is typical that the conference at Ann Arbor was jolted from a gloomy mood when Sir Charles asserted that, after all, it was "a jolly fine world." He has found it so himself, and in the course of a rich life he has done much to fortify his nation's pride in its history while yet furthering the cause of internationalism. It is as a diplomatic historian that Webster is most outstanding, though his knighthood came as recognition for his work in organizing the United Nations. As the author of pioneer studies of the Congress of Vienna, the foreign policies of Castlereagh and Palmerston, the League of Nations, Britain and the independence of Latin America, and now, the British air assault on the Reich, he enjoys the prestige and the serenity that come with achievement.

Charles Kingsley Webster was born on Easter Sunday, April 25, 1886, near Liverpool. That he was named for the eminent clergyman, novelist, and Christian socialist suggests something of his parents' outlook. His family was not wealthy, but they saw to it that he received a fine education—the grounding in classics that he recommended to scientists at Ann Arbor—at the Merchant Taylor's School in Crosby and at King's College, Cambridge, where he was appointed scholar in 1904 and fellow in 1909. At that time, as Webster later recalled,[2] Cambridge was about the only place in England where even a few scholars concerned themselves with the history of foreign policy. After reading widely in various fields he realized that this one held an attraction that could not be denied. Later he would maintain that he had simply been lucky, that he had begun the study of diplomacy on the eve of an explosion of interest in international affairs, almost at the same time that his good friend of the future, Bernadotte E. Schmitt, was doing so. In both cases talent and good fortune combined to produce great diplomatic historians.

Webster's researches drew him to the dim historical figure of Robert Stewart, Viscount Castlereagh after 1796 and Marquess of Londonderry after 1821, foreign minister of Great Britain from 1812 to 1822. Nearly all historians had neglected, belittled, or maligned Castlereagh. Yet the foreign office papers Webster saw gave an impression of a statesman of magnificent stature. Determined to be an archival historian, in fact almost snobbish about it, the young scholar studied the British documents avidly and with growing enthusiasm for his subject. Economies of the most stringent sort enabled him to finance further research expeditions to Paris, Vienna, Hannover, and St. Petersburg. Hard as he worked, he enjoyed it all hugely, for he has always had an immense appetite for life. He long loved to recount the way he had deluded the haughty custodians

---

[2] "The study of British foreign policy," *American historical review* (hereafter cited as *AHR*), XXX (1924–25), 728–37.

of the archives in Vienna by posing as a rich Englishman with important connections, whereupon they laid all their files before him. Also in Vienna he came under the influence of August Fournier and Alfred Pribram, who encouraged him more than anyone else to pursue his researches in diplomatic history.

The destruction of the unfortunate stereotype of Castlereagh was not a task to be undertaken casually. Webster took the most meticulous care in his first effort, an essay published in 1912,[3] to prove that the foreign minister had been high-principled and deft in managing British policy in connection with Spain and her rebellious American empire. In 1913 he read a paper before the Royal Historical Society in which with more boldness he praised Castlereagh's courage and statesmanship in forcing a settlement of the Polish-Saxon question at the Congress of Vienna.[4] Soon afterward, Alison Phillips brought out a book which, for almost the first time, included a favorable interpretation of Castlereagh, though he neglected to give Webster credit for his pioneer studies.[5] Even so, Webster had by then established himself as an authority, and in 1914 he was appointed professor of modern history in the University of Liverpool. At the same time he brought a protracted suit to a triumphant conclusion in marrying Miss Nora Harvey, whose inspiration and assistance he has unfailingly praised ever since.

[3] "Castlereagh and the Spanish colonies, 1815–1818," English historical review (hereafter cited as EHR), XXVII (1912), 78–95. The period 1818–22 he covered in another article of the same title but for the dates (ibid., XXX [1915], 631–45).

[4] "England and the Polish-Saxon problem at the Congress of Vienna," Transactions of the Royal Historical Society, 3d ser., VII (1913), 49–101.

[5] The confederation of Europe (London, 1914). In reviewing this book Harold Temperley caustically took Phillips to task for failing to acknowledge Webster's studies, with which he was sure the author was familiar (EHR, XXX [1915], 359–60).

The post at Liverpool, which Webster held from 1914 to 1922, was destined to involve little residence. His dismay over the outbreak of World War I was overshadowed by his moral outrage at the violation of Belgium. Traces of both emotions would appear in his future writings. Always he would value justice more than peace and admire Castlereagh and Palmerston for doing so. Soon Webster was in the army, a junior officer with a service organization. No one who knows him can doubt that this tall, forceful young scholar adapted himself with relish to the task of commanding imperious sergeants and other difficult personalities of the wartime service. He has always liked people and usually has his way with them. After two years he was drawn into the war office, for the British government had suddenly begun to appreciate historians. Webster took almost as much pleasure in being a man of action as in being a scholar. He made his will felt even in the bureaucracy. Before long he secured an assignment with the foreign office to prepare background material for the expected peace conference. His job was to compile a short account of the Congress of Vienna, about which, as he had once commented,[6] no comprehensive scholarly history had ever been written. Now, in May 1918, the task was his. In eleven weeks he wrote an excellent monograph which was long the standard work on the subject.

While *The Congress of Vienna, 1814–1815*[7] was destined to be exceedingly useful to teachers of history and to provide a basis for scholarly studies, it had no influence whatever on the Paris Peace Conference of 1919, or so Webster was fond of saying. President Wilson directed that there be no reference to the Congress of Vienna, so unfortunate

[6] "England and the Polish-Saxon problem at the Congress of Vienna," p. 49.

[7] London, 1919.

an affair did it seem to historians like himself.[8] Nor did professional scholars initially take much notice of Webster's book, though what they said was highly favorable.[9] It went through several printings, and since the more ambitious study planned by Fournier was never finished and Webster himself never had time to write a more elaborate account, the little monograph became a sort of classic. It was a model of neatness, with a chronology, a masterly survey of the background of the congress, its organization, labors, and results, together with a sketch of diplomatic developments to the end of 1815 and an appendix. Amazingly concentrated, the book was sober but not dull.

Most of the work derived from Webster's prewar archival investigations and the interpretations were uniquely personal. Two stood out: the commanding importance of Castlereagh in nearly every issue and the respectful treatment of the settlements of 1814 and 1815. If it seemed that the author had given too much credit to the British foreign minister, his future works would convince skeptics that his interpretation was sound. Never one to lose his balance, however, Webster bluntly depicted Castlereagh's preliminary defeat on the Polish-Saxon question, his disobedience of a flat command from the cabinet, and his dubious dealings regarding Sicily and Naples. The historian's implicit defense of the treaties of 1815 would seem more appropriate when the failure of those of 1919 came to be realized. Although he recapitulated the usual strictures against the earlier settlement, Webster pointed out that "the moving spirit of any age is seldom judged accurately by the men of

[8] C. K. Webster, The study of international politics (Cardiff and London, 1923), p. 17. This booklet is Webster's inaugural address at the University of Wales.

[9] Review by Ernest Satow, EHR, XXXIV (1919), 260–65; unsigned notice, AHR, XXV (1919–20), 137–38.

action who live in it."[10] And, he speculated: "Had any attempt been made to substitute for the contracts, written and unwritten, which had united Europe against Napoleon, the vague principles of nationality and democracy, so imperfectly understood alike by the peoples and the statesmen, the result would certainly have been disastrous."[11]

Webster's qualifications as a diplomatic historian were surely enhanced when he secured the position of secretary to the military section of the British delegation to the Paris Peace Conference. Still in uniform, as a captain and then as a major, he was supposed merely to supervise housekeeping details. This he did with gusto. It delighted him to see how large affairs might be affected by the distribution of hotel rooms, the manipulation of transportation privileges, and the placement of chairs. Petty matters, as his historical works would later show, often influenced the actions of eminent statesmen, at least those of less stature than Castlereagh and Palmerston. But Webster was also deeply involved with the issues of the conference. Wilson's "clear and resonant" voice across the Atlantic had moved him profoundly.[12] Apart from a passionate commitment to the president's program, the British historian was eager to further the causes of Poland and Zionism. In later years he liked to recall the consummate skill of his friend, Dr. Chaim Weizmann, who proved a master diplomatist.[13] Of course Webster could pretend to little influence at Paris, but he made many friends among the great and the near

10 The Congress of Vienna, 1814–1815, p. 146.

11 Ibid., p. 145.

12 "What the world owes to President Wilson," U.S. Congressional record, Senate, LXXII, Part 2 (January 10, 1930), 1349–52. Webster's speech was printed at the request of Senator Carter Glass of Virginia.

13 "The art and practice of diplomacy," U.S. Foreign service journal, November 1952, pp. 15–18. The same article had appeared in The Listener, February 28, 1952.

great. He had a high standing among the numerous historians who were "thick as bees" at the conference.[14] Most important of all, he observed the ways, both appalling and inspiring, in which matters of importance to humanity were handled. He was always inclined to defend the work of the treaty-makers of 1919. Once he told John Maynard Keynes to his face that he had caricatured the protagonists, especially Wilson. While Webster was invariably careful not to draw analogies of the past and present in his scholarly works, his experiences at Paris provided him with a new dimension for understanding the history of international affairs.

By the time he was demobilized Webster was well established as a historian of diplomacy. The period was one of intense concern with international relations, and the events of these postwar years made the educated public of Britain receptive to favorable appraisals of earlier statesmen who had won better results than Lloyd George was apparently obtaining. At the request of a group at Cambridge, Webster compiled a book of documents dealing with British policy in 1813–15, a period well studied from the Napoleonic side but comparatively little explored from the standpoint of the allied coalition. After consulting more than fifty thousand documents in the foreign office and the published papers of Castlereagh and Wellington, Webster produced a useful collection of dispatches.[15] It was helpful to scholars if scarcely a popular work. A short introductory essay gave him yet another opportunity to emphasize the high quality of Castlereagh's diplomacy, indeed his statesmanship. Also at this time Webster wrote two chapters in the *Cambridge history of British foreign policy, 1783–*

[14] The study of international politics, p. 11.
[15] British diplomacy, 1813–1815: select documents dealing with the reconstruction of Europe (London, 1921).

1919,[16] in which he dealt with the pacification of Europe in 1813–15 and the American war. Here again he demonstrated the greatness of Castlereagh in directing the final effort against Napoleon, though the author acknowledged that the unbending Tory was "the last man to cope intelligently" with the new forces unleashed by the wars[17] and that his cardinal error was "not that he ignored the principle of nationality, which was not ready for recognition, but that he placed no faith in popular institutions."[18] The chapter on the "futile and inconclusive"[19] struggle known in the United States as the War of 1812 was not among Webster's best efforts, as he well knew. An American historian praised his account but noted several minor flaws in his presentation of United States history.[20] This was not the last time that scholars across the Atlantic would find fault with Webster's handling of American history.

In 1922 Webster went to the University of Wales at Aberystwyth as the first Wilson Professor of International Affairs. His inaugural lecture dealt with a preoccupation of his own career, the historian as ally of the man of action.[21] He noted the longing of the human soul to understand itself through the study of history and the rarity with which anyone altogether rejected the past as a guide. Also he pondered the close but indefinable relationship between events and the labors of historians. The recent surge of respect shown by governments for historians he treated with a lightness that did not conceal the satisfaction he felt. Modern officials might apply historical knowledge imper-

16 Edited by Sir Adolphus Ward and G. P. Gooch (3 vols.; Cambridge and New York, 1922–23). Webster wrote chapters iv and v in Volume I.

17 Cambridge history of British foreign policy, I, 521.

18 Ibid., p. 519.   19 Ibid., p. 522.

20 Review by E. D. Adams, AHR, XXVIII (1922–23), 522, 525–26.

21 The study of international politics, passim.

fectly, but apply it they did. Yet to Webster the pathetic thing was the helplessness of statesmen, who generally meant well, in the face of public ignorance. Thus the main challenge was to promote the study of history by making it at once more popular, less nationalistic, and more scientific. Although Webster attempted all three of these possibly contradictory approaches, the last was part of a lifelong effort of his to press governments and prominent families into making their papers available to scholars. Speaking to the American Historical Association in Richmond, Virginia, in 1924, he repudiated Bismarck's famous dictum that official archives would yield few secrets. On the contrary, Webster insisted, rich materials awaited exploitation by historians, and at his suggestion the assembled scholars passed a resolution urging the automatic opening of official files after a specified period of years.[22]

By July 1924 Webster had completed the first volume of the long-promised study of Castlereagh's foreign policy.[23] That he elected to start with the second phase of his hero's career as foreign minister, the years 1815–22, reflected his own preoccupation with systems of international diplomacy, so much in his mind during the first years of the League of Nations. The book was based on three or four hundred thousand letters, dispatches, and memorandums in the archives of the major European capitals. While Castlereagh's private papers were not at that time available to Webster, it turned out, once they were, that they contained little to modify his original conclusions.[24] The author did not attempt a biography, for Castlereagh was too elusive

[22] "The study of British foreign policy," pp. 729–30; AHR, XXX (1924–25), 463 n.

[23] The foreign policy of Castlereagh, 1815–1822: Britain and the European alliance (London, 1925).

[24] Ibid., preface to 2d ed. (London, 1934).

for contemporary or historian to comprehend as an individual. Rather, he studied his foreign policy and frankly stated that the point of view was that of Britain. Yet the easy conclusion that Webster glorified his own country and made too much of his subject's importance would be dissipated as any fair-minded reader considered the evidence laid before him in these pages. The book was organized on a topical basis within chronological periods, with careful preliminary analyses of the background and characters and an appendix. It would be the same with Webster's future works. The scene must be laid, the actors characterized, and the action isolated, treated by unity of subject more than as segments of time. If the method was not ideal, it was the most satisfactory way to handle diplomatic history, as Schmitt was to demonstrate in his famous work on the coming of World War I.

Webster's style was graceful, balanced, and lucid to a degree not really attained in his previous studies and not to be surpassed in his later works. The most pleasing part of the book was the first chapter, where the author superbly set the stage for his account, describing the crown, the cabinet, parliament, and public opinion as factors in foreign affairs and then the character of Castlereagh and the diplomatic machine with which he worked. Here were fascinating sketches of individuals, sprightly, vivid, and, above all, accurate. Perhaps from his wide reading of novels Webster had sharpened his skill in brilliant characterization. Yet his human portraits were never wicked, even when he described personages he found repugnant, such as Metternich, Talleyrand, and Princess Lieven. Nor were they eulogistic or sentimental, as when he depicted Wellington, John Quincy Adams, and Canning, whom he admired. Only with royalty was he harsh, perhaps too much so. His style was never florid or pretentious, yet it conveyed the dignity of profound emotions and great events. While an exhilarating pace could scarcely be maintained as the author carried Castlereagh through all kinds of technical complexities, there was not a dull page in the book. Sometimes Webster tantalized the reader with allusions to fascinating matters he declined to elucidate. And a Victorian reluctance to discuss what he considered "filth" led him to gloss over many subjects which other writers would have explored with relish. Webster himself professed to take no particular pride in his style, claiming that he sought clarity above all and admitting that he so qualified his statements they lost color. Yet it is apparent that his writing is among the finest of its kind. The public appreciated it too. All his books sold well.

Webster's theme was more than the recognition of a great British statesman who had been dead for a century. He also sought to show how one of the earliest, perhaps the first, of international systems held the great powers in harmony for a few years. Castlereagh fathered the idea of diplomacy by conference, kept the method working for a time, and might have restored it once it broke down had he not died. It was a system his countrymen did not grasp and would have disapproved if they had. His successor, George Canning, exulted over the chance to wreck it. In handling this theme Webster emphasized the peculiar intimacy of the statesmen who had "shared trials and triumphs and even board and lodgings for long periods together"[25] while Napoleon was being overthrown. These men appreciated far better than succeeding generations how fragile and precious a thing peace was. By 1815 Castlereagh had acquired an ascendancy over these monarchs and ministers. It was his ambition to abolish the spirit of intrigue

[25] *Ibid.*, p. 64.

and suspicion from European diplomacy and to substitute trust and good will. The emotional Alexander I, the potential disturber of the equilibrium achieved at the Congress of Vienna, Castlereagh always seemed to read correctly and handle wisely. Webster offered a favorable interpretation of the tsar's purposes, which were much less sinister than many thought. Metternich he frankly scorned as false and vain. Castlereagh was not the Austrian's dupe; rather it was he "who led and Metternich who followed."[26] Both of course were reactionary, but they were not comic or malignant figures. They had seen what revolutions could do to society. Perhaps they were wiser than their liberal and nationalist detractors. Castlereagh's superintendence of European affairs shone at its best during the Congress of Aix-la-Chapelle in 1818. There he outmaneuvered his own countrymen, who disliked the idea of involving Britain in a permanent system of great power reunions, and rebuffed the tsar, who wished to transform that system into a grandiose and impossible machine for governing Europe. During the period of German restlessness in 1819–20 Castlereagh supported Austria subtly but effectively so as to deter Russian interference. When revolutions broke out in the Iberian nations in 1820 he won a complete if fleeting success by aligning the other powers against the tsar's plan for intervention. As usual, his sure-footed diplomacy attained its object, though he was painfully distracted by the difficulties of George IV with his queen at a time when foreign affairs demanded so much attention.

In 1821, however, Castlereagh sustained a grave defeat. Perhaps it was inevitable, Webster thought, that the international system would be disrupted by the temptation of the larger monarchies to interfere in the domestic affairs of the small powers. The revolutions in Italy brought Rus-

[26] *Ibid.*, p. 102.

sia and Austria together and resulted in intervention. Castlereagh had strongly denounced this policy and he, rather than Canning, had articulated the first British opposition to invoking the Holy Alliance for such purposes. There was still hope of restoring the co-operation of the great powers later in 1821. Castlereagh and Metternich met at Hannover and combined to keep the tsar from promoting intervention in Greece and in Spain and Portugal. The Greek problem was peculiarly tragic. Castlereagh, as Webster described him, was about the first British statesman to perceive the importance of preserving the Ottoman empire. Grievous as the sufferings of the Greeks were, to aid their insurrectionary efforts would "open a field for every ardent adventurer and political fanatic in Europe."[27] In the face of British and Austrian opposition the tsar drew back and peace was saved.

At this point in his account Webster recapitulated the role of his hero in the emancipation of the Spanish colonies. That Britain's policies were enlightened and Castlereagh's tactics dexterous he proved with abundant documentation, utilizing materials not available to him in his first studies. As Webster presented the situation, Spain might have saved her empire had her rulers heeded Castlereagh's advice to effect true reforms and open her ports. Since Spain refused this counsel, Britain declined to assist her and the revolutionary movements gained force. By 1818 the deadlock was complete. At Aix-la-Chapelle Castlereagh cleverly prevented the Spaniards from bringing pressure on the great powers for aid. What he sought was for Spain to accept his conditions, after which she might be supported by all Europe. Failing that, he anticipated the independence of Latin America but hoped to foster monarchical institutions there, something the United States would op-

27 Castlereagh as quoted, ibid., p. 377.

pose. With marvelous skill he played a double game, damp-
ening Russia's eagerness to intervene unconditionally while
at the same time employing the Russian threat to deter
American recognition of the republican regimes, at least
until after Florida was secured. In 1819 he also obstructed
a French scheme to send a prince to Buenos Aires. Thus
he kept matters in his own hands. Had he lived, Webster
believed, Castlereagh would have devised a program to
bring about the general recognition of Latin American independence and the creation of royalist governments oriented toward Europe. Then there would have been no
Monroe Doctrine of the defiant type that was announced
in 1823, fewer dramatics and less eloquence on the part
of the Americans and George Canning, and a sounder
order in Latin America.

Webster also enlarged on a point which G. M. Trevelyan
had recently made for the first time,[28] the pioneer work of
Castlereagh in preparing the basis for amicable British-
American relations. "Certainly no other British statesman
did more to lay the foundation of a hundred years peace
which few in either country at the time expected and certainly many did not desire,"[29] Webster judged, and related
the unobtrusive way Castlereagh supervised the negotiations regarding armaments on the Great Lakes and prickly
matters concerning Florida and Oregon. These were not
successes of the type to win the applause of contemporaries,
and they long escaped the notice of historians, "but they
are amongst the greatest achievements of the statesman."[30]
And while Castlereagh sometimes grew weary of Wilber-
force and the "Saints" regarding abolition of the slave

[28] British history in the nineteenth century, 1792–1901 (London, 1922),
pp. 177–78.

[29] The foreign policy of Castlereagh, 1815–1822, p. 437.

[30] Ibid., p. 453.

trade, his labors in that cause were sincere, practical, and successful.

The book concluded with Castlereagh's plans for the conference at Vienna in 1822, later held in Verona, and the complex program Webster believed he had for the settlement of Spanish, Greek, and Latin American problems. The poignant story of his mental collapse and suicide was told with exquisite taste. Webster has always denounced scandalous inferences about this tragedy. Castlereagh's mind, he insisted, gave way from the strain of overwork and nothing else. In closing his account the author traced the slow emergence of his subject's reputation from the obscurity imposed on it by the dazzling character of his successor, Canning, and the vilification of Whig and Liberal writers. And then, having recorded so thoroughly Castlereagh's successes, Webster summarized the case against him. He was temperamentally unable to enlist public support for his policies. His essentially reactionary attitudes placed him out of step with the forces of the future; he failed to associate his ideas with the deepest emotions of his age. If he attempted an impossible task with his system of international co-operation, however, "the end which he set before himself was one so noble, and the effort which he made to overcome his manifold and overwhelming difficulties was so gallant and persistent, that it is difficult to avoid paying tribute to his courageous statesmanship."[31] Introverted and reserved as he was, Castlereagh could never be known to us as a man. For his work, however, he was "entitled to the gratitude not only of his countrymen but of humanity."[32]

There was little professional historians could do with such a work but acclaim it, and this they did. So full was it of ideas and new information, or of facts stated in a

[31] Ibid., p. 502.   [32] Ibid., p. 504.

fresh manner, that R. B. Mowat found himself marking almost every line. No praise, he said, was too high for its scholarship.[33] Three future presidents of the American Historical Association—Dexter Perkins,[34] Samuel Eliot Morison,[35] and William L. Langer[36]—paid Webster splendid tributes in their reviews, though the first two fretted a little over his treatment of American history. Harold Laski mentioned, curiously enough, a certain heaviness in the way the author handled his materials but was greatly impressed with the book.[37] Schmitt has always admired it, and Webster has found more satisfaction in this work than in any of his others. The appearance of Harold Temperley's famous study of Canning[38] shortly after Webster's book came out inevitably brought comparisons of the two statesmen. It seems just to conclude that Castlereagh moved ahead of Canning in the esteem of historians.

Webster was now in the full tide of prestige and professional success. His restoration of Castlereagh caught the approval of the educated British public at a time when postwar disillusionment with the present made great characters of the past stand out all the more, especially when an unfair appraisal of long standing could be corrected. The historian was pressed with invitations. His professorship at Aberystwyth was ideal for his purposes, for he could do what he liked, go or stay as he chose. Since he always loved to travel, Webster accepted visiting professorships at the University of Vienna in 1926, the University of Calcutta in 1927, and Harvard in 1928–32. He did much lecturing

[33] EHR, XL (1925), 445–49.
[34] AHR, XXX (1924–25), 812–14.
[35] New republic, XLIII (July 8, 1925), 187–88.
[36] New York Herald-Tribune, October 4, 1925, p. 8.
[37] Nation, CXXI (December 9, 1925), 671–72.
[38] The foreign policy of Canning, 1822–1827 (London, 1925).

and sight-seeing in nearly every part of the world. A hearty extrovert, good company for himself and for nearly everyone else, he was an effective ambassador for his country, for the League of Nations, and for the promotion of education. He liked to prod governments into opening their files. Often he addressed groups of widely different types on international co-operation. Sometimes he offered courses or seminars. Always fond of doing justice to men who were not appreciated, he deliberately stunned a gathering in Vienna with a tribute to Freud, who was regarded as a charlatan by many of his fellow citizens.[39] In Washington he unsettled an audience with an eloquent speech in praise of Wilson at a time when his memory was not generally revered.[40]

The scholar was not lost in this rich variety of activities. Between 1924 and 1931 he found time to complete the story of Castlereagh's stewardship of British foreign affairs from 1812 to 1815. Most of the material he had collected before the struggle once known as the "Great War," but the opening of foreign archives after 1918 made it imperative for him to visit Dresden and Munich and to investigate again files in Paris, Vienna, and Berlin. Also the Londonderry papers were made available to him. Seldom able to make use of assistants other than copyists, Webster did most of the work himself. He found an ideal place to compose his narrative, at a Welsh farm, where for seven days a week during vacations he perused his notes in the morning, strode for much of the afternoon in country lanes and fields, and settled down for long evenings of writing. The manuscript was finished in January 1931. Like its twin volume, "Castlereagh Two," as he calls it, was a beautifully

[39] "Fifty years of change in historical teaching and research," Historical Association, Jubilee addresses (London, 1956), p. 33.
[40] "What the world owes to President Wilson," loc. cit.

made book, thoroughly documented, and tightly organized by topics within chronological divisions.[41] It was balanced, detached, and graced by the style that make his diplomatic histories pleasant reading. Here also were the opening chapter on the setting, the incisive analyses of the machinery of government written with a lightness that could come only from an unparalleled familiarity with the sources, and the graphic pen portraits of personalities. Castlereagh, whose career prior to 1812 was epitomized in a few pages, entered the scene in that year as a hard-minded politician whose potentialities for his new post of foreign minister were altogether unsuspected.

Before he allowed Castlereagh's activities in foreign affairs to monopolize the narrative, Webster emphasized the legacy of Pitt the Younger, whose "draft to Vorontzov" in 1804 outlined the reconstruction of Europe which Castlereagh, his pupil, would follow. Then the historian surveyed the situation as it was in 1812–13, when conditions were so fluid that a single false step might have permitted Napoleon to salvage his system. While Castlereagh was learning his job, the bungling of Aberdeen, Bentinck, and other diplomats threatened mischief. Even after the battle of Leipzig it was possible that Napoleon, whom Webster had once described as "the most successful soldier and statesman of modern Europe,"[42] might disrupt the allied coalition as he had on previous occasions. Decisive, then, was Castlereagh's trip to the continent in January 1814. The allies were hesitant to invade France, divided among themselves, and confused about war and peace aims. The British foreign minister alone saw clearly and thought straight. Exploiting his advantages to obtain Britain's war purposes—

[41] *The foreign policy of Castlereagh, 1812–1815: Britain and the reconstruction of Europe* (London, 1931).

[42] *British diplomacy, 1813–1815*, p. xxvii.

the exclusion of maritime rights from discussions in the future, assurance of a strong Netherlands, and disposition of the captured colonies as she wished—he freed himself to employ statesmanlike principles to bring the others to conclude the war and write a sound peace treaty. During the hectic weeks of early 1814, when discomforts, dangers, overconfidence, and panic confused the ranking officials of the several powers, Castlereagh steadied the coalition repeatedly. The Treaty of Chaumont in March 1814 was, as Webster presented it, perhaps the greatest victory of the impassive foreign minister. It was this agreement that assured the completion of the war and laid the basis for the co-operation of the great monarchies in the years to come.

After Chaumont events moved as Castlereagh hoped they would. Chiefly through his unobtrusive maneuvering the Bourbons were restored. The first Peace of Paris Webster pointedly praised for its moderation and wisdom. And while Alexander was making his disastrous visit to London and otherwise alienating his allies, Castlereagh quietly settled many awkward matters in ways beneficial to Britain and the stability of Europe. Already he was clear in his own mind that France must be treated considerately but restrained by strong border states, that Austria and not France should dominate Italy, and that Austria and Prussia should form a power center in the middle of Europe. Russia should have no more than her due. Above all, he was anxious to avoid reconstructing Europe so badly that a new war would follow after a short interval.

Webster treated the Congress of Vienna as he had before, but in more detail and with more authority. Again he stressed the courage and wisdom of Castlereagh, to whom all deferred after his striking victory in the Polish-Saxon crisis. These events he described with magisterial clarity, sometimes with accents of drama. Almost alone Castle-

reagh brought about the restoration of Louis XVIII following the Hundred Days and frustrated the efforts of others
to inflict a more severe treaty on France. Despite the confusion thrown into the situation by the tsar with that
piece of "sublime mysticism and nonsense,"[43] the Holy
Alliance, Castlereagh secured the Quadruple Alliance. Thus
the great powers remained bound to each other and ob-
ligated to continue the system of diplomacy by conference.
A masterful evaluation of Castlereagh and the Vienna settlement closed the book. After balancing praise and criticism, Webster ended his story with the judgment: "To the
overthrow of Britain's deadliest foe, and the making of the
new Europe in such a manner that Britain obtained the
longest interval of peace she had ever enjoyed, Castlereagh
contributed more than any other statesman of his time.
Such achievements should be sufficient to place him
for ever amongst the greatest foreign Ministers of his
country."[44]

Again laudatory comments showered on the historian.[45]
No serious flaws could be found in so careful a work, and
Webster's documentation and judiciousness were such that
no one could accuse him of eulogizing Castlereagh exces-
sively or brandishing the Union Jack. The facts spoke for
themselves. The appearance of this volume was less of an
event than his previous book, for Webster had already
ventilated his principal interpretations in earlier studies.
Also, in 1931 Britain and most of the world were preoc-
cupied with domestic economic affairs. Webster himself,
however, was still earnestly seeking to advance the cause

[43] The foreign policy of Castlereagh, 1812–1815, p. 482. The expression
was Castlereagh's.

[44] Ibid., p. 499.

[45] Review by R. B. Mowat, EHR, XLVII (1932), 133–35; review by
Dexter Perkins, AHR, XXXVII (1931–32), 323–25.

of the League of Nations. In two summer vacations in 1931 and 1932 he composed most of a survey he had long planned, to which Sidney Herbert contributed six chapters, dealing with the league.[46] Although it was not an ambitious work and was truly a labor of love, Webster found it difficult to write, for again he was breaking new ground. The authors traced the history of international organization, the construction of the league, the operation of its principal organs, and some of its failures and accomplishments. The tone was one of subdued pride and restrained optimism. Webster closed the study with an urgent summons to educate the multitudes to accommodate their national loyalties to an international outlook, and his final words were, "before it is too late."[47] It was already too late in 1933, when the book appeared. Nonetheless, it was a useful and respected popular study. Dexter Perkins wrote that its striking characteristic was the combination of sympathy and candor. "It exaggerates nothing," he said; "it does not extenuate League failures; it is remarkably dispassionate throughout." No other work on that organization, he believed, was so attuned to the historical mind.[48]

The volume on the League of Nations was dedicated in gratitude to Baron Davies, the principal founder of the chair Webster had held for ten years at the University of Wales and had now left. In 1932 he had gone to the London School of Economics in the University of London to become Stevenson Professor of International History. During the next generation he guided numerous graduate stu-

[46] The League of Nations in theory and practice (London and Boston, 1933).

[47] Ibid., p. 308.

[48] Review by Perkins, AHR, XL (1934–35), 342–43. See also review by P. B. Potter, American political science review, XXVII (1933), 481; review by W. L. Langer, Foreign affairs, XI (1933), 720.

dents, generously sharing with them his time, hospitality, and on occasion his funds. The gruff and intimidating manner he assumed invariably proved to be a fraud. Young scholars quickly perceived that they were being hazed, that no mentor could be more kindly or would do more for them, and Webster built up a devoted following. He was a renowned lecturer and despite a mock severity, a patient counselor. Despite his many satisfactions Webster was not happy in the late thirties. The collapse of the league and the approach of war, which he considered inevitable from 1936, depressed his ordinarily ebullient spirits for long periods.

The best escape from such broodings was to bury himself in the work he loved most, archival research. The career of another British foreign secretary excited his sympathies, that of Henry John Temple, Viscount Palmerston, whose place in history required redefinition rather than rehabilitation. The 1830's had not been well covered in diplomatic history, and Palmerston's promotion of constitutional government abroad seemed a fruitful subject to explore. Philip Guedalla urged Webster to undertake a definitive study, which he did after Lord Mount Temple made available to him, and to him alone, Palmerston's private papers at Broadlands. Webster set to work with his customary industry and all but completed the research by 1939. As early as 1934, when he delivered the Raleigh lecture on history,[49] and in 1938, when he read a paper at Zurich,[50] he presented his tentative interpretations. It was apparent he had found much to respect in the work of the diplomatist. A man of Webster's affirmative disposition could scarcely have de-

[49] "Palmerston, Metternich, and the European system, 1830–1841," Proceedings of the British Academy, XX (1934), 1–36.

[50] "Palmerston and the liberal movement, 1830–1841," Politica, III (1938), 299–323.

voted himself for long to a historical figure he did not admire.

Guedalla himself interrupted the researches on Palmerston when he invited Webster on behalf of the Ibero-American Institute of Great Britain to assemble a documentary collection dealing with Britain and the independence of Latin America. In his previous studies Webster had already handled this subject in a provocative fashion, but he was not particularly interested in Latin American history. He accepted the assignment, and with a fine discrimination which no one else was so qualified to exercise, picked documents out of the foreign office records covering the years from 1812 to 1830. A handsome set of two volumes was the product.[51] Much of the material was new, with many illuminating details concerning the attitude of Spain toward the revolted colonies, the policies of the great powers, the new nations, Britain's role, and the Monroe Doctrine. The selection of the dispatches pleased all the professional historians who reviewed the volumes.[52] The only regret was that the collection was not larger. A long introductory essay illustrated at their very best Webster's powers to summarize complicated diplomatic affairs. J. Fred Rippy called it "a brilliant survey" with which he was in complete agreement, though he raised a few queries about details of Latin American history,[53] where Webster was not truly an authority. And his treatment of the way the United States took advantage of Canning's proposal for joint action in

[51] Britain and the independence of Latin America (2 vols.; London, Toronto, and New York, 1938).

[52] Review by W. S. Robertson, AHR, XLIV (1938–39), 673–74; review by A. J. P. Taylor, Manchester Guardian, July 22, 1938, p. 7; review by J. Fred Rippy, Journal of modern history (hereafter cited as JMH), XI (1939), 544–45. Oddly, the Hispanic American historical review did not review this important work.

[53] Rippy, loc. cit.

1823 to issue the Monroe Doctrine on its own kindled some ire across the Atlantic.[54] One American historian who otherwise admired the work accused Webster of glossing over unedifying aspects of British policy,[55] a charge that brought a sharp denial from a British authority.[56] Webster was certainly no nationalist, least of all when he was writing history.[57] He simply chose periods in which British policy was triumphant and something to be proud of, as it was in the case of Latin American independence.

With the beginning of the war in 1939 Webster returned to government service. Soon he was in the United States, lecturing widely to university groups on the subject of peace after a British victory, which appeared extremely unlikely at the time. His talks were both inspiring and witty and he usually, though not always, succeeded in restraining himself in the face of provocation from Anglophobes and isolationists. As director of the British Library of Information in New York in 1941–42 he indulged his enormous affection for that city, in fact for the United States in general. But he felt miscast as a propagandist, and so he returned to England to supervise research at the foreign office. A fortunate change of apartments saved his papers and books from destruction in an air raid on London. Webster became involved in the planning for the United Nations and went to Dumbarton Oaks and San Francisco as a member of the

[54] A. P. Whitaker, *The United States and the independence of Latin America* (Baltimore, 1941), pp. 469–72; W. W. Kaufman, *British policy and the independence of Latin America, 1804–28* (New Haven, 1951), p. 228.

[55] Whitaker, p. 610.

[56] R. A. Humphries, *EHR*, LX (1945), 261.

[57] In delivering his inaugural address at the University of Liverpool in December 1914, Webster pleaded, despite his own and the general nationalistic fervor of the time, for objective instead of patriotic historical studies (*The study of nineteenth century diplomacy* [London, 1915], pp. 2–3).

British delegation. Working closely with Adlai Stevenson, his opposite number on the American side, he was recognized as one of the builders of the world organization. For these labors he was knighted in 1946 by King George VI.

By now there were so many demands on his time—university duties, book reviews, lectures, calls from the government and the United Nations, UNESCO activities, even radio broadcasting—that Sir Charles realized he could finish the Palmerston project only for the years 1830–41. Palmerston's subsequent career would have to be left to others. Pulling together his enormous collection of notes from Broadlands, the Public Record Office, and foreign archives and arranging them in twenty piles or more about his desk, he began to compose his account. Nearly all of the writing took place at the beloved farmhouse in Wales, where long walks in the countryside cleared his thoughts. In 1951 the two-volume set appeared.[58] The author followed his standard plan, beginning with a long opening chapter describing the factors of foreign policy and the machinery of government, followed by detailed treatment of diplomatic problems as unities, almost as separate monographs, an estimate of the statesman, and the inevitable appendix. Sir Charles confined his study to European affairs and the so-called Eastern Question. The reception of his work was extremely gratifying, though it was apparent that Palmerston had less stature than Castlereagh and that British foreign policy in 1830–41 dealt with less heroic issues than in the time of Castlereagh. Hence reviewers could admire Webster's scholarship without, as in the case of the Castlereagh studies, acclaiming a momentous new interpretation of a famous historical figure.[59]

[58] The foreign policy of Palmerston, 1830–1841: Britain, the liberal movement and the Eastern Question (London).

[59] Reviews by Paul Knaplund, Political science quarterly, LXVII (1952), 466–68; Frank J. Klingberg, JMH, XXVI (1954), 86–87; Paul Vaucher,

These books covered Palmerston's first two tours of duty as foreign minister, when he was at his best, before he developed his habits of preaching and hectoring and, sometimes, of blundering. Webster had indeed clarified the earlier career and softened the interpretation of his subject. An insignificant figure in public life until he was forty-six because, Webster believed but was unable to prove, of an attachment to a lady who was not free to marry him for many years, Palmerston learned quickly how to make the most of his office. While sound principles lay behind his diplomacy, he cleverly exploited the instruments of public opinion and outmaneuvered his opponents. A splendid description of his manners and methods, so different from those of the glacial Castlereagh, opened the story. It continued at a spirited pace with fine summaries of the liberal movement on the continent and of the Eastern Question. But soon the narrative broke in the bewildering and tedious details surrounding the creation of Belgium, where only the author's jibes at Talleyrand livened the account. It could scarcely have been otherwise, for the technical questions were appallingly complicated. More readable was the chapter on Palmerston's emergence as the principal exponent of liberalism in Europe as he clashed with the Eastern powers during the revolts in Poland, Italy, the Germanies, and Portugal. Next, the Eastern Question came into the account. Here Sir Charles defined the true nature of the Treaty of Unkiar Skelessi for perhaps the first time. He wrote large the success of Palmerston in convincing Tsar Nicholas I that Britain would defend her interests at Constantinople, thus bringing him to terms. Metternich, for whom Webster seldom had use in his studies on Castlereagh, came out as

---

Revue historique, CCIX (1953), 139–42; F. M. H. Markham, EHR, LXVII (1952), 421–23; W. T. Laprade, AHR, LVIII (1952–53), 107–9; and A. J. P. Taylor, Manchester Guardian, October 26, 1951, p. 5.

badly in these pages, and worse still when the subject shifted to Iberian affairs. Here Palmerston was peerless: sound in ideology, astute in method, and favored by fortune. Constitutionalism triumphed in Spain and Portugal and the neo-Holy Alliance was humiliated. In returning to the Eastern Question, Webster unraveled the complex story of the crisis of 1839–41, when the sultan undertook to chastise Mehemet Ali of Egypt, failed, died, and left the diplomats with a dangerous situation. Palmerston handled it superbly, though he hurt his French ally in the process. While Webster took care to support his interpretations, as he always did, some historians thought he was unfair to Louis Philippe and his ministers.[60] The final chapter assessed Palmerston's faults and achievements until 1841. Sir Charles concluded: "If the substantive is to have any meaning in social democracy, if Belgium and the Straits are to remain as independent areas, if the colossal mass of Russia can be contained and fitted into a world system, if effective international cooperation is to be obtained by the use of the Council table, these results will be due in part to Palmerston's work in these years."[61]

Sir Charles did not feel old when, in 1953, he was obliged to retire from his professorship at the age of sixty-seven. He had recently traveled to South America for UNESCO, where he had lost a row with the Perón dictatorship, and was serving the third of four terms as president of the British Academy. Now the government solicited his services to write the history of RAF Bomber Command's strategic offensive against Germany. Recognizing the unique character of the air war of 1939–45, and always susceptible to an opportunity to write on a glorious phase of his country's history, Webster accepted. It soon became apparent that

[60] Vaucher and Markham, loc. cit.
[61] The foreign policy of Palmerston, 1830–1841, II, 795.

199

the files were far more formidable than those of Castlereagh's and Palmerston's simpler times, and so he brought Frankland into the project as co-author. After working their way through British and captured German materials they visited the United States to consult papers at least as voluminous. They interviewed nearly every important surviving air force officer of righ rank. Webster proceeded as usual, exhaustively studying the background, principles, and personalities on the British side and mastering the materials on the enemy target system. It may be assumed with confidence that the study will be thorough, lucid, and full of opinions abundantly supported by evidence. If it is in the tradition of his other books, the work will be a unique contribution of high importance. A historian's historian who is also appreciated by the public, Sir Charles Webster hopes to crown his many studies on peacemaking by diplomacy with a tribute to Britain's gallant effort to make peace through air power.

DONALD F. LACH

RENÉ
GROUSSET
1885–1952

On a sunny spring morning in Paris, back in 1950, I was
seated on a wire-backed chair in the Parc Monceau. The
ubiquitous guardian had just collected the service charge
for my resting place when an elderly gentleman sank down
on a neighboring bench. After we had sat for a few minutes
quietly surveying the park's classical walks, I hesitantly addressed a question to my companion in meditation. "What,"
I asked him, "is that large house in the corner of the garden
supposed to be?" Already I had privately concluded that the
edifice in question, built sometime during the Second Empire, had now become an institution. So I was not surprised
when the old man replied: "That is the Cernuschi Museum
of Chinese art and antiquities run by the City of Paris."
But then, much to my surprise, he added, grinning: "Those
of us who live in the neighborhood call it 'M. Grousset's

Donald F. Lach is professor of modern history at the University of Chicago.

museum'!" René Grousset's name as a historian had long been known to me; this was the first time that I became aware of his popular renown.

Grousset was born at Aubais (Gard) on September 5, 1885.[1] His father, who died before his birth, had just previously joined the Faculty of Letters of the University of Grenoble.[2] Most of Grousset's younger years were spent in the quiet village of his birth located between Nîmes and Montpellier in southern France. In this region of the eastern Languedoc, Grousset's maternal relations were people of consequence. His grandfather, a propriétaire cultivateur, had held office as mayor of his village for forty years and his uncle had represented the department of La Lozère in the Chamber of Deputies. Grousset's education, after the elementary years, was obtained in Montpellier. He studied under Joseph Calmette, then a young medievalist. At the age of eighteen, in 1903, Grousset received the licentiate in history and geography. His health, which was to be poor for the rest of his life, prevented him from continuing his formal education.

The available materials are not entirely clear on how Grousset occupied himself in the decade following his

[1] To my research assistant, Miss Carol Rearick, I wish to extend my appreciation for her help in getting the widely scattered Grousset materials together and into my hands. I also wish to thank my colleagues, Professors Herrlee Creel, Mircea Eliade, and Earl Pritchard, for reading and commenting upon this paper.

For biographical details see Henri Massé in Larousse mensuel (1952), pp. 163–64, and the sketch by Jeannine Auboyer, curator of the Musée Guimet, in the special issue of France-Asie, IX, fasc. 88–89 (Saigon, 1953), pp. 781–84, devoted to essays and hommages reviewing the life and work of Grousset (hereafter cited as France-Asie).

[2] The elder René Grousset, an ancien élève of the École de Rome, was trained in Roman archeology and art. In the year of his son's birth and his own death, the senior Grousset published a monograph entitled Étude sur l'histoire des sarcophages chrétiens (Paris, 1885). Grousset's mother, after he reached maturity, retired to a convent in Montpellier.

graduation from the University of Montpellier. In retrospect it appears that, irrespective of whatever else he was engaged in during those years, he made the intellectual choices which were to guide his later activities.[3] Though trained as a medievalist, he also began to focus his attention upon the history and culture of Asia. This is not particularly surprising when one recalls that the Japanese victory over Russia in 1905 astonished the Western world and impelled many thoughtful Europeans to turn their eyes to the East. At the intellectual level Grousset seems to have derived encouragement for his changed perspective by reading Ernest Lavisse's lectures of 1890 broadly reviewing the political history of Europe.[4] In concluding sentences which Grousset would quote repeatedly in his later works, Lavisse had prophesied: "All strength gives out; the ability to maintain the lead in history is not a permanent attribute. Europe, which inherited it from Asia three thousand years ago, will perhaps not always keep it."[5]

Grousset, whose own education had followed traditional lines, meditated in these early years upon the inadequacies of the classical French curriculum, particularly its failure to take sufficient notice of Asia. And, like his father before him, he became a close student of art and archeology, evidently through conscientious independent study. That he was regarded as something more than an amateur of art is attested by his appointment in 1912 to the staff of the

[3] My deductions in this paragraph are made on the basis of the "Avertissement" preceding Volume I of Grousset's *Histoire de l'Asie* (Paris, 1922), from scattered remarks garnered from his later writings, and from conversations with Eliade.

[4] On Lavisse see my essay in B. E. Schmitt (ed.), *Some historians of modern Europe* (Chicago, 1942), pp. 240–55.

[5] *Vue générale de l'histoire politique de l'Europe* (Paris, 1890), p. 239. One of Grousset's earliest books, *Le réveil de l'Asie* (Paris, 1924), pointed out, also in prophetic sentences, what the burgeoning of nationalism could mean for Europe's supremacy in Asia.

Beaux Arts in Paris. Though Grousset never mastered any Asian language,[6] his growing knowledge and appreciation of art and archeology opened to him deep channels of understanding about Asian life. Mastery of Sanskrit or Chinese would certainly have contributed to his profundity on particular topics. Still, his command of art as a tool helped him to cut across linguistic boundaries, to concentrate upon the affinities of one civilization with the other, and to acquire a rare perspective on Asia as a whole.

Upon joining the Beaux Arts, Grousset was permitted by the director, Paul Léon, to continue with his scholarly pursuits. Just prior to the outbreak of war in 1914, he became a familiar figure in the reading room of the Bibliothèque Nationale. In the hours not devoted to administrative tasks or library research, Grousset worked at the composition of his comprehensive *Histoire de l'Asie*. I do not know when he first started writing it. Apparently, however, it was fairly well along by August 1914, when Grousset marched off to war. On March 5, 1915 he was gravely wounded at Beauséjour and for a time it even looked as if he would have to suffer the amputation of his right arm. For his distinguished war service, Grousset received the Croix de Guerre, and subsequently was decorated with the ribbon of the Légion d'Honneur. After the armistice he returned to his post at the Beaux Arts and resumed preparation of his first publication.

The three volumes of the *Histoire de l'Asie* appeared in 1922, the year of Lavisse's death. Like the older scholar, Grousset was interested throughout his life in the teaching of history. His stated intention in this work is to provide the schools of France and the educated public with a sur-

[6] See Georges Coedès' lecture delivered at the Académie des Sciences Coloniales (October 17, 1952) and printed as "La vie et l'œuvre de René Grousset," *France-Asie*, p. 814.

vey of Asia's history. He points out that "between the ancient history of the Orient (that is, of the Near East) and the history of European colonization in Asia" there existed a yawning chasm in French classical education. Asia, he laments, was not studied for itself but merely as a phase of European development. In his view, the general public had no conception of the grand strides which had been taken by French scholarship in uncovering Asia to the view of Europe. After naming many of the scholars who had previously contributed significantly to Oriental studies, Grousset observes:

This simple enumeration shows that it is not the materials which are lacking. . . . And in connection with these discoveries, general data have been acquired, landmarks have been discerned of which the public henceforward should take note in order to illuminate and mark the way for discoveries to come. And, moreover, if the hour for popularization [vulgarisation] will sound for the historical sciences only when the documentation contains no more uncertainties or lacunae, who would dare to write two handbook pages on the history of Christianity or the French Revolution? It is with these considerations in mind, and while apologizing for the boldness of our title as well as our temerity in undertaking an enterprise bound to be premature, that we endeavor to present a general survey of the history of Asia which is in many respects only a chronological table along with a summary of the latest published theses.[7]

Actually these volumes provide a more sophisticated and continuous narrative of Asian history than Grousset's prefatory remarks would indicate. The first volume, dealing with the ancient Orient and Islam, brings out the importance which Grousset attached to geography in the conditioning of peoples and civilizations and to art as a primary manifestation of and source for cultural achievements. The Latin Orient in the period of the Crusades and the role

[7] *Histoire de l'Asie*, I, ii–iii.

of Armenia in the Eastern Question also engage Grousset's attention and give a foretaste of some of the areas and problems which later increasingly engaged his attention. His second volume, which treats the early histories of India, China, and Indo-China, stresses the interconnections of these great Asian civilizations, particularly as they merge in Indo-China. The Mongol world, including its expansion in Asia from Genghis Khan to the sixteenth century, is the major topic of the third volume. This is followed by a brief history of China under the Mings and Manchus and a sketchy outline of Japanese history down to the Meiji Restoration of 1868.

Throughout the *Histoire de l'Asie*, Grousset sought to avail himself of the best monographic material then available. Inevitably he missed many works, particularly by foreign scholars, that are familiar to the initiated, and he was guilty of making a number of blunders on matters of fact. In their reviews the specialists, while noting some of Grousset's errors or questioning his emphases, were generally charitable in their comments on content and hearty in acclaiming his fearless desire to provide a general history which would bring Asia within the intellectual horizons of educated Europeans.[8] And, in terms of his own career, these first volumes contained the seedling ideas which would later blossom into full-sized books.

Grousset himself was acutely aware of the shortcomings in his pioneering effort, and he subsequently sought through a strenuous program of self-education to enrich his understanding of Asian scholarship. He began to attend the public lectures and private discussion sessions of the great

[8] For typical reviews of the time see Lucien Bouvat in *Journal asiatique*, CCVI (1925), 339–40, and P. Pelliot in *T'oung Pao*, XXII (1923), 56–57. For a later evaluation see P. Demiéville in *T'oung Pao*, XLII (1953), 411.

specialists (Sylvain Lévi, Paul Pelliot, and Henri Maspero) where they discoursed on their most recent findings or latest ideas. At their informal meetings Grousset was an observer and student. Much to the amusement of some in the group he would "discreetly pull from his pocket a tiny notebook and a tiny pencil, in order to take notes in his minuscule handwriting."[9] While continuing to learn and while fulfilling his duties at the Beaux Arts, he began publishing articles on the history and arts of Asia. In 1923, his ground-breaking *Histoire de la philosophie orientale*, another work of synthesis evidently prepared in connection with his study of Asian history, appeared in Paris. The following year he was elected to membership in the Société Asiatique.

Grousset gave up his post at the Beaux Arts in 1925 to become co-curator along with Joseph Hackin[10] of the Guimet Museum, the great center at the Place d'Iéna for Far Eastern art and archeology. Here he had available one of the world's best collections of Asian art and a convenient and excellent library. From this vantage point he was also able to keep in touch with the latest projects and developments in Oriental philology, archeology, and art history. Getting acquainted with his new post evidently kept Grousset from publishing at his earlier rate. The first three or four years at the Guimet, so far as his scholarly pursuits were concerned, seem to have been devoted to reading, reflection, and the collection of data on Far Eastern art and history. Some idea of the broad scope covered by his reading and a feeling for his critical ability can be obtained by perusing the bibliographical article which he published in

[9] From the necrology by Marcelle Lalou in *Journal asiatique*, CCXL (1952), 387.

[10] See Grousset's memorial article, "Un savant français: Joseph Hackin," *Revue de Paris*, LII (1945), 78–85.

the *Revue historique* for 1929.[11] Here, in commenting upon
Marcel Granet's *La civilisation chinoise* (Paris, 1929),
Grousset displays his usual broad-minded and positive in-
terest in approaches differing markedly from his own.
Granet's application of Durkheim's sociological theories to
the study of Chinese society wins his unqualified praise.
Grousset compares Granet's analysis to the ingenious dis-
section of Greek and Roman society presented in Fustel de
Coulanges' *La cité antique* (Strasbourg, 1864).

These years of reading and research yielded Grousset's
two-volume *Histoire de l'Extrême Orient* (Paris, 1929). Essentially this new work was an extension and revision of
the second volume of his *Histoire de l'Asie*, which dealt
with India, China and Indo-China as related and inter-
mingled civilizations. Japan, he comments in the preface, is
not treated because it can, by virtue of its insularity, be
easily handled separately. These new volumes are more
heavily documented, more qualified in their conclusions,
and better illustrated with historical maps and artistic reproductions than his first great effort. Though this new
work of synthesis at a scholarly level won for Grousset the
Stanislas Julien prize of the French Academy of Inscriptions, it received a cool reception elsewhere. For the general public its documentation (often in Chinese characters)
was too formidable; for the professionals Grousset's lack of
a firm philological footing (especially when he cited in
Chinese characters those sources which he obviously read
in translation) was only too apparent.

From this unfortunate experience Grousset learned that
his gifts were best adapted to synthesizing and popularizing

11 This was issued as a supplement to and continuation of the survey of
Oriental bibliography in Western languages published by the *Revue historique* in Volume II of the work entitled *Histoire et historiens depuis cin-
quante ans: méthodes, organisation et résultats du travail historique depuis
1876 à 1926* (Paris, 1928).

the monographs of the specialists.[12] This conclusion must have been reconfirmed for him by the warm reception accorded, by both laymen and scholars, to his four-volume series *Les civilisations de l'Orient* (Paris, 1929–30). These popular books, richly illustrated with artistic reproductions and bountifully supplied with quotations from the classical and popular literatures, were repeatedly reissued, translated into English,[13] and quoted far and wide. Another of his most popular works, *Sur les traces du Bouddha*,[14] first appeared in 1929. In his previous studies, Grousset had repeatedly pointed to Buddhism and Buddhist art as the fountainhead of "a vast current of humanism" which historically ran from the tip of Ceylon to the northernmost island of the Japanese archipelago. This book traces the travels of the Buddhist pilgrims, Hsüan-tsang and I-ching, across the Gobi desert, the Pamir plateau, and along the shores of southern Asia. Grousset paints in the background to their daring exploits by judicious use of striking literary and artistic sources. Clearly this was his kind of book, and the reviewers thought so too.[15] That he had learned his lesson well is further illustrated by the fact that he had his two-volume *Les philosophies indiennes* (Paris, 1931) annotated by Louis de La Vallée Poussin, the eminent authority on Buddhism and early Indian history.

Turning away from the Far East for a period, Grousset began work around 1929 on his monumental history of the Crusades. To prepare himself for this arduous undertaking,

[12] Demiéville, p. 412.

[13] By C. A. Phillips (New York, 1931–34).

[14] 2d ed., 1948. Translated into English by Mariette Leon as *In the footsteps of the Buddha* (London, 1932).

[15] For example see Pelliot's review of the original French edition in *T'oung Pao*, XXVII (1930), 106–8; or the review of the English translation in the *Times literary supplement* (June 16, 1932), p. 446.

he traveled in 1929–30 to Syria and Iran to familiarize himself with the terrain. This was his first trip to Asia, the
continent to which he had so far devoted his scholarly life.
But his interest in the Crusades doubtless went back to his
medieval studies at Montpellier and certainly his concern
with the Oriental background to the Crusades was clearly
apparent in the first volume of his *Histoire de l'Asie*. Moreover, in 1926 he had published a small study, *L'épopée des
Croisades*, which enjoyed an immediate popularity and
which is still used in its revised form[16] by those wanting
a short, intelligent, and atmospheric interpretation of the
crusading era.

The first volume of his great *Histoire des Croisades*
(Paris, 1934) deals with the anarchy of the Moslem world,
the First Crusade, and the foundation of the Kingdom of
Jerusalem. Most striking here is Grousset's determination,
evident on the first page of the book, to bring the Orient
into the history of the Crusades, not as an incidental factor
but as a substantial and necessary part of the whole story.
Whenever he could find them in translation, Grousset
used the Moslem sources to augment or reinforce his Latin
documentation. In 1935 the first volume was awarded the
Gobert grand prize of the Académie Française and the
second volume, after its appearance in 1935, was given the
Schlumberger prize of the Academy of Inscriptions. With
the publication in 1936 of the final volume, many reviewers
of the *Croisades* highly praised Grousset's panoramic and
scholarly presentation.[17] Even those who criticized him

---

[16] Second edition, 1939, revised in the light of his great work on the
Crusades published in the intervening years. In 1944 he published in the
series of short, popular books "Que sais-je?" another survey of the Crusades.
This was immediately translated into Spanish, as were its subsequent editions.

[17] For an appreciative review by his old teacher, Joseph Calmette, see
Annales du Midi, XLVIII (1936), 221–22; for a highly critical review

were generally in agreement with the conclusions stated in the preface to the third volume that the Crusades must be considered as part of the "Oriental Question," and that the internal history of the Levant and Persia must be taken fully into account in understanding the history of the Crusades and the Frankish kingdoms of the East.

While preparing the *Croisades*, Grousset was, as always, occupied with a host of other enterprises. In April 1933, he accepted an appointment as curator of the Cernuschi Museum, as successor to Ardenne de Tizac.[18] For the rest of his life he and his family occupied an elegant apartment on the top floor of the "petit hôtel" which houses the museum. In the first two years of his tenure he spent many of his waking hours laboring with architects and builders as they modernized, rehabilitated, and added new rooms to the building. Always a man of the world, Grousset used his many contacts in the higher levels of Parisian society to help acquire funds and new artistic treasures for the small museum. He finally organized his antiquary and collector friends into the Société des Amis du Musée Cernuschi as he worked successfully to build up collections on the great periods in Chinese art and to limit as much as possible the influence of those well-intentioned amateurs who wanted to load the museum with *chinoiseries*.

Grousset also continued to immerse himself in scholarly affairs. After serving with Gilbert Ferrand as co-editor of

which asserts that "these volumes make little or no contribution to our knowledge," see Frederic Duncalf in the *American historical review* (hereafter cited as *AHR*), XLI (1935–36), 124–26. A better-balanced review is that of Louis Halphen in *Revue historique* (hereafter cited as *RH*), CLXX-IX (1937), 154–56. In recent years Grousset's work has been superseded by S. Runciman, *A history of the Crusades* (3 vols.; Cambridge, 1951–54): see Claude Cahen in *RH*, CCXIV (1955), 328.

18 See for further details Vladime Elisseeff's account of Grousset's tenure as curator in *France-Asie*, pp. 829–35.

the *Journal asiatique*, he became its managing editor in 1936. He acted in this capacity for the next decade, and so was exposed constantly to the latest research in Oriental history and philology. That he continued reading widely and deeply is attested by the review article which he published in the *Revue historique* for 1937, a continuation of the similar article which had appeared eight years before.[19] A careful reading of this article, and of its scholarly digressions, reveals that Grousset, probably under Pelliot's influence, was concentrating on Mongol studies and the history of the steppe. In 1937 he published in collaboration with H. Desmoulin-Bernard a critical edition of the fourteenth-century travels across Asia of Odoric de Pordenone.[20] In the meantime he somehow found time, much to the mystification of his friends and colleagues, to collect and publish two excellent albums of Oriental art[21] and to rework with others his ill-fated history of the Far East, first published in 1929.[22] But all of these activities were only incidental to Grousset's major work of the years just prior to the outbreak of World War II.

L'empire des steppes, published on the eve of the war, is Grousset's main contribution to scholarship and scholarly synthesis. Down to the date of his death, it went through four editions; this was something of a record even for Grousset. Grand in conception, scholarly in detail, urbane in style, it is the kind of book every scholar hopes to write.

[19] See n. 11 above.

[20] *De Venise à Pékin au XIVe siècle: Odoric de Pordenone* (Paris, 1937).

[21] *L'art de l'Extrême-Orient: paysages, fleurs, animaux* (Paris, 1936), and *Les sculptures des Indes et de la Chine* (Paris, 1939).

[22] See p. 208 above. Written with the collaboration of J. Auboyer and J. Buhot, the two-volume work was published in revised form as Volume X of the *Histoire du Moyen Âge* in the *Histoire générale Gustave Glotz* under the title *L'Asie orientale des origines au XVe siècle* (Paris, 1941).

The preface possesses many of the qualities which run through the entire work. It begins:

Attila, Genghis Khan, Tamerlane . . . Their names are in all the records. The recitals of Occidental chroniclers, Chinese and Persian annalists have popularized their characters. They surge, these great barbarians, into the full light of civilized history and brusquely, within a few years, reduce the Roman world, the Iranian world, and the Chinese world to a heap of ruins. Their arrival, their motives, their disappearance seem inexplicable, so that the judgment of positive history itself differs but little from that of those ancient authors who see in them the scourge of God sent for the punishment of the old civilizations.

Yet never have any men been truer sons of the earth, explained by it, governed by environment, immediately "readable" in their motives and in their behavior by what we know of their way of life. The steppe has shaped those squat and stunted bodies, indomitable by reason of having overcome their physical surroundings. The bitter winds of the high plateaus, excessive cold and torrid heat, have molded those faces to narrow-lidded eyes, jutting cheek-bones, scanty beards, and have hardened those knotty torsos. The needs of a pastoral life, conditioned by moving flocks, have determined their nomadism, and the characteristics of the nomad economy have governed their contacts with sedentary peoples—contacts consisting either in timid borrowing or bloody raids.[23]

These two short paragraphs introduce a narrative that is sustained at an exciting, thoughtful, and provocative level for more than six hundred pages. Using the figures of the three great barbarian conquerors as pivotal points, Grousset tries to explain three millenniums of steppe history in terms of the rise and fall of the tides of barbarian power in the vast region stretching from Manchuria to Hungary. He sees this history as a drama of conflict between the pastoral societies of the steppe and the settled agricultural

[23] *L'empire des steppes: Attila, Gengis-Khan, Tamerlan* (Paris, 1939), p. 7. It was awarded prizes by the Academy of Inscriptions and the French Geographical Society.

civilizations surrounding them. Periodic forays by the
nomads, particularly when their flocks suffer from drought
or hunger, are for him "an inexorable law of human geography."[24] Equally natural and imperious are the rapid as-
similation of the conquering nomads by the settled society
and the rise to power in Persia, China, and India of erst-
while barbarian chieftains who then do their utmost to
strengthen and protect their newly adopted society against
the mounted warriors of subsequent invasions. Until the
sixteenth century, the archers on horseback maintain military superiority in their surging struggle with the surrounding civilizations. It is the invention of artillery in the sixteenth century which, in Grousset's view, enables the sedentary peoples to reverse the balance of military power and
to force the peoples of the steppe to halt their raids. But,
as he reminds us, "it is not more than three centuries since
the archers ceased to be world conquerors."[25]

About the incessant migrations of the nomads the records of the past are scanty and one-sided.[26] History, written
by the sedentary peoples, notices the nomads only when
the Great Wall or the Danubian fortresses are overrun by
the restless tribesmen. But about the internal backwash of
these flowing and ebbing tides, the historian who depends
primarily upon the annals of the settled people can learn
but little. As already observed, Grousset leans heavily upon
geography and climate to explain the movements within
the nomad world. He also uses extensively the evidences of
art, archeology, linguistics, and traditional literature to de-

24 Ibid., p. 9. For a discussion of the status of the theory of progressive
desiccation see Jung-Pang Lo, "The emergence of China as a sea power
. . . ," Far Eastern quarterly, XIV (1955), 495–97.

25 L'empire des steppes, p. 11.

26 See O. Lattimore, "Inner Asian frontiers: Chinese and Russian mar-
gins of expansion," Journal of economic history, VII (1947), 32.

scribe the civilizations of the Scythians, Huns, Turks, Mongols, and other steppe peoples.[27] By placing Asian and European records in juxtaposition, he makes more adroit use of the documents of the sedentary peoples than any previous writer on steppe history. In fact, the chronicles of Europe and the annals of Asia, when viewed from the vantage point he takes and when considered in relation to the other evidence he adduces, generally make much better sense than they do when considered exclusively in terms of the individual sedentary civilizations.[28] Even the silk route across Asia, as well known as it is to Asian and European historians alike, takes on new and interesting possibilities for research in cultural interchange when it is looked at in the context of steppe history.

As on previous occasions, Grousset again managed to derive several offspring publications from a parent study. In 1941 he published L'empire mongol as Volume VIII of Eugène Cavaignac's Histoire du monde. Three years later he issued a delightful biography of Genghis Khan[29] based, as was his chronology in the history of the steppe, upon the Pelliot and Haenisch renditions of the Secret history of the Mongols then available.[30] The publication in 1946

[27] For a discussion of his use of "steppe art" see the review by Solange Lemaître in Revue des arts asiatiques (Annales du Musée Guimet), XII (1938), 184–85. For an example of how later historians have used Grousset's delineation of the steppe peoples examine G. Vernadsky, The Mongols and Russia (New Haven, 1953) and H. D. Martin, The Rise of Chingis Khan and his conquest of North China (Baltimore, 1950).

[28] See the review by René Dussaud in Syria, XX (1939), 159.

[29] Le conquérant du monde—vie de Gengis-Khan (Paris, 1944). For a scholarly appraisal of the sources on the Mongol conqueror see Grousset's "État actuel des études sur l'histoire gengiskhanide," Bulletin du Comité International des Sciences Historiques, XII (1940–41), 22–40. To some of his contemporaries the biography of Genghis Khan looked like an indirect attack upon Hitler.

[30] For a critique of his Mongol studies see Eugène Cavaignac's article in France-Asie, p. 809.

of *L'empire du Levant—histoire de la question d'Orient* also owed much to several of his earlier works, including the history of the steppe. In fact, one of the features which distinguishes all his works on Asia published after 1939 is his ability to relate the history of the sedentary civilizations, such as China, to the complex series of migrations which they had to endure on their land frontiers.

World War II, as we have seen, did not bring a halt to Grousset's publication activities. In addition to seven books (including one collaborative effort),[31] six articles, at least, came out under his name. In 1941 he also began to lecture at the École Nationale des Langues Vivantes Orientales on the history and geography of the Far East. Like Granet, whose post he took over after the latter's death, Grousset was charged at the École with giving background lectures to students specializing in Far Eastern languages.[32] Apparently it was in connection with the preparations for his lectures that he wrote his *Histoire de la Chine* (Paris, 1942).[33] As is often the case with materials prepared for lectures, the chapters in this book have an internal coherence but are only sketchily related to each other. The style, as with most of Grousset's books intended for a popular audience, is captivating and replete with vivid characterizations. But references which involve comparison with European individuals and historical periods, striking as they

[31] *L'Europe orientale de 1081 à 1453* (Paris, 1945). This is Volume IX of the *Histoire générale Gustave Glotz.*

[32] See François Martini, "René Grousset à l'École des Langues Orientales," in *France-Asie*, pp. 869–71.

[33] Translated into English as *The rise and splendour of the Chinese empire* (Berkeley, 1953) and put out as a paperback in 1958. See the critical review by Arthur Wright in the *AHR*, LIX (1953), 212–13, as well as the attack in the *Times literary supplement* (May 9, 1952), p. 311, which chides Grousset for scampering "through the millennia breathlessly scattering names and dates."

sometimes are, tend to be misleading when used too frequently and without sufficient caution. Ch'in Shih-huang-ti is stereotyped as a "Chinese Caesar," Shensi as the "Chinese Wild West," and the minister Wei Yang as a "Chinese Richelieu." Vivid scenes extracted from Chinese literature and the classics are quoted uncritically, as Grousset seems almost carried away by his desire to be vivacious. Unlike most of his other works of popularization, this history of China is badly marred by the author's obvious desire to titillate his audience.[34]

Grousset continued to live and work at the Cernuschi during the German occupation of Paris. To appease the occupying forces, he put on several second-rate exhibitions at the museum. Meanwhile, he did his best to encourage the students to continue their Oriental studies by giving some of them a place of work and the necessary library facilities. In 1944, with the reorganization of the French museums, Grousset was made chief curator of the national museums. Meanwhile, of his Orientalist friends, Hackin perished in a ship torpedoed in 1941, Maspero expired in Buchenwald in 1945, and Pelliot, who had been active in the Paris Resistance movement, died shortly after the liberation of France.

The end of the war brought Grousset the greatest honor of his life. He was elected on February 14, 1946 to the Académie Française to occupy the seat vacated in 1942 by the death of André Bellessort, the literary critic and poet. Grousset was formally installed as one of the "Forty Immortals" on January 30, 1947. In his discourse of acceptance Grousset began by acknowledging his debt to the

[34] See the testimony of Bernard-Thierry who wrote about his lectures: "It seemed that Grousset knew Tamerlane or Genghis Khan intimately. Emperor Akbar held him under his spell. Marco Polo had confided his memories to him. The Buddha had whispered his teachings to him" ("René Grousset et les étudiants," *France-Asie*, p. 787).

great French specialists in Oriental studies and modestly
recognized that the honor was being paid less to him personally than to the distinguished achievements of French
Orientalism.[35] Henry Bordeaux, in his response, remarked
in a similar vein:

You will represent in our company a new historical school. Instead of being satisfied with a man or an epoch, with a Richelieu like Gabriel Hanotaux and M. le duc de la Force, with a
Napoleon like M. Louis Madelin, or even with cathedrals like
M. Émile Mâle, you feel impelled to deal with centuries, peoples, and entire continents. Thus you are reviving, with recent
documentation, the *Discours sur l'histoire universelle*.[36]

In making the analogy with Bossuet's hortatory discourse,
Bordeaux had in mind Grousset's *Bilan de l'histoire* (Paris,
1946).[37] Like the great bishop, Grousset here strikes his
balance on civilization from the viewpoint of a strict French
Catholic. Writing under the influence of wartime disillusionment, Grousset's retrospective survey leads him to the
pessimistic conclusion that "one day history will end, because mankind will be extinct."[38] As he looks upon the
charnel house of human history, Grousset is driven to
horror and intellectual despair. Left to his own devices,
man, he believes, is helpless and hopeless. Christianity,
reigning supreme over place and time, with its doctrine
of eternal salvation is still, as in ages past, the only hope
of mankind.

Were this Grousset's only message, his summation of
history could best be described as that of a "new Bossuet."
Such is not the case. For Grousset, unlike Bossuet, is su-

[35] *Discours de réception de M. René Grousset à l'Académie Française et réponse de M. Henry Bordeaux* (Paris, 1947), p. 3.
[36] *Ibid.*, p. 55.
[37] Translated into English as *The sum of history* (Oxford, 1951).
[38] *Ibid.*, p. 244.

premely conscious of Asia's contributions to the totality of civilization. But, as one reviewer remarks, his "argument is too abbreviated and hard to follow."[39] Indeed, to appreciate the *Bilan* fully it is almost necessary to have studied previously his major works on Asia, the Crusades, and the history of Oriental philosophy and art. Otherwise his conclusion that Asia has contributed to the human patrimony "the immense effort of Indian speculation and the great cosmic vision which fired the old Chinese painters of the tenth to fourteenth centuries"[40] is almost meaningless to the lay Western reader.

Grousset's generalizations about history, which he elevates to "historical laws" in his estimate of civilization, are neither very original nor very suggestive. "In human societies," he pessimistically concludes, "progress is generally made, at any given point, only at the price of more costly recession in other sectors."[41] Or, in much the same vein, "after a short period of triumph during which civilization conquers new domains, and a long quiet period in which it is content to exploit these conquests, there comes a period of deterioration which sets in quite early."[42] In addition to the triviality of such "laws," Grousset's *Bilan* is thrown out of balance by his determination to make the Germans the villains of European history, by his almost complete neglect of vital economic and technological factors, and by his insistence upon the transcendency of the Christian Gospel.[43]

Three years after publishing the *Bilan*, Grousset brought

[39] Reinhold Aris in *Contemporary review*, CLXXXII (1952), 378.

[40] *The sum of history*, p. 91.

[41] *Ibid.*, p. 4.   [42] *Ibid.*, p. 5.

[43] For a more favorable view see the comment of the Catholic magazine *Études*, CCLXXV (1952), 119–20, and of Daniel-Rops in *La table ronde*, No. 83 (November 1954), pp. 60–65.

out his *Figures de proue*,[44] another excursion into historical theory. Here he is concerned primarily with great individuals as makers of history, as the figures on the prow of man's ship of destiny. To those like the Marxists who believe that impersonal forces rule the world he addresses this question: "Is the direction taken by humanity the act of Man or men?"[45] His predisposition for seeing an era in terms of its leading figures is characteristic of a number of Grousset's earlier works, even though, as when he deals with the history of the steppe, he himself feels compelled to lean heavily upon impersonal factors like geography and climate. World history, as he proceeds to look at it here, is nonetheless depicted in terms of its great makers of decisions: Pericles, Alexander, Charlemagne, Frederick II, Charles V, Louis XIV, Napoleon, Bismarck, the Great Khans, and Akbar. Like Carlyle, Grousset contends that "there is an instant between the dying forces of the past and the still hesitant forces of the future, when the Hero is free to choose, master, it seems, of destiny. . . ."[46] Often the heroes of history seem to have labored in vain, but almost always such an impression is more appearance than reality. "It is not the work which fails, it is the worker."[47] From the time when his acts are performed, or decisions taken, the hero no longer controls them. Napoleon freed Europe of its old regimes by unleashing a nationalism which was turned against France; Roosevelt encouraged the nationalist aspirations of Asia only to have the new nations turn against the United States.

[44] Paris, 1949. These essays have been translated into German as *Schicksalsstunden der Geschichte* (Vienna, 1951). In preparing them Grousset was aided by his daughter, Ginette Lenclud. One of the saddest experiences of his personal and intellectual life was his daughter's premature death shortly before this book appeared. It is dedicated to his two grandchildren.

[45] *Figures de proue*, p. i.

[46] *Ibid.*, p. 328.   [47] *Ibid.*

Like the figurehead on the prow of an ancient vessel, the hero always plows the sea which lies ahead. But now, all the seas of our planet have been explored, all *terrae incognitae* removed from the maps, all peoples are known, and heroes are no longer to be expected. We approach the end of man's "animal history." We can learn no more about individual peoples, only about the unity of all peoples on our planet. While world unification brings world struggle with it, the hope also burgeons that the universal message of Christianity will provide this endangered world with its spiritual salvation.

Grousset's own life became more universal after the war. In 1949, he made his first visit to the Far East to participate in the ceremonies held at Tokyo to celebrate the reopening there of the Maison Franco-Japonaise.[48] On the return trip he enjoyed a short stopover at Angkor in Cambodia, where he visited the magnificent temples and ruins of the old Khmer capital, which he had frequently commented upon in his books.[49] Upon his return from the Far East, Grousset prepared for a trip to Canada. In 1950 he presented a series of lectures at the University of Montreal and in other Canadian cities. The following year he published *La Chine et son art* (Paris) which has been termed "the best manual of the history of Chinese art which exists today in any language."[50] And, about this time, only shortly before his final illness set in, Grousset accepted a charge from

[48] See the lecture which he delivered there, "La civilisation à travers l'histoire," as printed in *France-Asie*, pp. 761–77; also see his article "Au Japon" in *La revue des deux mondes* (March 1, 1951), pp. 3–21.

[49] For example see the scholarly account given in the popular volume on India in *The civilizations of the East* (New York, 1939), pp. 304–28; see also his article "La vocation historique de l'Indochine et l'œuvre française," *Revue de Paris*, LVI² (1949), 3–15.

[50] Demiéville, p. 413. This work was translated into Italian as *Storia dell'arte e della civiltà cinese* (Milan, 1959) and into English as *Chinese art and culture* (New York, 1959).

UNESCO to take responsibility as author-editor for preparing the third volume of A history of the scientific and cultural development of mankind which was then being projected. Grousset attended in 1952 one of the initial planning sessions, but death claimed him on September 12 before much could be accomplished on "his" volume in the monumental UNESCO series.[51]

Many details on the life and work of Grousset are missing from this short account.[52] It is not possible to compress more than forty years of restless and creative activity into a few pages. We can observe, however, that Grousset published significant scholarly and popular works which divide naturally into five major groupings: Far East, Central Asia, Near East and Crusades, histories of Oriental art and philosophy, and essays in the philosophy of history. About his working procedures a few conclusions also emerge. He began by publishing a general history of Asia and followed it with a general history of Oriental philosophy. His later works, seen from this perspective, may be looked upon as detailed expositions, modifications, and corrections of the several parts of his earliest general works.[53] As a consequence Grousset's bibliography is replete with small books and articles that are the children and even the grandchildren of parent volumes. While many of these offspring volumes inherit important characteristics from their progenitors, most of them, like the biography of Genghis Khan, are sufficiently unique to be worth studying in their own right.

[51] According to the testimony of my colleague, Louis Gottschalk, who is author-editor of Volume IV.

[52] No complete bibliography for Grousset is yet available. The list appended to France-Asie, pp. 935–38, is comprehensive but not complete. In addition to a number of striking omissions of important scholarly articles, it makes no attempt to list his numerous popular articles and was prepared before the appearance of the posthumous publications.

[53] See Mircea Eliade, "Apport de la synthèse," France-Asie, p. 327.

223

A review of his major works, as they appeared over a full generation, clearly reveals Grousset's preoccupations and biases. He was supremely conscious when dealing with Asia of the importance of thorough grounding in geography and art. Oriental literature and philosophy, which he was forced to use in translation, provided his works with rich illustrative material that he often employed to substantiate generalizations which had been drawn originally from his appraisals of Oriental art. While tolerant of differing approaches (such as that represented by Granet), Grousset relied heavily on the monographs of Oriental historians (like Pelliot) whose major interests were in philosophy and religious history. Perhaps this accounts in part for the relatively slight attention which he paid to economics, technology, and science. His profound interest in historical personalities and biography also helps to explain what sometimes amounts to a posture of impatience with impersonal forces in history, particularly when commenting on Europe's past. Such predilections also help to make clear why his excursions into the philosophy of history, brilliant and penetrating as they often are, rarely produce the comprehensive generalizations which might have placed Grousset in the company of Spengler and Toynbee.

"The main interest of oriental studies," Grousset wrote, "undoubtedly lies in the comparison of values which they make possible."[54] But from his own studies of the independent civilizations of Asia, he concluded that the human spirit remains one in all parts of the world. Such a verdict was based not only upon the conclusions emerging from his studies but upon his strong personal convictions as a Christian humanist. Though Grousset always insisted upon studying the various civilizations of Asia in their own terms, he was no religious, moral, or national relativist. For him

54 The sum of history, p. 124.

Asia was a yardstick against which the values and beliefs of the Occident could be measured. But, once he had done his measuring, his conviction gained in strength that the West, France, and Christianity were the prime movers of recorded history and the source from which humanity's salvation must flow to the rest of the world.[55]

Grousset will be remembered most for what he did to bring Asia and its arts to the attention of the French public. Through his books, both scholarly and popular, he provided the curious reader with a wealth of illustrative material in artistic reproductions, intelligently conceived maps, and occasional but excellent bibliographies. Even the specialists admitted that he was able to show them through his comprehensive grasp of Asian history how they differed from each other, what lacunae needed to be filled, and who might be called upon to fill them. Through his own works and those he inspired, Asia was introduced into the great general histories being laboriously prepared by the co-operative efforts of many French and foreign scholars.[56] As the curator of two of Paris' greatest museums and as editor of the Journal asiatique, he frequently encouraged

[55] Cf. the quotation from his obituary notice in the Times (London), September 15, 1952: "Oriental philosophy, history, religion, and art had early attracted him, but though he came to know these subjects with an intimacy few could surpass he never to the end of his life abandoned his deeply founded western culture nor his firmly based Christianity. Thus he remained in a sense outside his subject and, because he was able to take a detached view, proved an inimitable guide for western students of the Orient." Also cf. Daniel-Rops, p. 61, who observed that ". . . in discovering China, India, and their disorderly millennia, it was himself also that he discovered and set in order."

[56] Besides those already mentioned (the general histories edited by Glotz and Cavaignac), Grousset also contributed to two volumes in the Halphen and Sagnac series, "Peuples et civilisations": Vol. I, Les premières civilisations (Paris, 1926) and Vol. II, La Grèce et l'Orient, des guerres médiques à la conquête romaine (Paris, 1928; 2d ed., 1938). And he wrote the sections (I, 347–58, 359–90) on the "steppe" empires and peoples in Alexander von Randa, Das Handbuch der Weltgeschichte (2d ed.; Olten, 1958).

and inspired younger specialists with his passion for Oriental subjects.

Grousset was never in the ordinary sense a member of a recognized academic community. He knew and worked with many professors and students, but he also moved in the salon society of the capital.[57] As a man of erudition, affable manners and ready wit, he wandered easily from one level of life to the other. It was this quality which enabled him to bring Asia to the attention of influential artistic and political circles. Through his lectures at the Louvre and on the French radio, he relayed to the great public a measure of his personal enthusiasm for Asia. His books, written in an easy and exciting style, won many prizes of the learned academies and numerous readers from all walks of life. His death brought accolades to Paris from every quarter of the world, and in 1954 a special exhibition held in his honor at the Cernuschi brought to the small museum on loan some of the finest masterpieces of Oriental art.[58] Even after his death, a number of books continued to appear under his name and others are being contemplated.[59] But the greatest tribute to the man's talent comes from people, like my elderly companion in the Parc Monceau, who still continue to think of Asia as that remote quarter of the world which Grousset brought to life for them through his writings and art exhibitions.

[57] He produced the impression of being a "man of the world who had strayed in among the professors." See François Martini, France-Asie, p. 869.

[58] See the impressive catalogue of the exhibition called La découverte de l'Asie (Paris, 1954) prepared by V. Elisseeff, Grousset's successor as curator of the Cernuschi.

[59] A collection of humanistic essays from his nachgelassene Papiere was published at Paris in 1954 as L'homme et son histoire, and the following year there appeared La face de l'Asie, données permanentes et facteurs de renouvellement et deux chapitres complémentaires par Georges Deniker. It has also been suggested (Demiéville, p. 414, n. 1) that the excellent maps from Grousset's books, with the addition of those found in his papers, might be compiled and edited to produce a historical atlas of Asia.

WILLIAM H. MAEHL

ERICH
EYCK
1878—

Fame as a historian came late in life to Erich Eyck. He was
sixty-three when the first volume of his Bismarck biography appeared, and it was not till the close of World War II
that he achieved substantial recognition as a scholar. Not
what would be called a historian's historian, he had never
been associated with learned journals or been a professor.
He entered the archives from the law courts. Despite the
fact that he held a doctorate in history from the University
of Berlin, the main energies of his prime had been spent in
the fields of law, finance, journalism, and public administration. Were it not for the Nazi conquest of power, he might
never have written anything of lasting importance to historiography. All his principal writings came after 1933 and
were spread over a twenty-five-year period, mainly in his old
age.

William H. Maehl is professor of history at Nebraska Wesleyan
University.

Born in Berlin on December 7, 1878 into a middle-class
Jewish family, Erich was one of six brothers and sisters.[1]
His was a normal and happy boyhood. From his father, a
respected businessman and grain broker, he imbibed bour-
geois-liberal and latitudinarian teachings, while from his
cultivated and sensitive mother he derived his lifelong appreciation of Goethe and the classics. At the gymnasium
in Berlin Erich's interest in history was awakened early,
and upon graduation in 1897 he manifested his intention
of pursuing the study of history and literature. However,
when his father pointed out that unless he were prepared
to become a Christian convert he would have scant pros-
pect of appointment to any Prussian faculty, Erich decided
to follow the paternal advice and study law to earn a living.

Still, while preparing for the law, he devoted all his free
time to reading history and listening to eminent historians
—Delbrück, Schmoller, Paulsen, and Jastrow, among others
—at the University of Berlin. Of these, Delbrück had the
greatest influence upon his thinking, although Eyck never
was one of his seminar students. If, however, we look here
for some inspiration that was to lead Eyck to his later
revisionist position on Bismarck, we shall not find it. Eyck's
progressivism was rather the result of his admiration for
Friedrich Naumann and the leftist editor of the Nation,
Theodor Barth.[2] From them he learned to be critical of his

[1] Except where otherwise indicated, the biographical data in this essay
are based upon letters from Eyck to the author during 1959–60, which,
however, will not ordinarily be cited. Eyck's generous aid is gratefully
acknowledged.

[2] For Eyck's sentiments on Naumann and Barth see "A great German
liberal," Contemporary review, CLV (1939), 323–25. Their ideas were
freely discussed at the University Barth-Gothein Stammtisch, where Eyck
gathered with kindred democratic spirits, such as Theodor Heuss, the future president of the Bundesrepublik. See Theodor Heuss, "In alter
Freundschaft: zum 80. Geburtstage von Erich Eyck," Association of
Jewish Refugees information (hereafter cited as AJRI), December 1958,
p. 4.

emperor, although he did not dream of revolutionary opposition to the imperial government.

While still a junior barrister, Eyck completed work for and was awarded the Ph.D. in 1904 at Berlin. His dissertation, *Der Vereinstag deutscher Arbeitervereine, 1863–68,* harmonized with the interests of Jastrow[3] and Schmoller and reflected Eyck's, as well as the nation's, new and lively interest in the rising fourth estate. About this time he also passed his final bar examinations and, after a brief holiday in England, whose institutions he admired, commenced the practice of law in Berlin in 1906. He remained in that city until his emigration thirty-one years later. On May 12, 1910 he married Hedwig Kosterlitz, a Jewess of middle-class Silesian origin. She brought him the lasting love of a good woman, who was endowed richly with precisely those conciliatory and practical traits that Eyck himself lacked.[4] From this union issued two daughters and a son, all destined for the academic life.

A slight heart defect prevented Eyck's being inducted into the armed forces during World War I.[5] While continuing his practice and writing occasional popular history articles for such publications as *Die Hilfe,* of which Theodor Heuss was the editor, Eyck ran on the Progressive ticket in 1915 for the municipal council of Charlottenburg. He was elected and served in that body for four years. Also in 1915 Rudolf Ullstein, the publisher, intrusted him with the editing of "Recht und Leben," the Thursday legal supplement of the democratic *Vossische Zeitung.* He continued for many years to evaluate in that section the latest

[3] Jastrow is appraised in Eyck's "Erinnerung an Jastrow," *Deutsche Rundschau,* LXXXII (1956), 981–86.

[4] Frank Eyck to author, April 5, 1960.

[5] Mrs. Paul J. Alexander (née Lore Eyck) to author, March 28, 1960.

developments in public law with "calm objectivity" and an "incorruptible sense of justice."[6]

On the Charlottenburg council and later from 1928 to 1932 as Democratic alderman on the Berlin *Stadtverordnetenversammlung*, Eyck denounced insurrectionist tactics and monarchists. For him the empire was as extinct as the dodo, bolshevism was anathema, and the Weimar republic "the promised land." Moderate in his political views, Eyck often raised his voice at the Democratic Club, where in the early years of the republic Gessler, Rathenau, von Siemens, Preuss, Koch, and Stolper were wont to speak, to advise against radical or precipitate decisions that might later be regretted. In the twilight of the republic, Eyck did battle in the Berlin municipal council, as in the *Vossische Zeitung*, against unreconstructed militarists, Nazis, and Communists.[7]

He pilloried the old regime,[8] defended democratic parliamentarism, and contrasted the virtues of the republic with the glittering incompetence of the Wilhelmine government.[9] Of William II, for whom he had ineffable contempt, Eyck wrote: "In the old Reich the theory obtained that at the center of the political system was the monarch, firm as the north star. In reality, he followed an unpredictable course like a comet."[10] The question why the monarchy never made the transition from *Obrigkeits-* to true *Rechtsstaat* fascinated him. Its investigation led him in other articles to examine critically the German *Macht* con-

[6] Leo Engel, "Erinnerungen an Berlin," *AJRI*, December 1958, p. 4; Ernst Lemmer, "Gruss an den Politiker, Erich Eyck," *ibid.*

[7] Mrs. Alexander to author, March 28, 1960; Engel, p. 4; Heuss, p. 4; Eyck to author, October 30, 1959.

[8] *Die Monarchie Wilhelms II nach seinen Briefen, Randbemerkungen und den Zeugnissen seiner Freunde* (Berlin, 1924).

[9] E.g., see "Das System des Widerspruchs," *Vossische Zeitung*, October 2, 1924.

[10] *Ibid.*

cept, the constitutional position of the king-emperor, and the Bismarckian solution of the unification problem.[11] Gradually the suspicion grew in him that it was Bismarck who had diverted the German people from a better destiny. "Pompous submission" and "lyric servility" were all Bismarck had demanded of his pupils, and all creative political action had been impossible under that jealous master.[12] Even Frederick III had had to have recourse to cloak and dagger methods to find himself a spot in the sun out from under Bismarck's shadow.[13]

In 1933 Eyck was, as a Jew, removed from the editorial board of the *Vossische Zeitung*. While he remained technically *Rechtsanwalt am Berliner Kammergericht*, his clientele rapidly disappeared, and he was thrust into retirement. He was now free under perverse circumstances to devote himself entirely to the study of history, the first love of his youth. Falling back upon the extensive private library he had accumulated, he commenced not only his Bismarck research but also a biography of Gladstone. With this work he hoped to gain entrée into English intellectual circles. Having sent his children on ahead, he and his wife left Germany for London in 1937. There they opened a boarding house, the practical management of which devolved upon the self-sacrificing and capable Mrs. Eyck. Since she had a knack for handling people, the guest house succeeded, and Eyck was released from sordid cares to

[11] See "Wilhelm II," *ibid.*, October 28, 1925; "Rudolf von Bennigsen," *ibid.*, October 12, 1929; and "Eduard Lasker," *ibid.*

[12] "Bambergers geheime Tagebücher," *ibid.*, June 8, 1932. Cf. Freiherr von Roggenbach's remark that "all who were not Bismarck's foes were necessarily political cyphers alongside the only '1'" ("Der Kaiser der 99. Tage. Zum hundertsten Geburtstag Friedrichs III," *ibid.*, October 18, 1931).

[13] *Ibid.*; "Eduard Lasker," *ibid.*, October 12, 1929.

accomplish those historical projects which for years had tempted him.[14]

The "pleasant," laudatory Gladstone biography is not, in rhetoric or refinement of historical method, comparable to Eyck's later German studies.[15] Nonetheless, the work has a certain arabesque grace peculiar to all Eyck's writings; it rests upon an impressive bibliography; and the author's skill in weighing evidence is apparent throughout. Although Eyck prefers not to put Gladstone in the front rank of statesmen,[16] he recognizes in him qualities that have a universal appeal. Gladstone combined financial genius, a humanist's spirit—he was the author of a three-volume work on Homer—and a marvelous physical and intellectual energy which sustained him at the age of seventy-eight in the course of a three-and-one-half hour address on the Irish question. Furthermore, his idealism, love of liberty, and uncomplicated sympathy for the oppressed explain why he was "the first English statesman to recognize that it was England's duty to repair the injustice" done to Ireland.[17]

In the last years before World War II Eyck again visited the archives in Berlin to do necessary research on his projected biography of Bismarck, which, however, was mainly written in London and Oxford. It was destined to be the first half of a six-volume revisionist treatment of German history from 1848 to 1933. Up to then no historian had sculptured a complete Bismarck from the massive block

[14] Heuss p. 4; Frank Eyck to author, April 5, 1960.

[15] Gladstone (Zurich and Leipzig, 1938). Translated by B. Miall (London, 1938). Reviewed by E. Jones Parry, History, XXIV (1939), 95. Cf. the estimate by W. N. Medlicott in his "Tribute to the historian, Erich Eyck," AJRI (December 1958), p. 5.

[16] See his "Bismarck and Gladstone," Contemporary review, CLXX (1946), 343–48.

[17] Gladstone (English trans.), pp. 96, 120, 199, 311, 396–97, 432.

of new source materials published since World War I,
which had not been available to Karl Scheffler, C. G.
Robertson, and Erich Marcks when they wrote their biog-
raphies. Considering the vast literature on Bismarck,[18] any
sort of scholarly biography would have been a Herculean
feat. The three-volume study, indubitably Eyck's masterpiece, was published while World War II raged.[19] The first
comprehensive, critical treatment by a German liberal, it
made Eyck one of the world's foremost Bismarckian
scholars.

Eyck's preoccupation with writing history primarily for
the educated layman did not prejudice the extraordinary
job of selection, condensation, and synthesis that he performed. All the great collections were copiously used, and
it is apodictic that Eyck achieved a thorough mastery of
the sources.[20] Scholars generally concede this,[21] although
only skeletal footnotes are listed in the rear of each volume
and no serious bibliography of secondary literature is appended. Until the publication of Ludwig Reiner's more

[18] The literature on Bismarck up to 1930 was reviewed by Lawrence
Steefel, "Bismarck," Journal of modern history (hereafter cited as JMH),
II (1930), 74–95. More recent discussions are given by Wilhelm Mommsen, "Der Kampf um das Bismarck-Bild," Universitas, No. 3 (1950), 273–
80; Gerhard Ritter, "Das Bismarck problem," Merkur, IV (1950), 657–
76; Wilhelm Schüssler, "Noch einmal Bismarck und die Nationen," La
nouvelle Clio, II (1950), 432–55; Andreas Dorpalen, "The German historians and Bismarck," Review of politics, XV (1953), 53–67; Leonhard
von Muralt, "Bismarck-Forschung und Bismarck-Problem," Schweizer
Monatshefte, XXXIV (1954), 148–62; Walter Bussmann, Das Zeitalter
Bismarcks (Constance, 1957), pp. 251–74; and Maximilian von Hagen,
"Das Bismarckbild der Gegenwart," Zeitschrift für Politik, VI (1959),
79–83.

[19] Bismarck, Leben und Werk (Zurich, 1941–44), Vol. I (to 1864);
Vol. II (1864–71); Vol. III (1871–98).

[20] Medlicott, p. 5.

[21] Thus Hans Rothfels speaks of Eyck's "broad familiarity with the
huge monographic literature," "Problems of a Bismarck biography," Review of politics, IX (1947), 365.

orthodox biography,[22] Eyck's *Bismarck, Leben und Werk* was without a rival. Not since Erich Marcks's *Der Aufstieg des Reiches* (1920) had there been a comparable event in the historiography of the *Reichsgründung*. The measure of Eyck's achievement is best gauged not by the word of his admirers (of whom there are many), but by that of his critics, notably Hans Rothfels, who, notwithstanding numerous differences with Eyck's theses, admitted that "from the viewpoint of an overall coverage, the task could not have been mastered more successfully."[23]

The work is highly interpretative and entertaining. Metaphors and aphorisms of rare originality abound, while the author's opulent vocabulary shimmers on every page. In the first two volumes the emphasis is heavily on foreign affairs, in consonance with the *Primat der Aussenpolitik*. Not till Volume III, which deals with the period 1871–98 —an era when for Bismarck Germany was a satiated state— is the focus mainly on the internal political struggle. But even here certain aspects of German history have been neglected. The political perspective is that of one who indorses the *kleindeutsch* solution and rejects confederate or particularist accommodations of the German problem, such as have been favored by Franz Schnabel. As a matter of fact, Eyck's whole life disposed him to rally to the idea of the nation-state. Not only must the impressive military achievements of Prussia just before and during his time have convinced him, who was of West Prussian origin, that a *Kleindeutschland*, ineluctably dominated by North Germany, was the natural thing, but his secondary school training, studies under illustrious Prussian historians, and his career as successful attorney at the Prussian bar, determined that he should unconsciously absorb nationalism with his

22 *Bismarck* (3 vols.; Munich, 1956–59).
23 Rothfels, p. 367.

daily bread. The Jewish-liberal-idealist factor in his background mainly accounted for his aversion to militarism and
Hohenzollern autocracy. But the democratic constituent in
his makeup was rather a shield against, than an impellent
toward, acceptance of a neo-*Sacrum Imperium*. A *Gross-
deutschland* cast in medieval mold would not only have
seemed to him an anachronism but a Catholic-reactionary
encumbrance of liberty. Eyck's preference, therefore—evident in his Bismarck biography—is for a peaceable, democratic, and nationalist *kleindeutsch* solution in keeping with
the Frankfurt program of 1848. As one who applauds every
step taken in the nineteenth century toward the establishment of a body of uniform German law, Eyck does not
consider whether the liberal formula might not have produced a more highly centralized and, as Rothfels thinks,[24]
a more aggressively nationalist Germany than Bismarck's
loose-knit polity with its maxim of limited liability.[25]

Eyck's estimate of Bismarck is that he exemplified forti-
tude without rectitude, that he was at once the most tal-
ented and ruthless player in the immoral game of *Ragione
di Stato*.[26] Assuredly a man who would orient his life to

[24] *Ibid.*, pp. 370–71.

[25] Eyck's thesis on the possibility of a peaceful, liberal solution of the
problem of German unification can, thinks Dorpalen, neither be proved
nor disproved, but he insists that Bismarck "was devoid of all nationalist
ambitions" (pp. 55–56). Franz Schnabel, who is highly critical of the
kleindeutsch program, asserts that the Liberals were considerably more
nationalist and imperialist, especially as regards Northern and Eastern Europe, than was Bismarck ("Das Problem Bismarck," *Hochland* [October,
1949], pp. 6–9), while Ritter, pushing this line of thinking further, contends that the *Mitteleuropa* dream originated with the Liberals, not with
Bismarck, whose concept was rather of a *Reich der Mitte* ("Das Verhältnis
von Politik und Kriegsführung im bismarckischen Reich," *Deutschland und
Europa* [Düsseldorf, 1952], pp. 73–75). This is also the view that inspires
Henry Cord Meyer's *Mitteleuropa in German thought and action, 1845–
1945* (The Hague, 1955).

[26] See esp. *Bismarck*, I, 125, 162, 484; II, 212; III, 135, 332–33.

the boast that "I will make the kind of music I like or none at all" is no fit model of behavior. Yet Eyck cannot withhold his admiration for Bismarck's virtuosity. He cites with approval the words of the *Spectator:* "The policy of this man is contemptible, but his goals are great, his plans appropriate, and his abilities are marvelous."[27]

From the author's estimate of the man and his methods derives the central thesis of the study: precisely because Bismarck was a genius and possibly the greatest statesman in modern history, he was able to divert the stream of German history from its normal channel. While this thesis has not stirred up much heat in England,[28] it continues to outrage the historical confraternity in Germany for the obvious reason that the legacy of a united Germany and the reputation of its most celebrated statesman are both at stake.

Eyck's revisionist thesis posed a question which German scholars could not leave unanswered: was not the Bismarckian empire the progenitor of the Nazi Reich and indirectly the author of the world wars?[29] Answering in the wake of 1945 were such penitents as Meinecke, Kluke, Schnabel, Rassow, Lehmann, and Dehio. They turned their backs on Bismarck and parted company with those who, like Zechlin, A. O. Meyer, C. Becker, Ziekursch, Wahl, and Rothfels, would not see in him the Pied Piper of German history. Meinecke in particular now recognized re-

---

[27] Quoted in *ibid.,* I, 162. Cf. estimates in *ibid.,* I, 154; II, 341, 487; III, 343, 458–59. Of Bismarck's handling of the Hohenzollern candidature Eyck says: "Die Meisterschaft mit der er diese Falle gestellt hat, ist unvergleichlich. . . . Wer die Geschichte nur unter ästhetischen Gesichtspunkten betrachtet, muss Bismarck die höchste, uneingeschränkte Bewunderung zollen" (*ibid.,* II, 487). Elsewhere Eyck declares that Bismarck, one of the great men of history, was "not lovable or worthy of admiration . . . but, with all critical reservations, to be admired" (*ibid.,* III, 638).

[28] Medlicott, p. 5. [29] Rothfels, p. 367.

morsefully that "Germany's astonishing deviation from the main line of European development" began not with Hitler but with Bismarck.[30] A change of atmosphere, however, set in with the commencement of the "cold war" and the re-armament of the *Bundesrepublik*. Revisionism, of which Eyck had been the brightest luminary, began to recede be-fore the tidal wave of what Francis Loewenheim has called "a great Bismarck renaissance."[31] In their endeavor to de-tach and rescue German nationalism from the disgraceful failure of Nazism, Meyer, Leonhard von Muralt, Gerhard Ritter, Rothfels, Reiner, G. A. Rein, Martin Göhring, Wil-helm Mommsen, Wilhelm Schüssler, Otto Becker, Werner Frauendienst, and Maximilan von Hagen passed over to an attack on Eyck's interpretation.[32] They systematically sapped the hypothesis that the Bismarckian empire had transmitted lethal genes to the Weimar republic. In con-trast with the revisionists, the nationalist historians cele-

[30] Quoted by Medlicott, p. 5. Cf the tenor of the essays by Schnabel and Meinecke in Hans Kohn (ed.), *German history: some new German views* (Boston, 1954), pp. 65–93, 141–56, respectively; and Schnabel, "Das Problem Bismarck," pp. 6–9.

[31] *American historical review* (hereafter cited as *AHR*), LXI (1955–56), 459–60.

[32] Variations on the conservative, orthodox theme of Sybel and Marcks have been improvised with exceptional skill by Reiner (op. cit); Otto Becker, *Bismarcks Ringen um Deutschlands Gestaltung*, edited and com-pleted by Alexander Scharff (Heidelberg, 1958); A. O. Meyer, *Bismarck: der Mensch und der Staatsmann* (Stuttgart, 1949); Wilhelm Mommsen, *Bismarck: ein politisches Lebensbild* (Munich, 1959); Leonhard von Muralt, *Bismarcks Verantwortlichkeit* (Göttingen, 1955). Only a minority of German historians, led by Walter Goetz, conceded the merit of Eyck's approach (Eyck to author, October 30, 1959). Among the fairest reviews of Eyck's *Bismarck* were those by non-Germans: W. N. Medlicott, *His-tory*, N.S., XXXV (1950), 276–77; E. N. Anderson, *Journal of Central European affairs* (hereafter cited as *JCEA*) April 1946, pp. 85–90; Law-rence Steefel, *AHR*, XLIX (1943–44), 713–14; LI (1945–46), 501–2. But cf. Wolf Ulrich von Hassell, *Schweizer Monatshefte*, XXI (1942), 660–62; ibid., XXIV (1944), 245–47, and Eyck's reply in ibid., XXV (1945), 330–31.

brated once again, as in the days of Treitschke and Sybel, Bismarck's lofty Christian scruples, his sense of responsibility, and the correctness and rectitude of his policies. Their writings are, of course, proof not so much of their superior perception as of the end of the German *Machtvakuum*.

Among the important controversial theses advanced in Eyck's biography the following may be noted: (1) Austria's policy from 1864 to 1866 deserved to be condemned as criminal and stupid *Draufgängerpolitik*, to which any reasonable effort at agreement was to be preferred.[33] (2) Bismarck preferred the peaceful acquisition of Schleswig-Holstein but not at the cost of compromise with Austria; the view that he had decided on war against the latter before May 25, 1865, when he began in truth to sharpen the knife for the Austrian neck, is a *post hoc, ergo propter hoc* judgment.[34] (3) Until Königgrätz, Bismarck seriously entertained the idea of buying Napoleon III's aid with German Rhenish territory, but so did Austria.[35] (4) The years 1866–67 mark Bismarck's evolution from Prussian to German statesman.[36] (5) There was no "double offensive" in 1870, such as Ritter detects; the Franco-Prussian war was almost wholly of Bismarck's making, for he personally concocted the Hohenzollern candidature with the aim of weakening France and confronting the French emperor with the choice of war or overthrow of his dynasty.[37] (6) A

[33] *Bismarck*, II, 648.

[34] *Ibid.*, p. 16. To this Rothfels demurs (p. 374).

[35] *Bismarck*, II, 224.

[36] *Ibid.*, pp. 259–61, 366–67.

[37] *Ibid.*, pp. 367, 441, 448–49, 455–56, 475, 478, 481. Cf. Eyck, "Bismarck and the War of 1870," *Contemporary review*, CLVIII (1940), 196–202. Ritter's views on the genesis of the war are almost totally different from Eyck's, as emerges from their correspondence which this writer has been privileged to see (Eyck to Ritter, July 23, 1950; Ritter

main aim of the *Kulturkampf* and of the anti-Socialist laws was to weaken popular support for and thus cut the ground out from under the National Liberal party; by falling into the chancellor's trap, this party denied its constitutional principles and ruined all chance that it would ever secure a great mass following.[38] (7) After 1870 Bismarck tried as long as possible to avoid having to choose between Austria and Russia, but this option was in the long run ineluctable from the moment when Austria was driven by Bismarck to set foot in the Balkans.[39] (8) Bismarck circumvented a final choice between Austria and Russia only to commit the worse error of choosing between Russia and her archfoe, England.[40] (9) Bismarck's capital blunder was not to have

---

to Eyck, August 1, 1950). Nevertheless, Ritter has conceded that, however the Hohenzollern candidature may have originated. Bismarck exploited it to bring about the overthrow of Napoleon III ("Bismarck Problem," pp. 671–72). Affirming that France was on the diplomatic offensive in 1870, indeed ever since 1853, and that she would not have permitted peaceful unification of Germany, are Rothfels (p. 376), Wilhelm Mommsen, (*Neue politischer Literatur*, XI [1956–57], col. 127), and Wilhelm Schüssler (stated in Muralt, "Bismarck-Forschung," p. 156). The newest evidence from the German diplomatic archives, says Lawrence Steefel, "supports those who have held that the initiative came from Madrid," but it also shows that "the decision to accept was substantially influenced by Bismarck working through Lothar Bucher and Max von Versen" (*AHR*, LXIV [1958], 173). Eyck believes the newest documents support his view that Bismarck planned the war (Eyck to author, January 27, 1960), but Steefel insists that they contain so much new data as to render all previous works on the subject "practically worthless."

[38] *Bismarck*, III, 73, 93, 105, 135, 229. In contrast to Eyck, Walter Gagel in *Die Wahlrechtsfrage in der Geschichte der deutschen liberalen Parteien, 1848–1918* (Düsseldorf, 1958), pp. 172–74, and Thomas Nipperdey in "Die Organisation der bürgerlichen Parteien in Deutschland vor 1918," *Historische Zeitschrift* (hereafter cited as *HZ*), CLXXXV (1958), 567–68, argue that mobilization of the masses for political purposes hardly corresponded to the anti-popular *Honoratiorenpolitik* of the National Liberal party.

[39] *Bismarck*, III, 270, 345. Cf. also "Bismarck and Gladstone," p. 345.

[40] *Bismarck*, III, 340.

risked everything to make England the third partner of the Austro-German combination.[41]

That Eyck has objectively and responsibly examined the evidence is not doubted by this writer or by most American and English historians. However, some Germans, notably Muralt and Hagen, have charged Eyck with bias in the selection of sources and with distorting those he consulted. Stone by stone they have sought to tear down Eyck's monument. Hagen sums up his whole case against Eyck by averring that he "has submitted a Bismarck biography which we may not recognize as a portrait of our greatest statesman" and that Eyck has set Bismarck studies back almost to where they were one hundred years ago![42] Muralt too, without convincing corroboration, alleges misuse of sources so that Bismarck's entire significance is warped.[43] With this view Ritter now tends to concur,[44] although once upon a time he had hailed Eyck's work as "the first great Bismarck biography, resting upon critical and scientific research in the sources, to appear abroad"[45] and had also spoken in this vein in his capacity as president of the Deutscher Historikerverband to the Münchner Historikerkongress in September 1949.[46] To these distinguished historians, Eyck, the jurist (and hence "outsider"), is not only judge but prosecuting attorney too. Still, when we read Ritter's expression of concern in a personal letter to Eyck, not heretofore published—"Die Wirkung Ihres Buches auf

[41] Ibid., pp. 335, 338, 343, 347, 553. To Ritter, an Anglo-German-Austrian alliance "would really have been an anti-Russian option," the very thing Eyck claims Bismarck wanted to avoid (Ritter to Eyck, August 1, 1950).

[42] "Bismarckbild, " pp. 79–80. Only slightly less severe is the English scholar A. J. P. Taylor, who declares that Eyck's biography lacks "historical quality" (English historical review [hereafter cited as EHR], LVIII [1943], 113–15; LXI [1946], 109–12; and LXII [1947], 390–93).

[43] "Bismarck-Forschung," p. 150.   [45] Quoted in ibid., p. 150.

[44] Ibid., pp. 150–51.   [46] Ritter to Eyck, August 1, 1950.

241

das Ausland, fürchte ich, wird eine überwiegend negative
sein, indem sie das Cliché-Bild, das man sich dort seit
langem vom Verlauf deutscher Geschichte macht, noch
bestätigt und verhärtet"[47]—we are inclined to wonder
whether Eyck's more sardonic critics have not set their
courses solely by the star of nationalism and cannot forgive
him for having clipped the powerful wings and blunted the
steel beak of the German eagle.

Despite the inconveniences of air raids in World War II,
which often sent Eyck scurrying to the basement of the
British Museum, he brought his *Bismarck* to completion
and did the spade work for his study of the reign of William II, which was published in 1948. In these years too he
wrote—it would almost seem for recreation—a succinct history of eighteenth-century England, 1735–1806, as reflected
in the lives of Henry and Charles Fox and the two Pitts.

Pitt versus Fox[48] recalls the elegance of a Gainsborough
portrait when it does not bring to mind the gross realism
of Hogarth. The adroitness with which character is delineated, the absence of glaring aberrations of historical
judgment, and the rococo proportions of this narrative must
excite admiration. Nevertheless, one scholar has complained
that Eyck sacrificed historical clarity to biography.[49] While
space does not permit discussion of this work, it may be
argued that Eyck's aversion for the postwar policies of the
Earl of Chatham and his predilection for the liberty-loving
Charles Fox have engendered minor distortions.[50] Yet the
author's conclusion is well-established: "While it was the

[47] *Ibid.*

[48] *Die Pitts und die Foxs, Väter und Söhne, Zwei Paar verschlungener
Lebensläufe* (Zurich, 1946). Translated by Erich Northcott as *Pitt versus
Fox: father and son, 1735–1806* (London, 1950).

[49] M. A. Thomson, *History*, XXXVII (1952), 246–47.

[50] See *Pitt versus Fox*, pp. 158, 160, 261, 284.

spirit of the two Pitts . . . which triumphed over Napoleon
at Waterloo, . . . the spirit which gave nineteenth century
England her particular character and cast its spell upon so
many free minds in all the countries of Europe was that of
Charles Fox."[51]

Das persönliche Regiment Wilhelms II[52] is mainly a
tale of the sinuous diplomacy that set Germany on the
razor's edge in 1914. Despite the subtitle, Political history
of the German empire from 1890 to 1914, important political aspects, especially those relating to party evolution, have
been neglected. Nonetheless, this polished work is a formidable indictment of a "system which placed the fate of an
entire people in the hands of one man, and he a completely
incompetent one."[53] A vast range of correspondence and
printed source collections has been combed, and the assembled data has been given a consistent, if debatable,
interpretation.

The thesis of the "personal rule" of an incapable William II has elicited little opposition from German historians, who, unlike French, British, and American scholars,
prefer to fix ultimate responsibility on the man rather than
on the system and nation. While only Hans Helfritz has
demurred to Eyck's adverse estimate of the emperor, Walter Goetz, J. von Reichel, Meinecke, Fritz Hartung,
Frauendienst, and Günter Marzlik have all accepted it.[54]

[51] Ibid., p. 377.
[52] Subtitled Politische Geschichte des deutschen Kaiserreiches von 1890–
1914 (Zurich, 1948). In contrast with John L. Snell's favorable reaction
("Imperial Germany's tragic era, 1888–1918," JCEA, XVIII [1959], 384)
to this work, some authorities think it a brilliant failure. See H. Brunschwig, "L'Allemagne depuis Bismarck," Revue historique (hereafter cited
as RH), CCXI (1954), 322; S. B. Fay, AHR, LIV (1948–49), 596–97;
and A. J. P. Taylor, EHR, LXIV (1949), 115–17.
[53] Das persönliche Regiment Wilhelms II, p. 782.
[54] See Walter Goetz, "Kaiser Wilhelm II und die deutsche Geschichts-
schreibung," HZ, CLXXIX (1955), 265–78. Helfritz's unconvincing dis-
senting treatment is Wilhelm II, als Kaiser und König: eine historische
Studie (Zurich, 1954).

On the other hand, not so many Germans are ready to concur with the view, advanced by Hajo Holborn, Klemens von Klemperer, and J. Alden Nichols in the United States and England, that "the tragedy of the whole period, 1890–1914, stemmed from the limitations imposed upon it by the Bismarckian constitution."[55] Kluke, Rassow, Ritter, Herzfeld, and even Dehio object that personal incapacity and constitutional limitations are really *nihil ad rem*; the determining factor was deficient war capability: Germany simply did not have the requisite economic or military resources to justify the pursuit of *Weltmacht*.[56]

While there is in *Das persönliche Regiment* an abundance of flashing characterizations (e.g., Caprivi, Holstein, Eulenburg, Bülow, Delcassé, Edward VII, Grey, and Bethmann-Hollweg), it is the picture of William II, executed with consummate Italian artistry, that is the author's *chef d'œuvre*. The man who proclaimed with braggadocio at the outset of his reign, "We are fated for greatness, and I shall lead you to glorious days!" could not hew to the line but vacillated from day to day, while his insensate rodomontade prejudiced German interests in every diplomatic crisis from 1890 to 1914.[57] At one time William wrote on one of Metternich's dispatches: "If the English want to start a fight over the naval armaments race, well and good; we're not afraid." To which Eyck rejoins: "Who can, when he reads this heap of nonsense, still wonder at the collapse of an empire entrusted to such hands?"[58]

The poverty of German diplomatic talent is illustrated in Bülow, whose whole stock-in-trade was oratory and trans-

[55] The phrase is Klemens von Klemperer's (*JCEA*, XIX [1959], 311).

[56] Andreas Dorpalen, "The German Empire, 1871–1918" (manuscript read on December 29, 1959 at the annual meeting of the American Historical Association in Chicago).

[57] *Wilhelm II*, pp. 95, 125, 134, 140, 199, 395, 587–89, 619.

[58] *Ibid.*, p. 480. Cf. the more complex appraisal by Martin Göhring (*Bismarcks Erben*, 1890–1945 [Wiesbaden, 1958], p. 29).

parent flattery of the emperor. Bülow's unreliable *Denk-würdigkeiten*, upon which Eyck performs a minor operation, "revealed what a quantity of malice and poison this heart concealed."[59] In comparison with Joseph Chamberlain, who "thought like a statesman and who had a great vision of the future" of England in alliance with Germany, Bülow "thought like a petty merchant who demands first to see the color of his customer's money on the shop counter before producing his wares."[60] He was only an *homme d'expédients*. His flair for the well-turned phrase too often concealed capital errors in judgment, such as his classic underestimation of Italy's flirtation with France.[61] His worst blunder was to persist in the fatuous delusion that England would join the *Dreibund*, when he should have done everything in his power to achieve *any kind* of agreement with her. His policy of avoiding offense to Russia at all costs ended only in broken bones and tsarist ingratitude; in the end the artful improviser was forced to play *fortissimo* anyway at St. Petersburg during the Bosnian crisis, when "he cast the German sword into the scale of European decision."[62]

On the origins of World War I, Eyck stands with the most distinguished American exponent of the preponderant guilt of the Central powers, Bernadotte E. Schmitt. But to this writer, Eyck is something less than convincing when he argues that Sazonov, Kokovtsev, and the tsar in 1912 wished to preserve the peace;[63] and in the account of the July 1914 crisis, to which Eyck devotes almost one hundred pages and which closely follows Schmitt's classic interpretation, it would seem that the author lacks sufficient appre-

---

[59] *Wilhelm II*, p. 186.
[60] *Ibid.*, p. 225.   [61] *Ibid.*, p. 188.
[62] *Ibid.*, pp. 245, 263, 265, 312, 319, 428, 510, 533, 538.
[63] *Ibid.* p. 630.

ciation for the fact that whereas for Russia Serbia posed only a question of prestige, for Austria (because of the pan-Serb ambitions of the Pašić government and the terrorist tactics of the influential *Ujedinjenie ili Smrt*—"Union or Death"—the so-called "Black Hand") the Serbian problem was a matter of life or death.

Although it is admitted that neither William nor Bethmann wanted a European war[64]—the former regarded Francis Joseph's campaign against the Serbs as rather like his own against the Hottentots[65]—maximum condemnation is leveled not only against Austria, but Germany too. This may be because Eyck did not study the Russian documents as thoroughly as the German and Austrian. His verdict is just as severe as if William and his ministers had in fact with malice aforethought plotted a general war. While Eyck insists that "Austrian guilt cannot and should not be mitigated,"[66] on Germany he pontificates quite as pitilessly: "It is completely in order that she must bear responsibility for everything that issued from this error ["blank check" of July 5] and experience the consequence to the last measure."[67] He does not forgive Germany for supposing that Russia would sit by while Austria raped Serbia,[68] but, on the other hand, he does not ask whether Russia can be forgiven for ordering total mobilization when the Germans were mediating at her request in Vienna and when she knew with certainty that her action would beget German countermobilization, which would end the task of the diplomats.[69]

Well into his eighth decade Eyck continued his scholarly writing unabated. The year 1950 saw the appearance of

[64] *Ibid.* pp. 727, 739, 781.

[65] *Ibid.*, p. 727.

[66] *Ibid.*, pp. 745–46.

[67] *Ibid.*, pp. 781–82.

[68] *Ibid.*, p. 714.

[69] *Ibid.*, p. 783. Cf. S. B. Fay, AHR, LIV (1948–49), 597.

the one-volume English condensation of the Bismarck biography, incorporating viewpoints that Eyck had developed in a series of lectures given at Balliol College, Oxford.[70] While still eschewing historical journals, he continued to publish historical articles in magazines like the *Deutsche Rundschau* and the *Contemporary review*. In 1950–51 he delivered a series of lectures on eighteenth-century German history at the University College, London.[71] Finally, between 1954 and 1956 the two volumes of his *Geschichte der Weimarer Republik* appeared.[72] With his closing words on the accession of Hitler in 1933, Eyck said farewell to the German tragedy. He was then seventy-eight.

Eyck's history of the Weimar republic is marked by unfailing accuracy, surpassing grasp of foreign policy, broad familiarity with the printed sources, and an enviable understanding of legal-political problems, displayed, for instance, in the close analysis of the Helfferich and Barmat scandal trials. Almost all reviews, except in part that by A. J. P. Taylor, lauded this work.[73] Henry Brunschwig ventured the opinion that "this synthesis surpasses all previous ones,"[74]

[70] *Bismarck and the German Empire* (London and New York, 1950); also published as *Bismarck und das deutsche Reich* (Zurich, 1955). See reviews by Wilhelm Mommsen, *Neue politischer Literatur*, XI (1956–57), cols. 123–27; Hans Herzfeld, *HZ*, CLXXXIV (1957), 135–36; and A. J. P. Taylor, *New statesman and nation*, XL (1950), 204–5.

[71] Eyck to author, March 27, 1960.

[72] *Geschichte der Weimarer Republik*, Vol. I, *Vom Zusammenbruch des Kaisertums bis zur Wahl Hindenburgs* (Zurich, 1954); Vol. II, *Von der Konferenz von Locarno bis zu Hitlers Machtübernahme* (Zurich, 1956).

[73] Reviewed by S. W. Halperin, *AHR*, LX (1954–55), 361–62; LXIII (1957–58), 979–80; Fritz Hartung, *HZ*, CLXXXI (1956), 581–91; CLXXXIV (1957), 393–96; H. Brunschwig, *RH*, CCXVIII (1957), 393; A. J. P. Taylor, *EHR*, LXIX (1954), 689–90; LXXII (1957), 517–18; Klaus Epstein, *JMH*, XXXI (1959), 61; H. W. Ehrmann, *JCEA*, XV (1955), 297–98; D. Mende, *International affairs*, XXXI (1955), 227–28; G. Barraclough, *ibid.*, XXXIV (1958), 202; W. N. Medlicott, *Contemporary review*, CXCI (1957), 370–72; Erich Matthias, *Die neue Gesellschaft*, III (1956), 319.

[74] *RH*, CCXVIII, 393.

while Eric Kollman called it "the best written of the histories of the Weimar Republic."[75] Such criticism as there has been has stressed the study's neglect of certain parliamentary, social, and economic aspects of the history of the republic or, what is more damaging if vindicated, Eyck's biased selection of sources, deficient consultation of monographic literature, and ostentatious preoccupation with questions, as Fritz Hartung puts it, of "individual guilt."[76]

The viewpoint expressed in this study is still that of a nineteenth-century liberal-progressive, who has glimpsed in the Weimar republic his "promised land." While conceding the regrettable consequences of the November 1918 pact between the army's high command (OHL) and the German Socialists (SPD), Eyck does not so much condemn as seek to understand the necessity thereof.[77] When the leftist Independent Socialists (USPD) fell back for support upon the "street," there "was really nothing left for the government to do, if it wished to maintain itself, but to lean on the old army."[78] Eyck correctly explains the Socialist assumption of power in November 1918 on the basis of the SPD's repeated wartime proofs of readiness to assume political responsibility for the fate of the entire nation and not just the proletariat.[79] Some deficiencies, however, mar his analysis of the "revolution" and of the class composition of the workers' and soldiers' councils.

Wilson and the Treaty of Versailles are dissected with mildly hostile conclusions: the internal and external burdens piled on the young republic "made any impressive successes practically impossible from the start."[80] All the

[75] "Recent studies on the Weimar republic" (manuscript read on December 29, 1959 at the annual meeting of the American Historical Association in Chicago).
[76] HZ, CLXXXIV, 582.
[77] Gesch. d. Weimarer Republik, I, 17, 23, 33, 36–37, and 75.
[78] Ibid., pp. 75–76.   [79] Ibid., pp. 67, 70.
[80] Ibid., p. 100; also pp. 158, 164–66.

pros and cons of the Treaty of Rapallo (1922) are weighed with the conclusion that if the content was justifiable, the manner of negotiation was not, and the treaty must be blamed for a deterioration of Franco-German relations.[81] For the Ruhr crisis Eyck with nice impartiality divides the blame between Germany and France: if Germany deliberately defaulted on timber deliveries and was obdurately unwilling to make concessions to France's wish for security, French aggression and encouragement of Rhenish separatism fanned nationalist *revanche* sentiments in Germany.[82] The point is also made that since Germany by 1925 was rapidly becoming a republic without republicans, it was folly on the part of the SPD to vote with the German Nationalists to overthrow the Stresemann government. Ebert, whom Eyck deeply respected, was right when he foretold that the consequences of that ill-considered act would haunt the party and the republic for the next decade.[83]

The second volume, like the first, presents little that is new. In this narrative the only hero-statesman is Gustav Stresemann. We need not subscribe to Eyck's favorable verdict on the hotly disputed features of Stresemann's foreign policy to be able to appreciate the tact and skill with which they are delineated. Whatever Stresemann's earlier views may have been, he is not to be identified, Eyck insists, with Seeckt and the *Revanchekrieg* camp. Though Stresemann probably never ceased to hate and despise the Poles, he finally came to see that Germany needed peace above everything else and that European peace—West or

[81] *Ibid.*, pp. 280–82.
[82] *Ibid.*, pp. 311–14, 327, 371–72, 401–2.
[83] *Ibid.*, p. 376.

East—was indivisible.[84] In any case, he restored Germany
to a position of dignity, if not strength, which she had not
enjoyed since before the war.[85]

According to Eyck, the Socialists must bear heavy blame
for the fall of the republic, almost as much, it would seem,
as Hindenburg for his violations of the constitution and
encroachment upon the powers of the Reichstag. The SPD
was endemically indisposed to compromise with other parties. This may be traced to the circumstance that the SPD
"could not free itself from the ideology of class conflict
even though its own development had long since sum-
moned it to higher and more general tasks."[86] As does Karl
Bracher in his *Die Auflösung der Weimarer Republik*,[87]
Eyck charges that the SPD on March 27, 1930 destroyed
the existing cabinet coalition over a trivial difference with
the politically moderate but economically conservative German People's party (DVP) and other non-socialist government parties respecting unemployment insurance contribution rates.[88] In doing so, he seems not to have done justice
to Socialist alarm at the recent displacement of the focus
of power to the right in both the Catholic Center party
and the DVP.

The shadow of suspicion falls in this work on the spirit
of Heinrich Brüning's policies and on his methods. He too
stubbornly refused to compromise with the Socialists, while
his provocative policy toward Tardieu's France and his ill-
starred Austro-German customs union project contributed
neither to Germany's advancement nor to the pacification

[84] *Ibid.*, II, 273; also pp. 44–46, 271–72.
[85] *Ibid.*, p. 274.
[86] *Ibid.*, p. 75; also pp. 311–15, 564.
[87] (Stuttgart, 1955), pp. 289, 299–303, 358, 507.
[88] *Gesch. d. Weimarer Republik*, II, 314.

of Europe. Furthermore, Brüning was inordinately dependent upon and overawed by Hindenburg.[89]

In conclusion, two last shafts are sped at the Socialists. Severing, Prussian minister of the interior, should have finessed Papen's *Staatsstreich* of July 20, 1932 with the card of armed opposition by the Prussian police, for Hindenburg and Papen would have hesitated to plunge the nation into civil war.[90] Schleicher's sincere efforts to block the advent of Hitler foundered on the rejection of his overtures by the SPD, which "persisted in a useless and sterile opposition."[91]

All in all, Eyck's achievements in the field of German history entitle him to a place among the great historians of this century. No other living student of recent German history has been able to bring so awesome an undertaking to mere, let alone exquisite, completion. His writings bear the signature of the virtuoso. "I must make a confession to you," Eyck wrote me, "which will perhaps do me injury in the eyes of many historians; my ambition has been above all to be a good narrator. You will not misunderstand me nor think that I am assigning only subordinate importance to research and communicating the truth. I only mean that when these tasks have been accomplished, the writer of history is faced with the even more difficult one of presenting the results to the reader in a way that will interest him and in the proper places enthrall."[92] In Eyck's works, consequently, painstakingly mined data, reduced and cut with the aid of critical-analytical methods of research, are mounted in literary settings of rare beauty. We are left with the impression of French rather than German histori-

[89] *Ibid.*, pp. 319, 340–41, 377–78, 380, 393–94, 408, 478, 481–82. See the concurring opinion by Wolfgang Helbich, "Between Stresemann and Hitler: the foreign policy of the Brüning government," *World politics*, XII (1959), 40.

[90] *Gesch. d. Weimarer Republik*, II, 508–10.

[91] *Ibid.*, p. 565.   [92] Eyck to author, October 30, 1959.

cal genius. Though Eyck exhibits what Matthew Arnold called "the German genius for thoroughness," he does not bear one down with his massive erudition but sustains with pinions of style. He abjures the interminable sentence that is the curse of so much German prose. He possesses the epigrammatic touch. It is almost as much the allure as the acumen with which he has accomplished a needed reappraisal of recent German history that will insure him an honored place in twentieth-century historiography.

Considering what Eyck and his coreligionists have suffered at the hands of the Nazis, all praise must be given for the restraint and objectivity which distinguish his main works. No trace of "emigrant's malice" sullies a single one of the more than 3,000 pages of his German history. "I know only too well," he wrote, "what I assuredly owe to my German education and the German intellectual milieu, and I have too many honorable German friends who are suffused with the genuine spirit of humanity, to permit such sentiments to dictate to me or to allow myself to be influenced in my scientific work."[93]

The significance of Eyck as a historian, however, is not to be discovered solely in the magnitude of his undertaking, in his style, mastery of sources, or objectivity. It is also to be found in his democratic idealism. While he never developed a philosophy of history—he had tried to construct one on Hegel "but without visible success"[94]—he exhibits in rich degree the conscience and values of an enlightened European. In his thinking the public will, whose structural incarnation is the *Rechtsstaat*, is supreme, and he has erected it, irrespective of time, place, or nationality, into a Western political imperative. If the German people failed to develop initiative in public administration and were successively af-

[93] *Gesch. d. Weimarer Republik*, II, 9.
[94] Eyck to author, March 27, 1960.

flicted with a William II, a Hindenburg, and a Hitler, it was because popular sovereignty had been repudiated by Bismarck. "An administration which is united not by community of principles but solely by submission to its leader can only consist of minds which 'wheel into line like sergeants on parade', the sort of thing Bismarck demanded of his ambassadors."[95] In the unique metamorphosis through which the Reichstag and the political parties passed under Bismarck, the *volonté générale* was translated into *Gehorsamkeit*. The power of the "leader" was exalted. He came to dominate all, not so much because of his constitutional prerogatives, though these were important, but because of the universal fervor aroused by the legend of his infallibility. Since neither William nor Hindenburg could fill the void left by Bismarck, neither was able to exploit all the potentialities in his bequest. It was left to Hitler to revive the cabalistic *Führer* concept inherent in the German political tradition, for only he could pull the bow of Bismarck.

It may be an exaggeration to say that Eyck provoked a revolution in Bismarck studies, for revisionism has not prevailed in Germany. But he has compelled German historians to re-examine their "idols of the tribe." Furthermore, he has enriched our understanding of Bismarck and of the evolution of German constitutionalism. The verdict of posterity on Eyck's thesis of personal rule and resultant political immaturity of the German nation will probably not be rendered by the "renaissance" patriot historians. However, Eyck's views happen to be shared by most scholars in the Western world. For them, Eyck's service is that he has exhaustively charted the aberration of German political forms and usages from the democratic ideal. If his-

95 *Pitt versus Fox*, p. 158.

tory is, as Bolingbroke and Thucydides both said, "philosophy teaching by examples," the highest merit of Eyck's histories is that they have provided a mirror in which the German people might clearly see, as did Wilde's Dorian Gray, the progressively corrupting effects of ruthless methods and evil appetites.

FRED L. HADSEL

GEORGE PEABODY GOOCH

1873—

Some historians live but one life, and setting themselves on this single course they are judged by what they did in it alone. George Peabody Gooch, however, has led many historical lives. It requires only a quick glance at the major facets of his work to illustrate this. After graduating from Cambridge University in 1895, the young scholar turned to the history of political thought and soon thereafter published his prize-winning study, *English democratic ideas in the seventeenth century.*[1] Although he did not devote himself exclusively to political thought again, his interest in the field endured. In addition to the more popular study pub-

Fred L. Hadsel is First Secretary of the American Embassy in London.

[1] Initially entitled *The history of English democratic ideas in the seventeenth century* (Cambridge, 1898). The shorter title is used in the second edition, which has supplementary notes and appendices supplied by Harold J. Laski (Cambridge, 1927). The work was again reprinted in 1951.

lished eighteen years later, *Political thought in England: Bacon to Halifax*,[2] his writings are sprinkled with essays relating to the history of political ideas.[3] The history of ideas and the study of historians were closely linked in both his education and his scholarly activity, and it is not surprising that a second and extremely important facet of his career should reflect his interest in historiography. Beginning in the first decade of the twentieth century, with a chapter in the *Cambridge modern history*, and reaching maturity a few years later in his *History and historians in the nineteenth century*, this phase of Gooch's life witnessed perhaps his most enduring contribution to historical scholarship.[4] Having explored this area of learning, Gooch did not turn his back upon it, and historiographical essays of interest to students and scholars are scattered throughout the rest of his writings.[5]

Even before Gooch entered the field of historiography, he began writing on international affairs, as witnessed by publications at the time of the Boer War and later by his

[2] London, 1915. It was reprinted in 1923, 1926, 1929, 1933, and 1944. A new edition appeared in 1946 and was reissued in 1950 and 1955.

[3] For example: "German theories of the state," *Studies in modern history* (London, 1931), pp. 183–207; "Hobbes and the absolute state," *Studies in diplomacy and statecraft* (London, 1942), pp. 341–73; and "German ideas from Luther to Hitler," *Studies in German history* (London, 1948), pp. 1–36.

[4] "The growth of historical science," *The Cambridge modern history* (Cambridge, 1902–10), XII, 816–50; *History and historians in the nineteenth century* (London, 1913). The latter work has been reprinted many times and has also been translated into Italian, Spanish, and Japanese.

[5] For example: "The study of Bismarck," *Studies in modern history*, pp. 208–32; "German historical studies since the war," *ibid.*, pp. 233–76; "Ranke's interpretation of Germany history," *Studies in German history*, pp. 210–66; "Modern historiography," *Maria Theresa and other studies* (London, 1951), pp. 207–18; and "Voltaire as a historian," *Catherine the Great and other studies* (London, 1954), pp. 199–274.

slender *History of our times.*[6] After World War I, diplomacy came to dominate Gooch's interests. His *History of modern Europe, 1878–1919* and his contributions to the *Cambridge history of British foreign policy* marked the full flow of this historical life, of which his editorship of the *Documents on the origins of the war,* his *Recent revelations of European diplomacy,* and his *Before the war: studies in diplomacy,* were the major fruits.[7] Gooch's preoccupation with diplomacy, however, did not erase his interest in general European history. His early writings in this field had appeared in the *Cambridge modern history,* to which he contributed chapters on the impact of the French Revolution in Europe and on Anglo-Irish politics of the first part of the nineteenth century.[8] His major scholarly study, *Germany and the French Revolution,*[9] denoted the continuation of this interest, as did his *Germany*[10] and some of the essays found in *Studies in modern history* and *Studies in diplomacy and statecraft.*[11] This historical life was renewed again during World War II, when Gooch developed a ma-

[6] London, 1911. There have been numerous reprintings, as well as a second edition (1946) in which the period covered was extended to 1914.

[7] *History of modern Europe, 1878–1919* (London, 1923); "Continental agreements, 1902–1907," "Triple Alliance and Triple Entente, 1907–1914," and "The war and the peace, 1914–1919," *Cambridge history of British foreign policy, 1783–1919* (Cambridge, 1922–23), III, 294–538; with H. Temperley as co-editor, *British documents on the origins of the war, 1898–1914* (11 vols.; London, 1926–38); *Recent revelations of European diplomacy* (London, 1927); *Before the war: studies in diplomacy* (2 vols.; London, 1936–38).

[8] "Europe and the French Revolution," *The Cambridge modern history,* VII, 754–90; "Great Britain and Ireland, 1792–1818," *ibid.,* IX, 672–708; "Great Britain and Ireland, 1832–1841," *ibid.,* X, 655–84.

[9] London, 1920.   [10] London, 1925.

[11] For example: "The political background of Goethe's life," and "Germany's debt to the French Revolution," *Studies in modern history,* pp. 153–207; "The French Revolution as a world force," *Studies in diplomacy and statecraft,* pp. 291–310.

jor, but never exclusive, interest in the eighteenth century.
The first of these studies was *Frederick the Great* in 1944.
Maria Theresa, Catherine the Great, and *Louis XV* followed during the next twelve years. These publications were
interlarded with other volumes. *Courts and cabinets* dealt
with various members of European royalty from the standpoint of contemporary memoirs. *Studies in German history*
picked up certain personalities of the eighteenth and nineteenth centuries, and *The Second Empire* treated the court
of Emperor Napoleon III.[12]

Although these several aspects of Gooch's historical writing illustrate the remarkable spectrum of his activities, one
must add still another category that is a wide miscellany in
itself. Gooch's interests always were (and still are at eighty-
seven years of age) delightfully catholic. Throughout his
long career he was constantly inquiring into things outside
his major scholarly interests. Many of these inquiries, which
often first saw the light of day in speeches, were published
as articles in periodicals, as parts of collaborative books, or
as subsidiary chapters in his own works. Thus Gooch took
part in discussions of the League of Nations and contributed to three of the publications of the Geneva Institute of
International Relations, *Problems of peace.*[13] He wrote a

12 *Frederick the Great, the ruler, the writer, the man* (London, 1944);
*Maria Theresa and other studies; Catherine the Great and other studies;
Louis XV: the monarchy in decline* (London, 1956); *Courts and cabinets*
(London, 1944); *Studies in German History; The Second Empire* (Lon-
don, 1960).

13 These publications, authored by Gooch in collaboration with others,
are "1931–1932: an introductory survey," and "Some consequences of the
Sino-Japanese dispute," *Problems of peace,* 7th ser. (London, 1933), pp.
1–23, 252–63; "The growth of nationalism," *Pacification is not enough:
problems of peace,* 9th ser. (London, 1935), pp. 1–13; "1936–1937," and
"The breakdown of the collective system," *Geneva and the drift to war:
problems of peace,* 12th ser. (London, 1938), pp. 9–25, 58–74.

number of brochures on current diplomacy.[14] He explored lightly the role of autobiography and historical novels in the study of history, and he contributed to the running appraisal of civilization and public morality.[15] If these miscellaneous activities had been undertaken by a lesser historian, they might have been considered reasonably important. In Gooch's case, however, these essays are mainly significant because they reveal the breadth of his interests. In a sense they were Gooch's "table-talk," but by publishing them he opened his table to the world at large.

Gooch once remarked, when talking about his early years, that he had been very lucky to have been born with a warm heart, an inquiring mind, and an adequate income. This almost ingenuous explanation casts an appropriately gentle glow upon the youth and education of this distinguished historian. Even if one discounts the nostalgia which creeps into memoirs of childhood—and Gooch as a keen student of memoirs would be the first to admit this possibility—it can hardly be disputed that Gooch's own autobiography, Under six reigns, clearly attests the fortunate quality of his early education.[16]

Gooch was born in 1873 of a family which epitomized the Victorian era, for his father was a partner in a financial

[14] For example: Dictatorship in theory and practice (London, 1935), and British foreign policy since the war (London, 1936), a British historical pamphlet.

[15] For example: "Political autobiography," Studies in diplomacy and statecraft, pp. 227–90; "Historical novels," Maria Theresa, pp. 382–403; The unity of civilization (London, 1924), a League of Nations Union pamphlet; Politics and morals (London, 1935), based on the Merttens Lecture of 1935.

[16] (London, 1958), pp. 1–14. For a general view of Gooch, see also the admirable and friendly discussion by Felix E. Hirsch, "George Peabody Gooch," Journal of modern history (hereafter cited as JMH), XXVI (1954), 260–71. In addition, the author had several long conversations with Gooch in 1959–60.

firm and his mother the daughter of a clergyman. His parents' wealth and position in London opened to the young boy a variety of intellectual, religious, and cultural opportunities. When the determined physical education program of Eton proved unpalatable, young Gooch pursued his studies at King's College, a small Anglican institution in London. Home and school gave him a firm grounding in traditional studies, an active interest in religion, and a lively concern with the world at large. When he entered Cambridge, therefore, he was equipped, to use a phrase he often employed, to "warm both hands before the fire of life." He made much of his opportunity, hearing lectures on economic history by Cunningham, on constitutional developments by Prothero, and, above all, on political history by Seeley. Ecclesiastical subjects occupied his attention, as did political science. In this latter area, Gooch established his "allegiance to the thoughtful Liberalism of which Mill was the oracle," retaining this point of view the rest of his life.[17] Gooch looks back on his university years as a "sunny day in spring," not only because they were delightful but because they opened up so many doors to new thought and learning.[18]

During the years following his study at Cambridge, three events further shaped Gooch's intellectual efforts. In the autumn of 1895 he spent three months in Germany. There, intoxicated by the strong academic atmosphere of Berlin, he learned the German language, greatly expanded his knowledge of German institutions, and became a lifelong student of German history. In the spring of 1896 he met Lord Acton, whose broad grasp of history was welcomed by Gooch and whose guidance during the next five years did much to influence the young historian. In the autumn of

[17] *Under six reigns*, p. 20.   [18] *Ibid.*, p. 30.

261

1896 Gooch went to Paris, where at the Sorbonne and the
École Libre des Sciences Politiques he repeated the stimulating German experience. In this short span of years Gooch
learned directly from such giants as Treitschke, Gierke, Acton, Lavisse, and Sorel, and the long-term result was a continental breadth to his liberal approach to history.[19]

Gooch demonstrated his attachment to a liberal interpretation of history in his first work, *English democratic
ideas in the seventeenth century*, which he wrote in 1896–
97 as a counterpart to Figgis' *Divine right of kings*. Putting
aside the notion that history was past politics, Gooch set
out to follow in his own way Acton's classic charge that the
historian's task was "to view and to command the movement of ideas."[20] In this study Gooch described the influences from both home and abroad on seventeenth-century
English thought. He discussed the republicans, Levellers,
Diggers, and other extremists of the revolution and then
moved on to deal with the later decades of the century,
when the tide flowed strongly against this radicalism. Few
monographs of young scholars have survived as well as this
volume, which is enthusiastic, brilliant, full of acute interpretations, and still valid in most of its conclusions. Because
of his own liberalism, Gooch regarded with Whiggish tolerance even the more fanatic of the radicals. To be sure,
looking back after more than a half-century of further study
of the period, one notes that Gooch paid little attention to
economic or social background and that he therefore discussed his thinkers in something of a vacuum. But neither
this criticism nor the fact that scholars have now unearthed
additional archival material detracts from the enduring qual-

[19] *Ibid.*, pp. 32–55.

[20] Quoted in *ibid.*, p. 43. This attitude was also shown in his editing of
the *Annals of politics and culture, 1492–1899* (Cambridge, 1901). See
Hirsch, p. 260.

ity of the volume. This view was confirmed when another distinguished political thinker of a different persuasion, Harold J. Laski, sponsored and annotated a second edition in 1927. Today, after more printings, this essay in the grand manner still continues to inspire students of political thought.

While *English democratic ideas* reflected Gooch's attitude toward history, it was by no means the only illustration during these early years of his liberal point of view. He had already been attracted to the philosophy of the Liberal party, with its emphasis on individual rights, home rule for Ireland, free trade, and anti-imperialism. It was this last issue, however, that wrenched Gooch out of a life devoted largely to research and, for more than a decade, involved him directly in politics.

The South African crisis was the immediate occasion for the new direction in Gooch's life, and at the end of the century he was part of a band of young Liberals who under the leadership of Campbell-Bannerman criticized the imperialism of Joseph Chamberlain and attacked the conduct of the British government during the Boer War. In a pamphlet, *The war and its causes*,[21] which appeared at the beginning of the struggle, Gooch sought to explain the historical background and attitudes of the Boers. Two years later he contributed a chapter on imperialism to Masterman's *Heart of empire*, in which he elaborated the liberal criticisms of jingoism.[22] In 1903 he was adopted as a parliamentary candidate by the Bath Liberal organization, and in 1906, after the party as a whole regained the initiative during the dispute over protectionism, he was elected to the House of Commons. This first-hand experience during

[21] London, 1899.

[22] C. F. G. Masterman (ed.), *The heart of empire* (London, 1901), pp. 308–97. See also *Under six reigns*, pp. 85–87.

a period of major reform at home and increasing involvement abroad confirmed his liberal philosophy and broadened his knowledge of men and issues. While Gooch was too junior to play a leading role in the Commons and was not to sit again after his defeat in 1910,[23] there can be no doubt that his excursion into politics gave him a sureness of touch, to say nothing of a direct acquaintance with leading personalities, when he came to write about this period of history.

While Gooch's parliamentary career was over, another career opened up to him the following year. In 1911, the editor of the liberal monthly, the *Contemporary review*, died. Dr. Scott Lidgett and Gooch became the new editors. Lidgett, a nonconformist theologian, dealt mainly with religious and cultural contributions, while Gooch occupied himself with political and international questions. This collaboration continued for some thirty years, after which Gooch assumed full responsibility for the journal. Only in 1960, after forty-nine years of editorship, did Gooch give up the guidance of the periodical. However, he intends to continue as one of its contributors.

Directing the attention of readers of the *Review* to a broad spectrum of interests, Gooch secured as contributors a brilliant group of diplomats, statesmen, journalists, and academicians. Only gradually, however, did Gooch himself begin to write for the *Review*. After his first article in 1915, he limited himself to an occasional book review, appreciation or essay until after the war, when the number of his contributions increased. Although Gooch considered himself a man of cool blood and, like his admired Ranke, a

[23] Gooch tried three times between 1910 and 1914 to re-enter parliament, but the tide turned against his group of Liberals. In retrospect, he has affirmed to the author that his retirement from active political life was one of the best things that happened to him. The wealth of his writings supports this view.

non-active participant in political affairs, he could not remain silent during the rise of Fascism and Nazism in Europe. During the late twenties he welcomed distinguished Italian refugees as contributors, and he spoke out editorially against the Nazi leadership of Germany in 1934.[24] During and after World War II, Gooch became a major contributor to the Review. Many of his essays and almost all of his more recent books first appeared there in serial form. In spite of the radical change in the times, neither Gooch nor the Contemporary review abandoned any part of the liberal point of view. As he once remarked to the author, the world may have changed since the heyday of liberalism, but his outlook on life had not. He espouses today the same creed he believed in fifty years ago.

While for some the editing of the Contemporary review might have been a major preoccupation, it was only an incidental activity for a man of Gooch's temperament and energy. The initial years of editorship were also years of intense historical scholarship. They witnessed the completion of his History and historians in the nineteenth century, published in 1913.[25] Gooch had first taken up the subject at the suggestion of the editor of the Cambridge modern history, who wished to conclude the last volume of the series with a chapter on the "Growth of the historical sciences." The young historian had done considerable research

[24] Based on an address to the Sociological Society, in which he had been active since its establishment early in the century, his first article in the Contemporary review (CVII [1915], 743–53) is entitled "German theories of the state." A warm appreciation of Lord Morley appeared in December 1917, as did one of Lord Courtney in June 1918. Gooch later undertook as a labor of love the Life of Lord Courtney (London, 1920). After the war, essays on a variety of topics were increasingly frequent in the periodical he edited. For Gooch's views on Fascism and Nazism, see "Salvemini and the Fascists," Contemporary review, CXXIX (1926), 181–85, and "The terror in Germany," ibid., CXLVI (1934), 129–36.

[25] See note 4 above.

in preparing this 34-page essay, which appeared in 1910. In fact, the approach and organization which marked the article were repeated in full three years later. In this volume, which Gooch declares is his favorite,[26] he sought to assess the achievements of historical research during the nineteenth century, to portray the masters of the craft, to trace the development of scientific method, to measure the influences which contributed to outstanding works, and to analyze the effects of these writings upon their times.[27]

In pursuing this ambitious objective, Gooch dealt with some five hundred writers, ranging in his treatment from a brief and often witty comment to an entire chapter. Displaying a remarkable knowledge of German historians, he traced the emergence of the liberal and later the Prussian schools. With perhaps a bit less enthusiasm, he treated the romantic and then the national historians of France. After a sympathetic survey of English writers, Gooch passed to brief discussions of the historians of other countries. His concluding chapters dealt with various historical subjects and the historians associated with them. Gooch moved through this forest of writers and their works with consummate grace. Praising wherever possible, he gloried in the emergence of history as a scientific art in much the same manner as his great predecessors were enthralled by the particular subjects with which they dealt. He left no doubt that his hero was the man of cool detachment, Leopold von Ranke. Gooch summarized Ranke's contributions, aside from his many historical works, as threefold: in describing an event "wie es eigentlich gewesen," he sought to disregard current passions; while not the first to use archives, he established the necessity of basing work on

[26] See *Under six reigns*, pp. 165–66. Gooch corroborated this in conversations with the author.

[27] See the preface to the first edition of *History and historians*.

contemporaneous sources; he founded the science of historical evidence.[28] While not discounting Ranke's role in nineteenth-century historiography, historians today recognize that he fell short of his goal in his own works and almost naïvely minimized the subjectivity in which we are all immersed. Gooch, however, never wavered in his admiration for the great German.[29] He has remained confident that a dispassionate historian can discover the past and that this goal can be achieved without preconceived theories by the pragmatic use of historical method as it evolved during the nineteenth century.

Reviewers of *History and historians* almost all hailed the work as a major contribution to historiography, although one writer caviled at both Gooch and Ranke for thinking that scientific history could be written in the manner they advocated.[30] While queries were raised about its organization (which involved some duplication in time and country) and footnotes (which never fascinated Gooch), the work has splendidly survived the principal test of time. In reprints and new editions it continues to be the best treatment of the subject. No one else, moreover, is likely to match the author's knowledge and grasp of nineteenth-century historians. For these two reasons, *History and historians* is probably Gooch's most enduring historical contribution.

During the next four decades Gooch often returned to historiography, and from his industrious pen there came a

[28] *Ibid.*, 2d ed., pp. 96–97.
[29] See his "Ranke's interpretation of German history," *Studies in German history*, pp. 210–66; "Modern historiography," *Maria Theresa*, pp. 219–58. This viewpoint was also reaffirmed in conversations with the author.
[30] See the reviews by James T. Shotwell, *American historical review* (hereafter cited as *AHR*), XIX (1913–14), 151–53; A. F. Pollard, *English historical review* (hereafter cited as *EHR*), XXVIII (1913), 753–58; Lord Cromer, *Spectator* (April 26, 1913), pp. 715–17; unsigned review, *Nation*, XCVII (1913), 208–10.

number of essays in this general category. For example, he wrote about his mentor, Acton, and his colleague, Harold Temperley.[31] He published a survey of studies on the French Revolution and another on Bismarck.[32] And he wrote a series of essays on eighteenth-century writers of history, notably Voltaire, Mirabeau, and Frederick the Great.[33] The most considerable contribution in this field made by Gooch in later years was *Recent revelations of European diplomacy*, first published as a book in 1927 and revised periodically until 1940.[34] This volume, which he called a "causerie" rather than a bibliography, is both historiography, in that he discussed and evaluated authors, and bibliography, in that he surveyed the documents, memoirs, and derivative works in all the countries concerned. One of the handful of best-informed scholars on this subject, Gooch brought his charm, wit, and sympathetic understanding to bear on a survey which otherwise might have been turgid and contentious. While far more specialized than his *History and historians*, and not seriously contending with it as a work of historiography, *Recent revelations* is nevertheless in its own way indispensable to the student of pre-1914 diplomacy. This fact was recognized by distinguished historians at the time. In reviewing the first edition, B. E. Schmitt praised it highly, and in

[31] "Lord Acton: apostle of liberty," *Foreign affairs*, XXX (1952), 517–30, and "Harold Temperley," *Proceedings of the British Academy*, XXV (1939), 41 ff. Both are reprinted in *Maria Theresa*, pp. 332–47, 348–81.

[32] "Study of the French Revolution" appeared first as a pamphlet in 1920 and later, expanded, in *Studies in modern history*, pp. 117–52. "The study of Bismarck," *ibid.*, pp. 233–67, was republished with an additional chapter as "Bismarck's table talk," *Studies in German history*, pp. 300–91.

[33] "Voltaire as historian," *Catherine the Great*, pp. 199–274; "Mirabeau's secret letters from Berlin" and "Mirabeau on the Prussian monarch," *Studies in German history*, pp. 75–118. A chapter in *Frederick the Great*, pp. 298–327, deals with the Prussian ruler as a historian.

[34] See note 7 above.

commenting on the last edition, S. B. Fay described it as a "truly prodigious accomplishment."[35] As perspectives change and interests shift, *Recent revelations* will undoubtedly become more dated. It is unlikely, however, to be replaced; for while younger scholars may know the period well, they can hardly bring to the subject either Gooch's first-hand knowledge of the people involved or his direct experience with the documentation.

Recent revelations, however, was only an incidental part of Gooch's work in diplomatic history, and aside from his historiographical studies he has made his most important contribution in this field. From the days of the Boer War and his active participation in British politics, Gooch had been interested in diplomacy. Almost half of his popular book, *History of our time*, first published in 1911, dealt with recent international relations. World War I deeply moved Gooch, for not only did he have personal and intellectual associations with liberal elements in Germany, but he was induced to search for an explanation of the origins of the holocaust which affronted his humanitarian outlook on life. Except for an occasional address or a lesser bit of writing during the war years, however, he stayed clear of the passionate controversy over its causes. As the war wore on, Gooch gradually identified himself with those groups which favored a league of nations and supported a moderate settlement with Germany.[36]

Gooch's major efforts in diplomatic history began after the war, when he become co-editor of the *Cambridge history of British foreign policy*, to which he contributed in 1923 three significant chapters dealing with European diplomatic history from 1902 through the war.[37] In the same

[35] B. E. Schmitt, *AHR*, XXXII (1926–27), 879–80; S. B. Fay, *JMH*, XIII (1941), 410.

[36] *Under six reigns*, pp. 172–83.

[37] Gooch's principal diplomatic works are cited in note 7 above.

year he published a general diplomatic history of Europe from 1878 to 1919, which was a projection of the standard textbook by Fyffe on European history from 1792 to 1878. The next year Gooch was invited to become the senior editor of the government's series, *British documents on the origins of the war.* In carrying out this prolonged task— the eleven volumes appeared between 1926 and 1938— Gooch not only reviewed the official diplomatic correspondence of the foreign office but also examined the personal files of the leading British participants. While reviewers of these documents commented on the problems posed by topical organization (as in this case) and chronological organization (as in the case of the French documents), or made suggestions about details, they all agreed that the editors were as impartial as humanly possible and as thorough as their high reputation would lead scholars to expect.[38]

On the basis of this rich experience, Gooch published in 1936 and 1938 his two volumes entitled *Before the war: studies in diplomacy,* in which he dealt in some detail with European international relations between 1898 and 1914. While the *Cambridge history,* the *British documents,* and *Before the war* represent the peaks of Gooch's work in this field, they were accompanied by a number of lesser publications. Thus half the essays in *Studies in diplomacy and statecraft* are in the area of international relations, as is one in *Studies in German history.*[39]

[38] See the reviews by S. B. Fay, *AHR,* XLI (1935–36), 751–53, XLII (1936–37), 332–34, XLIV (1938–39), 626–27; R. J. Sontag, *JMH,* VI (1934), 215–17; and R. B. Mowat, *EHR,* LIV (1939), 148–51.

[39] These essays were written or rewritten between 1920 and 1940. "Franco-German relations, 1871–1914," "The diplomatic background of the First World War," "British policy before the War of 1914, in the light of the archives," "Prince Bülow and his memoirs," "Kiderlen-Wächter, the man of Agadir," and "British foreign policy, 1919–1939" appeared in *Studies in diplomacy and statecraft,* pp. 2–226. "Holstein: oracle of the Wilhelmstrasse," is in *Studies in German history,* pp. 391–512.

In examining Gooch's major diplomatic works, we need to ask two closely related questions: What was his approach to the pre-1914 policies of the European powers, and what lasting contribution did he make to the study of this period? For all of Gooch's deftness and tact—and his pen was held by a sensitive hand in a velvet glove—he was very English in his approach to the coming of World War I. As one of the editors of the Cambridge history of British foreign policy, he signified his intention of combining adherence to truth with "an avowed regard for the interests and above all the honour of Great Britain."[40] His own assumptions with respect to the requirements of British policy tallied with those of Lansdowne and Grey.[41] But at the same time he sought to apply Rankean standards of impartiality to the intricate diplomacy of the period.

The primary task of the historian as he saw it was to explain rather than judge.[42] Although he did make critical evaluations of the prewar figures, such as Bethmann-Hollweg and even Grey, he tried so conscientiously to explain the circumstances in which they acted that the net effect was one of sympathy for almost all the statesmen he dealt with.[43] Gooch emphasized the individual. In his eyes, the various foreign ministers were not mere reflections of national culture, economic interests, or psychological im-

[40] Preface to the first volume of the Cambridge history of British foreign policy.

[41] For example, Gooch agrees with Lansdowne that the latter did not offer an alliance in May-June 1905 to France: Before the war: studies in diplomacy, I, 176–77. He likewise indorses Grey's reasoning on Britain's entry into the war (ibid., pp. 131–33, and Studies in diplomacy and statecraft, pp. 103–7).

[42] Gooch stressed this point of view repeatedly, e.g., in Before the war, II, v.

[43] This did not escape the critical notice of other authorities in the field. See for example B. E. Schmitt's review of Before the war, AHR, XLIV (1938–39), 627–29.

pulses. Rather, they were intelligent men, able significantly to affect the destinies of their countries. As a result, prewar diplomacy, in Gooch's eyes, was largely a matter of personal judgment, and his approach was almost biographical. *Before the war: studies in diplomacy* is completely cast in this mold. It gains much from its focus on the leading diplomats, but nevertheless it does give an impression of men acting in something of a vacuum. This is reinforced by Gooch's practice of letting the individual speak for himself wherever possible. On the other hand, while Gooch would not overlook a telling remark to give the portrait perspective, he was such a master at weaving the fabric of a personality that it is this tapestry which especially attracts the reader's attention.

How was the war of 1914 unleashed and who was guilty of causing it? Gooch was unwilling to condemn any one power. During the period of intense feeling over German war guilt immediately after the war, he emphasized the multiple responsibilities for the conflict. He elaborated this point of view in the *Cambridge history of British foreign policy*, before he had worked through the documents, and he continued to hold it with only slight refinements afterward.[44] Thus, while he continued to apportion immediate responsibility between Austria-Hungary and Russia, he later recognized more clearly the causal element of Bethmann-Hollweg's weakness (although not as much as some would wish). His later researches also clarified the greater share of France in creating the dangerous situation of July 1914 through encouragement of Russian designs. Gooch, however, declined to sit in final judgment on the question of exact war guilt, except to attribute the ultimate

---

[44] *Cambridge history of British foreign policy*, III, 486–508; *History of modern Europe, 1878–1919*, pp. 557–59; *Before the war*, II, v and passim; *Studies in diplomacy and statecraft*, p. 104.

cause of the war to international anarchy, the absence of international machinery, the doctrine of unfettered sovereignty, and the assumption that grave disputes could only be settled by the sword. His point of view was in harmony with his lifelong desire to achieve Rankean detachment. But it suggests, of course, that in the world as we know it even this ideal has its limitations.

Gooch's enduring contributions to the study of diplomacy are easily pointed out. He added in significant measure to the quality of the documentation, and he provided an indispensable guide to its use. He also illuminated the documents through his own writings. By bringing into play his insight and style, he made the principal personalities live as few writers have been able to do. At the same time, it was entirely natural that he should have been a moderate revisionist. He thought that excessive penalties on the Weimar republic would be self-defeating, and he was therefore a critic of the Treaty of Versailles.[45] In this, as in his attitude toward the war-guilt question, Gooch held throughout the following decades the views which he adopted right after the end of hostilities. It need only be observed that most of what Gooch believed in the early postwar period came to be the virtual consensus on these matters in later years.

Another of Gooch's historical lives concerns general European history. This interest first showed itself in chapters of the *Cambridge modern history* dealing with the French Revolution and the early nineteenth century. When World War I cut across his life, he found leisure to write his first full volume on the period, *Germany and the French Revolution*.[46] In this solid piece of scholarship, which still com-

---

[45] *Cambridge history of British foreign policy*, III, 509–38. Gooch expressed this point of view in numerous speeches and articles as well.

[46] London, 1920.

mands respect, Gooch sought to document the influence of the revolution by painting a panorama of the ferment among German intellectual and political leaders of the time.[47] Such an approach illustrated his view that history includes the entire human adventure, thus again placing him among those who like Acton saw the past broadly rather than among the political historians of the Seeley persuasion. This study not only showed the results of Gooch's work on *History and historians*, for some of the early writers are discussed in both books, but it provided background for his *Germany* published in 1925.[48] The latter work, partly a history and partly a survey of the institutions of the Weimar republic, revealed Gooch's deep sympathy with the liberal tradition in Germany. Because so much of it is a description of contemporaneous conditions, it has suffered rather badly with the passage of time and the addition of perspective.

Two decades intervened before Gooch returned to general history. This period of his life, which began with the publication of *Frederick the Great* in 1944, saw him write three other studies of eighteenth-century autocrats: *Maria Theresa, Catherine the Great,* and *Louis XV*. It also saw the appearance of his *Courts and cabinets* and *Studies in German history* and concludes—perhaps only temporarily— with his latest book, published in the spring of 1960, *The Second Empire*.[49] Although none of these involved archival research—and Gooch made it clear that in no instance was he trying to produce a definitive biography of his subject— they are all based on contemporary sources, either the

---

[47] *Germany and the French Revolution,* pp. v–vi. Incidentally, the second portion of the work (pp. 367–514), which deals with the political effects, is less satisfactory.

[48] Guy Stanton Ford hailed this work as the best book about Germany since 1914 (*AHR*, XXXI [1925–26], 525–26).

[49] See note 12 above.

letters of the person concerned or the observations of ac-
quaintances. In reviewing *Frederick the Great*, Ferdinand
Schevill remarked that this approach had "the effect of
making the reader a direct participant in the events."[50]
These portraits are also without exception highly personal
presentations in which Gooch's interest in the role of individuals found its fullest expression. As John B. Wolf
said of *Louis XV*, not only did Gooch brilliantly use the
memoirs of the times, but a book such as this was a "devastating response to the historical 'physicists' who attempt
to explain the historical process solely in terms of abstract
forces. . . ."[51]

Moreover, Gooch set out in these volumes to entertain
the intelligent reader. Those who criticize him for not
writing definitive history mistakenly think that a *doyen*
of historians—as Gooch undoubtedly is—must be only a
dispenser of footnotes and a researcher of archives. They
do not appreciate the shafts of sunlight which Gooch cast
into what might otherwise be a dull landscape of historical
events.

Gooch's various essays and observations on the world he
has lived in are scattered about like odd pieces left in the
studio of an artist. They were occasionally popular treat-
ments or second looks at problems with which he had once
dealt more extensively. More frequently, they were originally addresses or lectures that were later redone for publication.[52] As incidental contributions they often confirm what
was indicated in other writings, but, being incidental, they

[50] *JMH*, XX (1948), 167–68.

[51] *Ibid.*, XXIX (1957), 263.

[52] Two widely different examples are "Cambridge Chair of Modern History," *Studies in modern history*, pp. 268–89, and "German views of the
state," *The German mind and outlook*, co-edited by Gooch (London,
1945), pp. 1–42.

do not add much to our understanding of Gooch as a historian.

One exception is "Politics and morals," which he delivered as the Merttens Lecture in London in 1935.[53] It deals with the problems posed for society by Machiavelli. Quoting with approval John Stuart Mill's view that democracy is an expression of faith in the power of mankind to learn from experience, Gooch contended that Machiavelli drew an unfair picture of man's nature and ignored the power of moral forces in the world. Moreover, he held that Machiavellian principles were no longer valid when nations had established ordered liberty in their internal affairs. While admitting that the problem was far more complex in the international sphere, Gooch argued that by recognizing the unity of civilization and the need for effective institutions to prevent aggression, it would also be possible to abandon Machiavellian principles in the relations among nations. It is indicative of Gooch's confidence in mankind that he should have elaborated this optimistic outlook at a time when the shadow of Hitler was cast across the civilization that Gooch loved and represented. It is equally indicative of Gooch's lifelong adherence to this point of view that in his reminiscences published more than two decades later he should have expressed the same confidence in his fellow men.[54]

Writing of the charity which Gooch displayed in his life and work, his distinguished colleague C. V. Wedgwood correctly affirmed that he "stood in a great humane tradition."[55] Appropriately, moreover, this comment was followed by the wistful question: who can follow in his foot-

[53] Published as a pamphlet in 1935 and reprinted in Studies in diplomacy and statecraft, pp. 311–40.

[54] Under six reigns, pp. 327–28.

[55] Review of Under six reigns, Time and tide, XL (1959), 77.

steps? Gooch has established no school. To be sure, he was not a teacher. But this is not the reason. Rather, the explanation must be sought in the major change which has taken place during the past half-century in both the training of historians and the philosophic milieu in which they develop. Liberal historians such as George Peabody Gooch are no longer being produced. The fact that the times call forth a different kind of scholar should not, however, dim our appreciation of the contribution which Gooch has made to historiography or the erudition which he so gracefully displays in his many writings.

PALMER A. THROOP

LUCIEN FEBVRE

1878–1956

The laborious and fruitful life of Lucien Febvre ended in 1956. His passing brought to a close the career of a man who had wielded an enormous influence in the world of historians. Shortly after Febvre's death, Fernand Braudel, long and closely associated with the master, proclaimed him the only great French historian since Michelet.[1] Another friend declared that it was Febvre who kept France in the avant-garde of a "history renewed and radiating toward the other social sciences."[2] Febvre's accomplishments are indubitably most impressive, impressive enough to deserve a long and detailed study.

Febvre was born into a cultivated French family in 1878

Palmer A. Throop is professor of history at the University of Michigan.

[1] Fernand Braudel, "Lucien Febvre," *Annales* (*Économies, sociétés, civilisations*) (hereafter cited as *Annales*), XI (1956), 291.

[2] Georges Friedmann, "Lucien Febvre toujours vivant," *Annales*, XII (1957), 5.

and received his primary education at Nantes, although he always identified himself with Franche-Comté. He completed his long and thorough training in history in 1911 at the age of thirty-three, brilliantly sustaining a thesis, "Philippe II et la Franche-Comté," written under Monod. His first university position was on the faculty of letters in Dijon, where his career was interrupted by military service, begun in 1914 and lasting throughout World War I. He was then called to Strasbourg for the installation of a French university in "liberated" Alsace. Here he was joined in 1920 by Marc Bloch, and out of a close friendship grew their joint editorship of the Annales d'histoire économique et sociale, founded in 1929. Already he had come under the influence of Henri Berr, always intent upon systematizing and enriching historical synthesis. In these early years Pirenne also was an inspiring friend and example, serving on the Comité de Rédaction at the inception of the Annales.[3]

The Annales were always the center of Febvre's life, and he succeeded in keeping the journal alive through depressions, attacks, and World War II with several changes in title. It was his crusader's sword in seeking victories for "la vieille Clio." The journal was founded for the purpose of bringing together historians, economists, sociologists, geographers, and other social scientists for an exchange of views and the cross-fertilization of method.[4] After twenty years Febvre could say with pride that no one in France con-

[3] Fernand Braudel, "Présence de Lucien Febvre," Hommage à Lucien Febvre: éventail de l'histoire vivante offert par l'amitié d'historiens, linguistes, géographes, économistes, sociologues, ethnologues (Paris, 1953), pp. 1–16; Pierre Mandrou, "Lucien Febvre (1878–1956)," Revue universitaire (hereafter cited as RU), LXVI (1957), 3–7; Annales d'histoire économique et sociale (hereafter cited as AHES), I, (1929), 1, 2.

[4] Marc Bloch and Lucien Febvre, "À nos lecteurs," AHES, I (1929), 1, 2.

tested the fecundity of the *Annales;* their revolutionary leadership was more than justified by their solid contributions to history.[5]

In 1933 Febvre became professor of history at the Collège de France. He also undertook the editorship of the *Encyclopédie française,* contributing many articles himself to this ambitious endeavor to give a unified and authoritative interpretation of learning in contemporary France. He did not live to bring out the volume on history, although due homage is paid him for inspiring this interesting assessment of the most recent historical methodologies.[6] Febvre was also active on the commission for the reform of teaching in France. From 1945 to 1950 he served as a representative of his country in UNESCO, going on many cultural missions to thirty countries in all.[7] In this long and successful life the establishment of the sixth section of the École des Hautes Études under his leadership was a triumph he very much relished.[8] As a testimony to his far-reaching influence he was presented on his seventy-fifth birthday with a volume entitled *Hommage à Lucien Febvre: éventail de l'histoire vivante offert par l'amitié d'historiens, linguistes, géographes, économistes, sociologues, ethnologues.*[9]

The position of leadership Febvre achieved in so many areas reveals the force of his personality and thought. He was feared and disliked because of the cutting wit and ruthlessness of his reviews. Although those near him insisted that he was not "un homme dur,"[10] his writings re-

[5] "Vingt ans après," *Annales,* IV (1949), 1–3.

[6] Gaston Berger in *Encyclopédie française,* XX (Paris, 1959), 20.02–5.

[7] Mandrou, pp. 3–7.   [8] "Vingt ans après," *Annales,* IV, 2, 3.

[9] The astonishing range of these articles indicates the wide influence of Febvre.

[10] Braudel, "Présence de Lucien Febvre," p. 4.

veal a vehement advocate and ferocious defender of his concept of history, a concept that became richer as the years passed. Febvre repeatedly gave masterly demonstrations of a history intent upon revealing intricate relationships, upon deepening an understanding of the complexities of man.

His thesis, *Philippe II et la Franche-Comté*,[11] was already a model of historical sophistication so far as methodology is concerned. He successfully demonstrated "the multiple action of profound causes"[12] during the second half of the sixteenth century that brought about extraordinary changes in Franche-Comté. Around 1550 this little province was going its own way, relatively prosperous and quiet, when the advent of Philip II altered everything.[13] The conflict resulting from the attempt to impose Catholic reforms and monarchical absolutism upon Franche-Comté was not merely a local episode of a great political struggle. It represented also the battle between two rival classes, the nobility and the bourgeoisie, for power and influence.[14] To disentangle these complexities Febvre began with an analysis of the geography of Franche-Comté and its relation to the economics of the second half of the sixteenth century.[15] Febvre had already published a detailed study, in large part geographical, of Franche-Comté,[16] and to this section of his thesis he brought a concise mastery.

Next followed a section devoted to the political history of Franche-Comté through the reign of Charles V. Then came one of the most original parts of the book, an account of the social conditions of the nobility, the bourgeoisie, and the peasants through the reign of Philip II,

[11] Paris, 1911.
[12] *Philippe II et la Franche-Comté*, p. vii.
[13] *Ibid.*, p. ix.
[14] *Ibid.*, p. x.
[15] *Ibid.*, pp. 3–37, 93–118.
[16] *Les régions de la France: la Franche-Comté* (Paris, 1905).

with relationships to geographical and economic factors clearly indicated. The complex pattern was then skilfully developed by showing the interrelationships of political and religious factors, particularly the impact of Philip II's absolutism and the Catholic Reformation upon provincial liberties.[17] The concluding chapter showed Franche-Comté poverty-stricken and exhausted, ruined by Philip's policies.[18] The tale of a small, once prosperous region coming under great external political and religious forces which very much complicated the economic and social factors already in play, unfolds like a great tragedy. Febvre had a dramatic sense that made this meticulously documented study[19] of a minor French province vivid and alive.

Philippe II et la Franche-Comté was followed in 1912 by a history of Franche-Comté in which the leading motif was the growth and development of the bourgeoisie in relation to some of the great movements and revolutions that swept Europe.[20] This, obviously, is a larger canvas, and the principal lines of development are necessarily more briefly sketched. It was also at this time (1912–13) that Febvre undertook to write an introduction to historical geography for the series "Évolution de l'humanité" edited by Berr. The war interrupted this work, which was taken up again in 1919 and published in 1922 with the collaboration of Lionel Bataillon.[21]

Here Febvre demolished with characteristic vigor various geographical determinisms. Throughout the book he main-

[17] *Philippe II et la Franche-Comté*, pp. 123–390, 400–572.

[18] *Ibid.*, pp. 744–77.

[19] Febvre also published a collection entitled *Notes et documents sur la réforme et l'inquisition en Franche-Comté* (Paris, 1911).

[20] *Histoire de la Franche-Comté* (Paris, 1912).

[21] *La terre et l'évolution humaine* ("L'évolution de l'humanité," Vol. IV [Paris, 1922]).

tained that man is faced with possibilities, not necessities, in connection with the problem of adapting himself to his geographical environment.[22] Mountains, plains, or other geographical entities possess no unity as such that universally determines cultures and psychological types.[23] Indeed, to hunt for the influence of nature on man, of soil on history, is fantastic. *Influence* is a word that belongs to astrology. True problems must be observed in terms of relations. What relations do human societies today have with their geographical milieu? That is the fundamental and only problem of human geography.[24] A deepened and first-hand knowledge of the natural milieu and a knowledge of the development of human society—these are the fundamental bases of all serious and effective human geography. Always between men and the natural milieu there is the *idea*.[25]

Here we have an application of Febvre's theory of causation, shared with Berr, that is fundamental to an understanding of his work. There are three categories in historical causation: contingency, necessity, and logic or *idea*. Contingency or chance is "a phenomenon which is an effect neither of a law nor a will, but a coincidence of series of independent phenomena, and which thus is not and cannot be foreseen by the human mind."[26] Social institutions constitute a more permanent element, since they contain repetitive aspects and thus sharply limit contingency—here necessity comes into the picture. At this level the historian can profit from the work of sociologists in making his synthesis, although he must always be aware of the play of contingency in the institution and in the role of the in-

[22] *Ibid.* See especially pp. 216–25.   [24] *Ibid.*, pp. 438–39.

[23] *Ibid.*, pp. 241–83.   [25] *Ibid.*, p. 442.

[26] Febvre and Berr, "History," *Encyclopaedia of the social sciences*, VII (New York, 1935), 361.

dividual, "the intermediary between chance and necessity."[27] Finally there is the effect of ideas both on individuals and institutions; it is thought that "weaves its thread continuously or repairs it when it breaks." Febvre felt that in the *idea* the evolution of humanity found its inmost and characteristic expression.[28] The historian must note the play of these orders of causation and must avoid sacrificing any one of them to the other two.[29]

Febvre gave a most suggestive demonstration of the interaction of geography, the *idea*, and institutions in his book on the Rhine, which he wrote in collaboration with a geographer, Albert Demangeon. Febvre had already smashed orthodox ideas concerning frontiers in *La terre et l'évolution* by insisting there were no natural boundaries; nature imposed nothing on the political organization of men. There was simply the adaptation of men to possibilities.[30] A river might make a convenient line on the map, but it was not a deep ditch that separated men. On the contrary, it was a route that connected them.[31] The Mediterranean had been the common matrix of ancient civilizations.[32] Similarly the Rhine had been a matrix in the expansion of Rome. Both sides of the great river had felt the impact of Roman civilization. Again, both sides had been subjected to the same sort of Germanic force after the collapse of Rome; and again, the Rhine has been a great road in the expansion of Christianity.[33] Thus Febvre and Demangeon saw this waterway as a great binding and connecting force that was economic and cultural in character

[27] *Ibid.*, p. 365.　　[28] *Ibid.*, p. 362.　　[29] *Ibid.*, p. 365.

[30] *La terre et l'évolution*, pp. 360–83.

[31] *Ibid.*, p. 364.

[32] Albert Demangeon and Lucien Febvre, *Le Rhin: problèmes d'histoire et d'économie* (Paris, 1935), p. 72.

[33] *Ibid.*, pp. 3–72.

and that operated persistently even in modern times in spite of national passions.[34]

Although Febvre seems to have to become aware of historical complexities through the study of human geography and never lost his interest in it,[35] he became increasingly concerned with the psychology of leaders—political, literary and religious—of the sixteenth century. Psychology he came to consider the most valid base of history, and he seemed to think that progress in "collective psychology" would largely determine the progress of history.[36] Apparently Febvre thought that historians could make great contributions to collective psychology, contributions that could be largely independent of psychological theory, of which he appeared suspicious.[37] His first major contribution in this field was a psychological study of Luther, a work of popularization.[38] Here he wished to attack what he considered a major problem of history: the nature of the relations between the individual and his society, between personal initiative and social necessity.[39]

In undertaking to cope with this question, Febvre endeavored to show how Luther's first mystical religious protest, made upon the basis of mystical meditation, changed

[34] Ibid., p. 291.

[35] Febvre hailed as a "manifesto" of intellectual history the impressive book by Fernand Braudel, La Méditerranée et le monde méditerranéen à l'époque de Philippe II (Paris, 1949), in which Braudel put Spanish politics under Philip II in a geographical and cultural frame of reference. "Vers une autre histoire," Revue de métaphysique et de morale, LIV (1949), 240, 241.

[36] Febvre and Berr, p. 365.

[37] Un destin: Martin Luther (Paris, 1928), pp. 43, 44.

[38] Febvre described his work on Luther as a "travail de vulgarisation" (p. 10). He considered popularization part of the duty of a professional historian; it should not be left to journalists and amateurs. See "Face au vent," Annales, I (1946), 8.

[39] Un destin: Martin Luther, p. 9.

under the pressure of circumstances. Perhaps Febvre was drawn to the problem because the plaster-saint legend of Luther had been thoroughly demolished by Father Henry Suso Denifle, O.P., archivist at the Vatican, in 1904.[40] This erudite Dominican had pointed out that Luther's own account in later life of his early attitudes toward the Roman church did not agree with the documentary evidence of his youthful development and protest.[41] Febvre, taking this evidence and yet other data contributed by Protestant scholars, painted a portrait of a Luther completely absorbed in a religious search during his young manhood. His trip to Rome had not started him on the reformer's path. His anguished soul, in his quest for the certainty of salvation, brought him to a conviction, professed as if it were a revelation, of the sinner's total inability to achieve salvation through good works, a conviction of the necessity of accepting his helplessness as something deserved. The sinner could be saved only by throwing himself completely upon the mercy of God, who could regenerate him. This individualistic doctrine Luther preached with an exalted and idealistic fervor that brought explosive results which he had not foreseen. Febvre remarked the psychological similarity of Luther's experience to the conversion of St. Paul, as interpreted by Nietzsche.[42]

The crisis that sprang from the controversy over indulgences was striking. Febvre showed that earlier and even more radical protests against the sale of indulgences had not brought tremendous social explosions.[43] Why was Germany in 1517 a tinderbox ready to burst into flames? Febvre tried to give a sketch of the economic, social, and political conditions of Germany that made the reaction to Luther's doctrine comprehensible. Germany was prepared,

[40] Ibid., p. 26.
[41] Ibid., pp. 27–56.

[42] Ibid., pp. 57–79.
[43] Ibid., pp. 83–91.

and printing made it possible for Luther's ideas to spread with great rapidity.[44] The readiness of the middle class, above all, made Luther's protest a revolution; the readiness of the peasants made it a tragedy.[45]

It was the *idea* of Luther's doctrine playing upon the necessities of social and economic institutions that made Luther a dramatic figure of great intensity. Febvre's description of the crisis resulting from the peasant's rebellion was almost as romantically vivid as one from the pen of Michelet. Although Luther lost control of the protest he had begun, Febvre showed that there was never any inconsistency in his thought so far as secular control of the Lutheran church was concerned. There were inevitable changes and compromises, however, resulting from the revolts and wars.[46] Febvre was at his best in describing the mature Luther, who wrote almost entirely in German and propounded German lower-class proverbs. Luther's adaptation to his more restricted sphere revealed the influence of his origins, education, and political convictions.[47] Altogether, Febvre fulfilled in masterly fashion his purpose of showing the reciprocal relations between a man of singular vitality and the tremendous social forces that created the Reformation.

Fascinated by these complexities, Febvre never ceased his attempts "to understand and make understandable" the extraordinary figures of the sixteenth century. He chose some of the most difficult and controversial. Besides numerous articles on humanists and religious leaders, Febvre wrote three remarkable studies of "historical psychology" in book form. Two of these were finished during the war

[44] *Ibid.*, pp. 104–27.

[45] Febvre held, however, that it was Melanchthon particularly who adapted Luther's thought to the needs of the bourgeoisie. See *ibid.*, p. 291.

[46] *Ibid.*, pp. 225–91.   [47] *Ibid.*, pp. 275, 293–304.

287

years, which he spent teaching in Paris: *Origène et Des Périers* and *Le problème de l'incroyance au XVIe siècle: la religion de Rabelais*.[48]

Febvre's study of Des Périers, whose curiously impious dialogues have puzzled scholars from the eighteenth century to the present, demonstrated most convincingly the origin of his incredulity: Origen's *Contra Celsum*, a pious defense of Christianity against the attack of the pagan philosopher Celsus. Des Périers, according to Febvre, differed radically from other contemporary skeptics, who considered the New Testament inspired not by a God but by a very erudite man. Des Périers, on the contrary, considered Christ a poor, ignorant, mediocre man—a trickster. This viewpoint could come from only one ancient source— Celsus—known only through Origen's attack, *Contra Celsum*, an attack that Des Périers turned into a *Pro Celso*.[49] It was Des Périers' *Cymbalum Mundi*, published at the end of 1537 or the beginning of 1538, that was the real "introduction à la vie libertine" in France and not Bodin's *Heptaplomeres*, published sixty years later.[50]

Remarkable as this study was, it was surpassed by Febvre's masterpiece of intellectual history, *Le problème de l'incroyance au XVIe siècle*. Startled by the verdict of an editor of Rabelais, Abel Lefranc, that the learned doctor was a militant atheist, Febvre endeavored to find the scope of Rabelais' belief by checking all possible evidence. First of all, what did his contemporary humanists think of him in their literary, religious, and personal battles? The evi-

[48] A specialist in the sixteenth century, Marcel Bataillon, immediately saw the implication of these books for historical method. See Bataillon, "Le problème de l'incroyance au XVIe siècle d'après Lucien Febvre," *Mélanges d'histoire sociale*, V (1944), 26.

[49] *Origène et Des Périers, ou l'énigme du Cymbalum Mundi* (Paris, 1942), pp. 128, 129.

[50] *Ibid.*, pp. 130, 131.

dence was difficult and picturesque, but brought no conviction of atheism. The testimony from contemporary
theologians proved that atheism was a derogatory word
used in a very wide sense. Febvre made it clear how indispensable the history of "smear" words was in intellectual
history. To get Rabelais' religious convictions from his
literary works as well as from the pertinent documents
required great finesse, and the difficulties attending the
use of literature for the history of ideas were instructively
demonstrated.[51]

The most original section of the book, "The limit of
skepticism in the sixteenth century," took up the relation
of religious belief to private, professional, and public life
in order to determine what was representative and typical.
The problem of the man who might not be representative
of his time, the precursor, was discussed most suggestively.
Des Périers was clearly an example. Then came remarkable
studies of what in the early sixteenth century the possible
sources of skepticism might be: philosophy, science, oc-
cultism. This investigation of the range of possibilities of
Rabelais' conceptual equipment was Febvre's most original
contribution. The conclusion was forcefully drawn that
skepticism had its own forms in every age and that Rabelais
could not have been the sort of skeptic Abel Lefranc had
indicated. On the contrary, the evidence seemed to point
to Erasmus as the most probable source of Rabelais' religious beliefs.[52]

Febvre's success in placing Rabelais in his authentic intellectual milieu was a masterful triumph in his lifelong
war on anachronism, the abomination of historical abomi-
nations in his eyes. What Febvre called historical psychol-

[51] Le problème de l'incroyance au XVIᵉ siècle: la religion de Rabelais
("L'évolution de l'humanité," Vol. LIII [Paris, 1947]), pp. 1–361.
[52] Ibid., pp. 329 ff.

ogy was a matter of giving accurate information concerning emotions, beliefs, and motivations in their proper contemporary context. He never tired of warning historians that they must not read their own emotional reactions and motivations into the past. This was a distortion that robbed history of its prime value as a means of understanding man in the current of his time under many and varied relationships. He wrote with cutting irony:

Anachronism, the perpetual and irritating anachronism of men who project themselves into the past with their own sentiments, ideas, moral and intellectual prejudices, and who, having made a travesty of Ramses II . . . Julius Caesar, Charlemagne, Philip II, and even Louis XIV on the model of Dupont or Durand of 1938, find in their heroes what they have just put into them, are pleasantly astonished at their discovery, and conclude their "analysis" with a disconcerting platitude: "Thus man is always the same."[53]

Febvre repeatedly demonstrated that man was capable of remarkable variations. His one long study of a Renaissance lady revealed a few that were even more astonishing than man's—variations that he did not succeed too well in resolving into a unifying theme. Challenged by psychological mysteries, Febvre undertook to explain Marguerite de Navarre in his book *Autour de l'Heptaméron: amour sacré, amour profane*. This sister of Francis I of France presented two aspects: a deeply sensitive woman, protector of those dallying with religious reform, submitting herself to religious disciplines, and a worldly woman, who, after pious austerities, and in her full maturity, wrote sensuous and even bawdy tales, the Heptameron. Nor did all of Febvre's skill heal this psychological schism. Febvre painted Marguerite's spiritual development with the aid, for the most part, of a brief, too brief, dedicatory letter by Capiton.

[53] "Psychologie et l'histoire," *Encyclopédie française*, VIII, 8.12–6.

With very little evidence he traces two spiritual crises: one which left her disillusioned with traditional ascetic practices and another which left her disenchanted with philosophy so that she threw herself with great intensity into deep faith in Christ.[54]

And then came the Heptameron. . . . To give Marguerite spiritual continuity, Febvre made a determined effort to transform this lusty collection of tales into a didactic work of deep moral philosophy. Marguerite, he insisted, did not see men through books or texts, Greeks or Romans, Catholic moralists or Protestant theologians. She gave the world around her a clear, disabused, honest, and scrupulous look. She was without blind indulgence or fanatical severity. She possessed "the honesty of a great lady of true nobility, or real delicacy of soul." Febvre sincerely convinced himself of Marguerite's "profound unity," realized in her religion.[55] But, lacking a wide range of documents, he has been most successful in deepening the mystery. His treatment was impressionistic when compared to his study of Rabelais; he did not scrutinize all the possibilities inherent in contemporary opinion in order to determine probabilities.

Febvre's last contribution to historical method came in a book written almost completely by another: L'apparition du livre. In 1953 Febvre asked Henri-Jean Martin, librarian of the Bibliothèque Nationale, to write a book according to a plan which Febvre had conceived and which he intended to amplify. The first chapters were carried out according to plan, but Febvre's death in 1956 ended the collaboration. However, Martin generously ascribed the inspiration and conception of this splendid book to Febvre, an inspiration and conception he has fulfilled remarkably

[54] Autour de l'Heptaméron: amour sacré, amour profane (Paris, 1944), pp. 135–56.

[55] Ibid., pp. 202–11.

291

well.[56] Febvre himself was extremely well qualified to plan a history of printing; he had edited the volume of the *Encyclopédie française* dedicated to the subject.[57] The history of a technological process gave new scope for Febvre's powers of synthesis. In the preface Febvre declared his intention of studying the impact that printing had upon various developments in the fifteenth and sixteenth centuries. Above all, how did the press affect humanism, literature, the Reformation? How did it fit into the economic organization of the time?[58]

This book exemplifies admirably Febvre's belief that specialists should work together under guiding hypotheses to bring new light. Anne Basanoff, Henri Bernard-Maître, Moché Catane, Marie-Roberte Guignard, and Marcel Thomas, all contributed to the success of this collective enterprise. For example, the conditions under which books were reproduced immediately before printing were described by Thomas, head of the manuscript division of the Bibliothèque Nationale.[59] Then the appearance of paper and the overcoming of technical difficulties were discussed.[60] The relations of the press to the economics of the period were carefully and statistically presented.[61] Febvre's concepts of "collective psychology" vitalized large sections of the book, particularly those chapters, some of which he had reworked himself,[62] concerned with "the little world of the book"—vivid descriptions of fifteenth- and sixteenth-century printshops and the daily life of various types of printers.[63] The place that the humanist printer and the philo-

[56] Febvre and Martin, *L'apparition du livre* (Paris, 1958), p. vii.

[57] *Encyclopédie française*, XVIII (Paris, 1939).

[58] *L'apparition du livre*, pp. xxiii–xxix.

[59] *Ibid.*, pp. 1–24.

[60] *Ibid.*, pp. 27–108.

[61] *Ibid.*, pp. 162–93.

[62] *Ibid.*, p. vii.

[63] *Ibid.*, pp. 194–216.

sophical bookshop, frequently attached to the press, had in the intellectual world makes the ferment of the fifteenth and sixteenth centuries far more comprehensible.[64] This posthumous work is an eloquent tribute to Febvre's ideal of history: "to understand and to make understandable."

Febvre fought valiantly for this ideal throughout his life, and in 1953 published a collection of articles which he entitled Combats pour l'histoire.[65] With the same purpose of demonstrating his concepts of history, Febvre had collected a group of articles on the religious problems of the sixteenth century for which he proposed to write a preface. The preface did not get written, but Fernand Braudel brought out the articles, grouped as Febvre had planned, under the title Au coeur religieux du XVIe siècle.[66]

Out of this rich thought concerning the French Renaissance and Reformation Febvre constantly developed his concepts of methodology and periodization. His association with Henri Berr proves that at an early age he was concerned about problems of synthesis. Aside from his dissertation, published when he was thirty-three and still a model of historical synthesis, his great books came in his maturity: his Martin Luther appeared when he was fifty, his masterpieces, Origène et Des Périers and Le problème de l'incroyance au XVIe siècle were completed when he was sixtysix. His books were episodes, although important ones, in a busy life as an editor. It was as an editor, fighting to establish new standards, new norms of competence, that he made himself a very real force in French historical scholarship. Febvre felt deeply and intensely the need for a renovation of historical method. It is apparent in all of Febvre's editorial work that he was extraordinarily sensitive to the crises—political, economic, social, and intellectual—of his

[64] Ibid., pp. 217–55.   [65] Paris, 1953.   [66] Paris, 1957.

293

world. Not only was he involved in two painfully disruptive
world wars; he felt himself very much involved in the intellectual maladjustments of the twentieth century. History he
knew was passing through a severe crisis. The ferocious attacks to which it was being subjected on all sides, the uncertainties and irresolution that historians manifested, were
not, he felt sure, the consequences of a sickness peculiar to
"la vieille Clio" herself. Her ills were but the particular aspect of a general crisis, one of the results of a quite recent
transformation of the attitude of men of science in regard
to science. There was a unity in knowledge, Febvre insisted
—not in the subject matter, but in method, conceptions of
relationships and validity. There was an attitude common
to all scholars, whatever their specialty, in regard to the
particular objects of their study.[67]

In the last thirty years science had changed radically.
After four hundred years of elaborating laws, scientists no
longer spoke of law; at times they spoke of frequencies.
Every day, Febvre pointed out, our ideas were losing their
character as essences and were taking on the character of instruments. *Savoir* was being reduced to *pouvoir*. Was liberty also outdated?[68] Concepts of determinism and contingency had all changed profoundly. Old ideas were being
eliminated, willy-nilly. To demonstrate the "pull" of ideas
Febvre, always a master of Gallic irony, did not lose the
opportunity of showing how Paul Valéry, notoriously con-
temptuous of history, described in 1894 a da Vinci who
believed in the continuous in science as did the scientists of
1894. After the recent scientific upheaval, Valéry created
another da Vinci, this time a precursor of the discontinu-
ous at the end of the fifteenth century. "Not that we are
going to inflict upon Valéry," Febvre added, "the posthu-

[67] "Sur Einstein et sur l'histoire," *Annales*, X (1955), 306.
[68] *Ibid.*, p. 312.

mous insult of taking him for a historian, even of Leo-
nardo."[69]

Febvre was always aroused to a magnificent fury at
charges of history's backwardness so far as conceptual equipment was concerned:

Are we historians obstinately to remain alone, apart, at the
rear, poor cripples clinging to a bumpy ambulance on washed-
out roads? For half a century I have exhausted my lungs asking
this question. Out of bad temper? . . . I have no hatred of men.
I have it for laziness, inertia, stagnation. And this hatred proceeds only from my fervor for history.
    Let them watch out, those who in 1955, retarded rag-pickers
of Clio, stubbornly take their subjects from the garbage heap.
. . . Don't they feel how fast the wheel turns and leaves them
out of the game? Don't they perceive around them . . . this
extraordinary pullulation of defective philosophies of history . . .
this flood of *vues d'ensemble* in ten, twenty, even fifty or a
hundred pages on the past, present, and future of humanity. . . ?
With no solid bases. Without knowledge honestly acquired.
Puffed and swollen imaginations. . . . A great art of flattering
the curiosities of the public, of provoking them, of going out
to meet them. A total scorn for professional historians, these
pedants, these grotesques, these monopolists of sinister ennui
. . . in a word (and a dangerous one), these useless specimens.
    These are the bitter fruits engendered by a history indifferent
to the subjects it treats, seizing without discrimination anything
. . . that comes in a pack of documents: antiquated in its methods and procedures; young only in its juvenile deficiencies of
style.
    . . . One does not take the trouble to criticize their work.
Their work is ignored; they are ignored. It is because they never
answer the questions that are tormenting their contemporaries.
They leave this duty to the writers whom they (the public)
question concerning . . . the anxieties of the day. And the writers
have no scruples about responding: of difficulties they suspect
nothing.—"Pardon, the savant does not have to satisfy such
desires."—What has he to do then? Make napkin rings to pass

[69] *Ibid.*, p. 309.

295

the time, like an old retired customs official? And to admire himself enormously for his successes?

Einstein has not disdained to answer questions of the men of his time. . . .

So long as we stubbornly remain in our studies, shutters closed, curtains drawn, en *tête à tête* with our notes—so long as we refuse to open our eyes on life, to cultivate a history which, not daring to ask vital questions, will not be able to furnish any nourishment to our contemporaries in these times of unrest and growing malaise, we will be without any influence on the world which surrounds us.[70]

This acid invective against *histoire historisante* on the one hand and ignorant or inadequately grounded popularizers on the other recurred constantly throughout Febvre's career. He spared no one. Spengler to Febvre was an amateur whose amazing success was best explained by the stupidly pedestrian history of the Germans, whose capacity for obscurity and inanity accounted for their failure to enlighten their troubled contemporaries. Toynbee was also an opportunist without the benefit of rigorous and critical thought in regard to civilization. His control of sources was deficient.[71] Even distinguished and capable historians of philosophy were reproached for not putting their histories in a social context.[72]

Repeatedly the professional historian was sternly held responsible for all inadequacies.

We protest when they (the public) take X, Y, or Z for historians. Fine. But what do we offer them to read—that is readable? We enclose ourselves in our academic problems. . . . And

[70] *Ibid.*, pp. 310, 311.

[71] "De Spengler à Toynbee: quelques philosophies opportunistes de l'histoire," *Revue de métaphysique et de morale*, XLIII (1936), 573–602.

[72] Review of Étienne Gilson, *Les métamorphoses de la cité de Dieu*, in *Annales*, IX (1954), 374; "Histoire des idées, histoire des sociétés: une question de climat," *Annales*, I (1946), 159–61; "Dualisme en philosophie," *ibid.*, III (1948), 181.

we repeat with pride: "It is our dignity. It is our honor. Besides, is it not in solving, in complete objectivity of mind, purely theoretical problems that the physicist finally contributes to the solutions of practical problems?"—Perhaps the physicist. Historians, no! Distinction between theory and practice makes no sense for them. They cannot invoke it. History, their history, is nothing if it does not nourish human societies from whom they derive their origin and development. . . . The historian seems to take a perverse and unhealthy pleasure in making this nourishment disgusting. This he does under the pretext of honesty. He must realize, finally, that cooking can be both honest and appetizing. . . . The day when he becomes aware of this, on that day something will be changed in the world of Clio. But that is not the important thing. Something will be changed in the mentality of our contemporaries. Who can be indifferent to that?[73]

It is this pressing awareness of, one is almost inclined to say obsession with, the social usefulness of history, that weaves in and out of Febvre's reviews, articles, and books. It made him ruthless, even with honest and competent historians, who string together minute details without a working hypothesis.

When one does not know what one is looking for, one does not know what one finds. Without hypotheses, no scientific work is possible. All nature is founded on the postulate that nature is explicable. Man, the object of history, is a part of nature. Man is for history what the rock is for the mineralogist, the animal for the biologist, the star for the astro-physicist: something to explain. To make understandable. Thus something to think about! You go to the archives. You collect facts. You arrange them. History is made. You have performed your trick.

Histoire historisante demands little. Too little. Too little for me and for many others besides me. That is all our complaint, but it is real. The complaint of those who need ideas. Ideas, those brave little women of whom Nietzsche speaks, who do not let themselves be possessed by men with frog's blood.[74]

[73] "Un feuilleton ou comment vulgariser l'histoire," *Annales*, I (1946), 156, 157.
[74] "Sur une forme d'histoire qui n'est pas la nôtre," *Annales*, III (1948), 22–24.

Febvre was so convinced that history could contribute to the solution of pressing questions of the present that he felt the necessity of constituting batteries of historians for co-operative research guided and directed by an organizing hypothesis that related to contemporary problems.[75] Only with the aid of hypotheses could the historian be guided toward new relationships. And these relationships must be conceived in terms of modern economics, modern sociology, modern psychology. He wrote:

We never find ourselves before facts impartially classified which we are free to combine as we wish. We find old selections, more or less arbitrary, of events and interpretations—collections of ideas and documents that have become classic: in short, "great problems" posed, sometimes centuries ago, under the sway of habits, ideas, and needs that have ceased to be ours.[76]

It was in order to guard against this ever present danger of defining problems in terms of old and discredited concepts that Febvre repeatedly sounded his warnings. Contemporary experience and an awareness of contemporary problems were indispensable. He urged:

Plunge into life. Intellectual life. Historians should be geographers, jurists, sociologists, and psychologists. Nor should they close their eyes to the great currents of physical science.[77]

Febvre held that a crusading ardor, such as his, on behalf of extending the boundaries and relevancies of history would in no way compromise the independence of his beloved discipline. On the contrary, he was convinced that

[75] "Vers une autre histoire," Revue de métaphysique et morale, LIV (1949), 242. Febvre here is amplifying a point made by Marc Bloch. According to Bloch, the complexity and variety of evidence demanded for the solution of great problems required crews of specialists working toward a common goal. No one person can master all the necessary auxiliary sciences; those now required are quite inadequate even for the novice. See Marc Bloch, Apologie pour l'histoire ou métier d'historien (Paris, 1949), p. 28.

[76] "Les origines de la réforme française et le problème des causes de la réforme," Au cœur religieux du XVIe siècle, pp. 7, 8.

[77] "Vivre l'histoire," Mélanges d'histoire sociale, III (1943), 16, 17.

history had much to contribute because it was concerned with the plight of man specifically at a certain time and place. According to a remark once made by Berr, there was the contingent milieu of belief and the progressive milieu of reason.

Febvre would concede this [Berr observed], but he does not wish to give too much to (generalized) man. His historical sense is so scrupulous, his vision so sharp, that he is inclined to insist more upon diversity than similarity, upon change rather than continuity and progress.[78]

Febvre was quite aware that the solutions of the past could not be those of the present. On the other hand, he believed that we would flounder less blindly in the midst of complicated situations if we knew their origins. On one occasion he exclaimed: "To understand well how the past differs from the present: what a school of flexibility for the man familiar with history!"[79]

Firm in his conviction, along with his old friend Marc Bloch, that history makes for justice by training one to weigh evidence, and for peace by bringing charitable understanding rather than nationalistic pride to conflicting interests,[80] Febvre devoted the latter part of his life to cultural missions in UNESCO. His conception of a universal history to which every historian should contribute through central guiding hypotheses[81] was that of a man dedicated to the possibility of a more fraternal world.

[78] Berr, in Le problème de l'incroyance, p. xxvii.

[79] "Face au vent," p. 7.

[80] Bloch, pp. 66, 67. Bloch's book was dedicated to Lucien Febvre in 1941, but remains incomplete because Bloch was executed by the Germans. In the dedication Bloch wrote of the ideals that he had in common with Febvre. Febvre's work and life confirm them.

[81] Febvre and Berr, "History," p. 367. It should also be remarked that Febvre considered this sort of universal history a way of achieving objectivity (ibid.).